Religion and Authoritarianism
Cooperation, Conflict, and the Consequences

This book provides a rare window into the micropolitics of contemporary authoritarian rule through a comparison of religious-state relations in Russia and China – two countries with long histories of religious repression and even longer experiences with authoritarian politics. Drawing on extensive fieldwork in multiple sites in these countries, this book explores what religious and political authority want from one another, how they negotiate the terms of their relationship, and how cooperative or conflicting their interactions are. This comparison reveals that although tensions exist between the two sides, there is also ample room for mutually beneficial interaction. Religious communities and their authoritarian overseers are cooperating around the core issue of politics – namely, the struggle for money, power, and prestige – and becoming unexpected allies in the process.

Karrie J. Koesel is Assistant Professor of Political Science at the University of Oregon, where she specializes in the study of contemporary Chinese and Russian politics, authoritarianism, and religion and politics. Her work has appeared in *Perspectives on Politics*, *The China Quarterly*, and *Post-Soviet Affairs*. Koesel's research has been supported by grants from the John Templeton Foundation, the Social Science Research Council, the Fulbright program, the International Research & Exchanges Board, the Einaudi Center and East Asia Program at Cornell University, and the University of Oregon. In 2010, she was the recipient of the American Political Science Association Aaron Wildavsky Award for the best dissertation in religion and politics.

Cambridge Studies in Social Theory, Religion and Politics

Editors

David C. Leege
University of Notre Dame

Kenneth D. Wald
University of Florida, Gainesville

Richard L. Wood
University of New Mexico

The most enduring and illuminating bodies of late nineteenth-century social theory – by Marx, Weber, Durkheim, and others – emphasized the integration of religion, polity, and economy through time and place. Once a staple of classic social theory, however, religion gradually lost the interest of many social scientists during the twentieth century. The recent emergence of phenomena such as Solidarity in Poland; the dissolution of the Soviet empire; various South American, southern African, and South Asian liberation movements; the Christian Right in the United States; and Al Qaeda have reawakened scholarly interest in religiously based political conflict. At the same time, fundamental questions are once again being asked about the role of religion in stable political regimes, public policies, and constitutional orders. The series Cambridge Studies in Social Theory, Religion and Politics will produce volumes that study religion and politics by drawing upon classic social theory and more recent social scientific research traditions. Books in the series offer theoretically grounded, comparative, empirical studies that raise "big" questions about a timely subject that has long engaged the best minds in social science.

Titles in the Series:

Religion and Authoritarianism

Cooperation, Conflict, and the Consequences

KARRIE J. KOESEL

University of Oregon

CAMBRIDGE
UNIVERSITY PRESS

CAMBRIDGE
UNIVERSITY PRESS

University Printing House, Cambridge CB2 8BS, United Kingdom

One Liberty Plaza, 20th Floor, New York, NY 10006, USA

477 Williamstown Road, Port Melbourne, VIC 3207, Australia

314-321, 3rd Floor, Plot 3, Splendor Forum, Jasola District Centre, New Delhi - 110025, India

79 Anson Road, #06-04/06, Singapore 079906

Cambridge University Press is part of the University of Cambridge.

It furthers the University's mission by disseminating knowledge in the pursuit of education, learning and research at the highest international levels of excellence.

www.cambridge.org
Information on this title: www.cambridge.org/9781107684072

© Karrie J. Koesel 2014

First published 2014

A catalogue record for this publication is available from the British Library

Library of Congress Cataloging in Publication data
Koesel, Karrie J., 1974– author.
Religion and authoritarianism : cooperation, conflict, and the consequences / Karrie J. Koesel.
  pages cm – (Cambridge studies in social theory, religion and politics)
ISBN 978-1-107-03706-9 (hardback) – ISBN 978-1-107-68407-2 (pbk.)
  1. Religion and state – Russia (Federation) 2. Religion and state – China. I. Title. II. Series:
Cambridge studies in social theory, religion and politics.
BL65.S8K59 2013
322´.10947–dc23   2013024283

ISBN 978-1-107-03706-9 Hardback
ISBN 978-1-107-68407-2 Paperback

To Patrick, Sasha, and Addi

Those who say religion has nothing to do with politics do not know what religion is.

– Mahatma Gandhi

Contents

List of Figure, Table, and Illustrations

Figure

Table

Illustrations

Acknowledgments

Writing a book is a long, collaborative endeavor and I owe many a debt of gratitude. The greatest are to my mentors, Valerie J. Bunce, Elizabeth J. Perry, Sidney Tarrow, and Kenneth Roberts. It is undoubtedly a privilege to study in the company of such extraordinary scholars, and I have greatly benefited from their wisdom, criticism, and friendship. I am especially indebted to Val Bunce for her invaluable feedback on countless drafts, unwavering support for the comparative project, and encouragement to ask big, important questions.

I am also extremely grateful to the series editors, David C. Leege, Kenneth Wald, and Richard L. Wood. It was truly a pleasure to work with such dedicated editors and generous scholars, who offered both rich feedback and a considerable amount of autonomy to ensure the book remained my own. I also wish to thank Lew Bateman and Cambridge University Press for their professionalism in bringing the manuscript to press.

Over the many years, numerous colleagues raised crucial questions and shared valuable insights that have strengthened the book. A special thanks goes to Tony Gill, who showed an early interest in the project, offered indispensible advice, and even included me in his *Research on Religion* podcast. I also benefited a great deal from many individuals who graciously offered their time and expertise, including Febe Armanios, Ameya Balsekar, Allen Carlson, Matt Evangelista, Felix Giron, Dev Gupta, Ron Herring, Denise Ho, Brooks Jessup, Jeanne Kormina, Toby Lincoln, Dave Luesink, Don Miller, Andy Mertha, Sasha Panchenko, David Patel, Tsveta Petrova, Maria Repnikova, Andres Rodriguez, Cole Roskam, Rachel Stern, Tariq Thachil, Wang Jianping, and Zhang Xin. I am also particularly indebted to my colleagues at the University of Oregon who offered advice on key chapters and provided enormous support.

During field research in Russia and China, I was the beneficiary of many institutions and individuals. I was graciously hosted by the Moscow Carnegie

Center, the Linguistic University of Nizhny Novgorod, and Kazan State University in Russia. In China, the foreign affairs departments at the Shanghai Academy of Social Science and Jilin University helped me gain my footing and facilitate my research. Additionally, I owe an enormous debt to those who helped me negotiate local landscapes with their time and expertise – in particular, Rafiq Abdrakhmanov, Cai Rong, Ilya Gerasimov, Zukhra Khusnutdinova, Larisa Levanova Kempbell, Li Xiangping, Li Yihai, Ma Lei, Marina Mogilner, Rafiq Mukhametshin, Rosa Musina, Aigul Sabirova, Alexander Sergounin, Olga Senjutkina, Wang Caibo, Wang Jianhui, Xiao Ke, Xiao Yu, Xia Yu, Xi Tianyang, Yang He, Zhou Shu, and Zhou Yi. To the many courageous and dedicated individuals in China and Russia who took risks to share their stories, so that we may all better understand the politics of religion under authoritarian rule, I am especially grateful.

Field research for this project was generously supported by numerous organizations. I thank the John Templeton Foundation and the Pentecostal and Charismatic Research Initiative (PCRI), the Center for Religion and Civic Culture at the University of Southern California, the International Research & Exchanges Board (IREX-IARO), the Fulbright-IIE Program in China, the Social Science Research Council (SSRC) Eurasia Program, the Institute of European Studies and East Asia Program at Cornell University, and the University of Oregon Political Science Department.

And lastly, I want to express my warmest thanks to my family, especially to my parents, Fred and Judy Koesel, for their unconditional love and support. I also remain impossibly indebted to Patrick W. Deegan for his steadfast encouragement and intellect, which has enriched this book. And finally to my Sasha and Addi for reminding me what is important and why – this book is dedicated to them.

I

Introduction: The Politics of Religion

Religion is the opiate of the people.

– Karl Marx

In the summer of 1999, I made the familiar walk through a crowded market in the northeastern city of Changchun, China. Like most mornings, the market noise was deafening as shoppers haggled with farmers over vegetables pedaled in from the countryside before dawn. As I slipped through the crowds and into a neighboring park, the morning became unusually quiet. Gone were the hundreds of ballroom dancers with their scratchy record player, the martial artists practicing sword fighting, the retirees walking backward, and the tai chi masters training their devoted students. For the first time in almost two years, the park was alarmingly empty.

Later that day, I bumped into a student and asked if the park had closed for renovations. "No" she explained, "it's open, but empty because of Falun Gong." A recent editorial in the *People's Daily* had denounced the quasi-religious group as an "evil cult" (*xiejiao*), and the local government was beginning to crack down on their activities. In fact, the local campaign was expected to be particularly severe because Changchun was the hometown of Falun Gong's founder, Li Hongzhi, and the park was considered a popular place to meet and recruit members.

At the time, it seemed strange that other associational groups would also self-censor their activities or that local cadres might confuse the lively energy of ballroom dancing with the more somber Falun Gong meditations. However, over the following weeks, the extent of the crackdown became evident – even the local Avon and Amway salespeople had been targeted for their "cultlike" activities. Apparently, the door-to-door selling of lipstick and laundry detergent was under investigation for being part of a pyramid scheme, behavior that local officials associated with cults. In many ways, the campaign against Falun Gong

I

is a familiar story about the politics of religion under authoritarian rule, the quickly shifting political winds, the coercive reach of the state, and the reverberations felt across civil society. This book tells a different story: one in which the relationship between religious and political authority is far more complex.

This book examines the political consequences of growing religiosity in countries where politics is repressive and religious freedoms have yet to be well defined. It explores religious-state relations across different authoritarian settings, detailing how autocratic state actors manage religious groups and, just as importantly, how religious communities navigate state and society from the political margins. More specifically, this study analyzes what religious and political authorities want from one another, how they negotiate the terms of their relationship, and, as a result, how cooperative or conflictual are their interactions.

At present, the literature suggests several reasons to expect conflictual if not outright hostile relations between religious communities and their authoritarian overseers. First, religion and the state represent competing centers of authority. Most modern states, including autocratic ones, tend to base their legitimacy on the secular principles of delivering stability, order, and economic growth, whereas religion claims a "higher" authority that transcends the state and its leaders.[1] For those in power, therefore, religious groups raise the fundamental question of loyalty. Another reason to expect religious-state tension is that authoritarian leaders often lack popular legitimacy to rule. As a result, they seek to co-opt religious institutions (and leaders) as well as incorporate religious symbols, titles, and rituals into the regime to enhance their base of support and legitimize their position.[2] Indeed, the instrumental use of religion has proved to be one of the most effective tools of state-building because "challenges to the state will be classified as sins – political dissent will be identified as sacrilege, for the state rules with divine right."[3]

A third reason to expect religious-state conflict highlights the role of civil society in authoritarian political contexts. As the extensive literature on civil society indicates, some of the key functions of associational groups are to balance against state power, articulate shared interests, stimulate civic participation, and socialize democratic norms.[4] In authoritarian regimes, however,

---

[1] See Gill (1998); Moen and Gustafson (1992); Bellah and Hammond (1980).

[2] Toft, Philpott, and Shah (2011); Linz (1996 [2004]); Johnston and Figa (1988).

[3] Stark and Bainbridge (1985: 508); see also Seul (1999); Berger (1967: 22).

[4] There is an extensive literature on civil society. See, for example, Henderson (2003); Howard (2003); Chambers and Kymlicka (2002); Krishna (2002); Gibson (2001); Ottaway and Carothers (2000); de Tocqueville (2000 [1835]); Diamond (1999, 1994); Schmitter (1997); Putnam (1993); Przeworski (1992). Within this scholarship, some influential scholars of civil society, such as Robert Putman, have been hesitant to include religious associations into the ranks of civil society because they tend to be hierarchical and are organized in nondemocratic ways. The argument here is that religious groups do not engender the same kind of democratic norms as secular associations. However, in recent scholarship, Robert Putnam and David Campell (2010) found that religion can promote a healthy civil society, particularly in democratic regimes. For example, religious Americans are three to four times more likely to be involved in their community than

the ability of civil society groups to fulfill these responsibilities can be limited. Autocratic rulers are generally assumed to control if not dominate all aspects of associational life. Civil society groups are seen as "illegitimate" and "inauthentic" because they do not function as mechanisms for collective empowerment or a buffer between state and society as their democratic counterparts do. Thus, civil society is often relegated to little more than a wolf in sheep's clothing – a tool of the regime to identify dissidents, socialize potential troublemakers, tame opposition, solicit support from groups outside the ruling elite, and promote and reinforce state policies and leaders.[5]

At the same time, studies of authoritarianism identify another function of civil society in that political context: to challenge autocratic rule.[6] Religious groups, as members of civil society, may be particularly threatening to authoritarian leaders because of their perceived ability to mobilize, especially at the grassroots. This is because religion is not simply a body of beliefs but also a community of believers.[7] In authoritarian regimes, religious communities tend to represent the most diverse and robust forms of associational life outside of the state. They are voluntary organizations that cut across cleavages. They are endowed with resources and dedicated supporters, often led by charismatic leaders, and tied to larger domestic and transnational networks.[8] In other words, religious communities have a distinct set of resources that make them particularly good at mobilization – a toolkit that authoritarian elites and their allies view as extremely threatening.[9]

Indeed, religious entities have frequently played a prominent role in mobilizing against authoritarian rule. Not only did the 1979 Iranian Revolution topple a secular shah (replacing one form of authoritarianism with another), but also during the third wave of democratization (1970–90s), many Catholic leaders across Latin America, Africa, and Asia used their moral authority to condemn authoritarian governments, mobilize opposition, and promote political change.[10] At the same time, the struggle against communism in

---

nonbelievers. In fact, people of faith are also more likely to volunteer for community projects, attend public meetings, vote in local elections, participate in protest demonstrations and political rallies, and donate time and money to secular and religious causes.

[5] For discussions of civil society under authoritarian rule, see, for example, Hildebrandt (2011); Jamal (2007); Wedeen (2007); Brownlee (2007); Riley (2005); Foster (2001); Wiktorowicz (2001); Leahy (2000); Linz (2000); Bunce (1999); Frolic (1997); Brook and Frolic (1997); White et al. (1996).

[6] See especially, Havel, Keane, and Lukes (1985); Chirot (1991); Bernhard (1993); Kubik (1994); Scott (1997); but see also S. Berman (1997); Encarnacion (2003).

[7] Scott (2005).

[8] See especially Smith (1996); also Philpott (2007); Wald et al. (2005); Rudolph (1997).

[9] Acemoglu and Robinson (2006); Huard (2000).

[10] Of course, there is variation among religious actors during the third wave, and some remained neutral while others were pro-authoritarian. For a more detailed discussion of religion during this time, see Toft, Philpott, and Shah (2011); Gill (2002, 1998); Linz (1996 [2004]); Borer (1998); Kamrava and O'Mora (1998); Fleet and Smith (1997); Cavendish (1995); Huntington (1991); Mainwaring and Wilde (1989); Mainwaring (1986). More generally, see Haynes (2009) for a discussion of religion and democratization.

Eastern Europe took multiple forms.[11] Imprisoned religious leaders in Hungary became international martyrs of Stalinist repression, and religious institutions sought subtle strategies of subversion through policy reforms.[12] In contrast, the Catholic Church in Poland took a more assertive stance as both a symbol of national resistance and resource to coordinate the anticommunist opposition; for example, churches were one of the few places where large, diverse groups could gather without attracting attention.[13] Even in regimes where autocratic rulers have remained entrenched and religious movements are not necessarily democratic in their outlook, religious communities may still pose threats to dictatorship as demonstrated by the 2007 Buddhist uprisings in Myanmar (Burma) and the role of Friday prayers in mobilizing opposition during the Arab Spring.[14] Thus, whether religious groups are dominated by the authoritarian state or leading the charge against it, the relationship is assumed to be antagonistic.

This leads to one final reason why religion may be a cause of concern for authoritarian power holders: religious ideas and identities are often closely associated with violence.[15] Religious beliefs, for instance, are the triggers for present-day communal conflicts across the authoritarian world, including violence in Afghanistan, Algeria, Chad, China, Egypt, Lebanon, Russia, Sri Lanka, and Sudan. Religious identities have also contributed to regime collapse. Recall, for instance, the disturbing precedent from the late 1980s and early 1990s when a tide of nationalism swept across the Soviet Union and minority movements pressed for greater rights if not outright independence. Many of these struggles for self-determination had strong religious overtones that hardened overtime and fueled violent conflict, as in the case of the former Yugoslavia.[16] The history lesson for authoritarian leaders is clear: religion should be suppressed or contained – and certainly never ignored.

Although there are many reasons to expect contention between religious communities and their authoritarian overseers, this book demonstrates that the relationship is not necessarily one of a predatory state penetrating and dominating religious communities. Nor is it one of subversive religious groups mobilizing against dictators and the current political order. Instead, I argue that across the authoritarian world, a dynamic process of exchange is at play such that innovative government officials and active religious leaders negotiate the rules that govern their relationship. Conflict can certainly emerge from this interaction, but there is also ample room for cooperation.

---

[11] Weigel (1992).

[12] Wittenberg (2006); Ramet (1998).

[13] Morawska (1987); see also Osa (1989).

[14] Hliang (2008); Patel and Bunce (2012); Toft, Philpott, and Shah (2011: 14, 214); also see Armanios (2012) on evangelical mobilization in Egypt.

[15] See, for example, Juergensmeyer (2003); Fox (2002); Lijphart (1977). Similarly, Monica Duffy Toft (2007) finds religious civil wars to be more violent, last longer, and reoccur more frequently than secular civil wars.

[16] See Beissinger (2003); Kahn (2000); Treisman (1997); Evans (1997a); Sells (1996).

ARGUMENTS AND IMPLICATIONS

The central argument of this book is that even in repressive political settings, religious and regime actors have needs that converge in many ways and can develop mutually reinforcing and supportive relations. Although the interests of religious and political authority differ, each side has a set of resources at its disposal that can be offered to the other to minimize uncertainty and meet strategic needs. For instance, government officials may attempt to establish cooperative relations with religious communities as a means of preserving political power, governing more efficiently, and diffusing local conflicts. At the same time, religious leaders may seek vertical alliances with the regime to safeguard their survival, gain access to resources, and promote their spiritual agenda.

This book therefore moves beyond a domination-resistance explanation of religious-state relations and instead offers an interests-based theory of interaction. I argue that a combination of uncertainty, pressing needs, and transferable resources set the stage for unexpected and innovative partnerships to occur locally. When these conditions are present in authoritarian regimes, religious communities and their local overseers can be seen trading favors, offering promises of reciprocal support, and exchanging a variety of resources. Specifically, religious and political authority will bargain over the key issues of politics – namely, the distribution of money, power, and prestige. However, where these conditions do not apply, such as in extremely repressive regimes where there is no space for religious expression, in political contexts in which religious groups have already captured the state, or in locales where religious identities are linked to separatist movements, we would expect religious-state interaction to play out quite differently.[17]

This study of religion and authoritarianism seeks to make several contributions, both empirical and theoretical. The first is to detail the nature of religious-state relations in authoritarian regimes and the likelihood of conflict and cooperation between the two. Although it is widely recognized that religion and political authority interact, there is little empirical work that explores in a systematic or comparative way how these interactions take place across the authoritarian world and what the political consequences for those involved might be.[18] Therefore, one central task of this book is to theorize the conditions under which autocratic overseers support or suppress and politicize or depoliticize religious groups, and under what conditions they simply tolerate them.

---

[17] The central argument that religious and local regime actors choose cooperation over conflict should travel widely across the authoritarian world; however, this is not to suggest that context is irrelevant. The authoritarian club is diverse, and many regimes have wildly different political realities at the subnational level. Therefore, in deeply divided societies where religion overlaps with minority identity and Center-local struggles are ongoing, the arguments and analysis presented here may not apply.

[18] Notable exceptions include Grim and Finke (2011); Toft, Philpott, and Shah (2011); Marsh (2011); Gill (2008); Linz (1996 [2004]); Ramet (1998, 1992).

A second and equally important task is to present a clear and detailed account of how different religious organizations attempt to protect and promote their interests and values within restrictive environments. In accomplishing these two tasks, this book both brings a much-needed comparative perspective to the study of state-society relations under autocracy and provides a rare window into the micropolitics of contemporary authoritarianism. This book also takes an important empirical step toward providing a more systematic understanding of the various points of contact between religious groups and the state, or what Jose Casanova calls the "deprivatization" of religion – in which religion abandons its assigned place in the private sphere and enters the undifferentiated public sphere.[19] This step not only advances our theoretical understanding of the complex and intertwining relationship between religion and the state, but in the process also highlights the changing boundaries between public and private and cultural and political arenas of cooperation and contestation under authoritarian rule.

This book is also squarely situated in the theoretical debates of comparative and international politics on authoritarian resilience and durability. More specifically, this book weighs in on important questions, such as the following: Do religious groups function as a constraint on or partner to authoritarian power holders? Is the growth of religious associational life an indicator of weakness or sign of impeding crisis for authoritarian elites? Do religious groups contribute to political liberalization or the strengthening of authoritarian rule? Can they play both roles at the same time?

In addressing these and other questions, the arguments and evidence presented here build on a growing body of scholarship that emphasizes the innovative nature of authoritarian leaders – that is, rather than relying solely on domination and coercion to remain in power, autocrats are creative and innovative stewards of their power.[20] This book reveals that within the authoritarian bag of tricks is also cooperation – an instrument that rarely makes the headlines but that political elites frequently use to solidify their rule.[21] The findings of this study contribute to this literature in three distinct ways. One is by studying authoritarianism locally and shedding light on the inner workings of the contemporary authoritarian project. Another is by adding cooperation to the toolkit authoritarian leaders use to channel regime interest and maintain, if not enhance, their powers. The third is by bringing two groups of neglected actors to the discussion – namely, religious communities and local government

---

[19] Casanova (1994: 65–6).

[20] See, for example, Koesel and Bunce (2013); Svolik (2012); Dobson (2012); Bueno de Mesquita and Smith (2011); Dickson (2011); Stockmann and Gallagher (2011); Hertog (2010); Lorentzen (2010); Wright (2010); Egorov, Guriev, and Sonon (2009); Gandhi and Lust-Okar (2009); Gandhi (2008); Shambaugh (2008); Brownlee (2007); Solomon (2007); Gandhi and Przeworski (2006); Lust-Okar (2006); Magaloni (2006); Albrecht (2005); Bueno de Mesquita and Downs (2005); Nathan (2003); Wintrobe (2001); Quinlivan (1999); Zartman (1998).

[21] But see Gandhi (2008) on cooperation in authoritarian regimes.

officials – and in the process detailing how and why autocratic elites reach out to these unlikely allies to support the authoritarian project.

At the same time, the book encourages us to rethink some of the key assumptions about the role of civil society under authoritarian rule. Instead of functioning as a force for destabilization and political change, this study demonstrates how and to what extent religious communities function as a partner to authoritarian power holders. It suggests that we should not hastily assume religious communities, as members of civil society, provide a counter to authoritarian leaders. Nor should we assume a robust associational life is necessarily an indicator of regime weakness or will have a democratizing effect.[22] Rather, this book reveals that local religious-state interaction can indirectly reinforce the authoritarian status quo from the bottom up.

COMPARING AUTOCRACY, COMPARING RELIGION

This study is explicitly comparative in nature and examines the politics of religion within two large and resilient authoritarian regimes, Russia and China. A paired comparison of these countries is instructive for several reasons.[23] First, Russia and China are both authoritarian regimes of great theoretical and empirical significance. They are influential in their regions, in the larger authoritarian community, and on the global stage. Second, they are both "difficult cases" to expect collaborative and mutually empowering relations between religious and state actors. Not only do these countries share histories of communism and extreme hostility toward religion, but their recent religious revivals have also been closely monitored and managed by government authorities.[24] Over the past three decades, Moscow and Beijing have established legal frameworks outlining acceptable religious confessions and setting parameters on religious

[22] Levine (2008: 214).
[23] On paired comparison, see Tarrow (2010, 1999); Brady and Collier (2004). On the importance comparing China to other countries, see Kennedy (2011), especially chapter 1.
[24] Several recent studies have remarked on the diverse revival of religious practices in these countries. See, for example, F. Yang (2012); Chau (2011, 2005a); Goossaert and Palmer (2011); Marsh (2011); Madsen (2011, 2010); Fielder (2010); Ashiwa and Wank (2009); Frose (2008, 2004); Malashenko and Filatov (2005); Bays (2003); Filatov (2002); Kipnis (2001); Dunch (2001); E. Chao (1999); J. Liu, Luo, and Yan (1999); Ying (1999); Kääriäinen (1998); Gautier (1997); K. K. Chan and Hunter (1994); Greeley (1994); Hunter and K.K. Chan (1993). Also, see C. K. Yang (1961) for earlier discussions of religion in China. For more on communist campaigns to eradicate religion in the Soviet Union and China, see Goossaert and Palmer (2011); Froese (2008); Knox (2005); Z. Luo (1991). Attempts to suppress religion, however, are not confined to the communist period. During the republican era in China, political elites argued that the eradication of "superstition" was crucial to making modern citizens; see Nedostup (2009); Wah (2004). Moreover, the pre-communist periods in both Russia and China were characterized with state-supported religious monopolies, marginalization of religious minorities, and the rise of religious groups that sought challenge imperial rule. See, for example, Seiwert (2003); Spence (1996); Shek (1990); Ter Haar (1992); Harrell and Perry (1982); Chesneaux (1972).

activities to ensure that religious groups align with regime interests. Religious policies have been written and revised to allow for greater religious expression while containing the expansion and limiting the independence of religious groups. Religious associational life is tolerated, but never as entirely independent or as an equal partner to the state.[25]

These same religious policies have also created an uneven playing field among religious actors across both countries. In Russia, federal laws have created a hierarchy of religions with the Orthodox Church regaining its pre-revolutionary position of power with full legal protections and access to special state subsidies. Other religious communities, such as Muslims and Jews, are classified in a second tier as "traditional religions," which grants them legal protection but limited access to government benefits. All other religious groups are relegated to a third tier of "foreign religions," receiving only a pro forma guarantee of freedom of worship and no state support. Here, the implication is that religious groups farther down the hierarchy are more likely to face marginalization from both the state and the protected Orthodox majority.

The Chinese state is considerably more restrictive. Government policies limit legal religious activities to five traditions – Buddhism, Taoism, Islam, Protestantism, and Catholicism – and the regime has institutionalized patriotic associations to oversee each religion. Religious communities operating outside of these faiths and state-sponsored associations have no legal protections, are subject to state persecution, and must often operate underground.[26] In addition, some religious traditions in China are viewed with greater suspicion than others. Christianity, in particular, is closely associated with national victimization during the late nineteenth century; whereas Buddhism, and to a lesser degree Taoism, have positioned themselves as having deep, historic ties integral to Chinese culture.[27]

A Russia-China comparison is additionally instructive because the management of religion in both countries is a local game.[28] Although Moscow and Beijing have introduced legal frameworks of religious activity, it is at the local

---

[25] See Marsh (2011); Fox (2008: 167–9, 189–91); Spiegel (2004); Potter (2003); Elliott and Corrado (1999); Witte and Bourdeaux (1999); Gunn (1999).

[26] There are several religious traditions operating outside of state-defined parameters in China; see F. Yang (2006). On underground Protestants, see Koesel (2013); Vala (2009); Wielander (2009); J. Yu (2008); Vala and O'Brien (2007); Kindopp (2004b); F. Yang (2005). On the Catholic Church, see Madsen (1998); Leung (1992). On popular religious communities, see Chau (2005a); Bruun (2003).

[27] On the cultural positing of Buddhism and Taoism, see Ji (2012–13: 21–22); Ashiwa and Wank (2009: 11–12); F. Yang (2004: 114); on Chinese victimization, see Gries (2007).

[28] There is considerable literature suggesting the importance of local politics in both Russia and China. See, for example, Gel'man and Ross (2010); Ruble, Koehn, and Popson (2001); Oakes (2000); S. Li and Tang (2000); Stoner-Weiss (1999); Petro (1999); Treisman (1999, 1997); Gladney (1998); Stoner-Weiss (1997); Goodman (1995); Jia and Lin (1994); Shue (1988).

level where the political management of religion largely takes place – and as a consequence, where the relationship between the state and religion is defined. For instance, across Russia and China, it is local officials who grant permission for the construction of a new mosque, church, or temple; decide whether religious communities are eligible for state funding for the reconstruction of religious landmarks; and even determine whether religious activities, such as tent revivals and the public showings of films, are legal and protected by the law or "cultlike" and subject to suppression.[29] It is also the case that the strength of religious associational life is often the greatest at the local level – here religion is most embedded in the community, the distance to those in power is reduced, and religious actors have an increased possibility of becoming important political players.[30] Thus, religious-state interaction in these countries is most evident and observable locally.

Russia and China also share a number of differences that provide analytical leverage in explaining when and why religious and political authority cooperate or collide. To start with, they have distinct political cultures and belong to different "civilizations"; furthermore, their divergent pathways from communism have resulted in the development of very different types of authoritarianism.[31] Russia's sharp break with communism and dual transition toward liberal democracy and capitalism has been followed by what can best be described as a process of de-democratization under Vladimir Putin – economic and political power has been consolidated in the executive branch, one party has a monopoly on political institutions, opposition is rarely tolerated, elections are orchestrated rather than competitive, elected officials take their cues from the Kremlin, and civil society is kept on a short leash. Russia, in effect, has transitioned into a "competitive authoritarian" political system that maintains democratic procedures without true democratic practices.[32] In contrast, China has not deviated from classic authoritarian politics in the post-Mao era. The Chinese Communist Party (CCP) has maintained a monopoly on political power and ensured the continuity of borders by reimagining itself and deemphasizing the role of ideology.[33] Thus, Russia and China are both

---

[29] See Potter (2003); Elliott and Corrado (1999); Witte and Bourdeaux (1999).

[30] Brook and Frolic (1997: 11).

[31] Huntington (1993); Freedom House ranks Russia as "partially free" from 1991 through 2004 and "not free" from 2005 through 2013. During this period, China is consistently rated as "not free." Freedom House scores are available at http://www.freedomhouse.org (last accessed August 13, 2013).

[32] Levitsky and Way (2010); Taylor (2011).

[33] As Richard Madsen (1993: 183) reminds us, "even though the communist party still governs China, and may do so for quite some time . . . it is ideologically dead: it can no longer plausibly claim to represent a historical vanguard, and to stay in power it must adopt economic policies that contradict its basic principles." Also see Shambaugh (2008: 6) on the eclecticism of the Chinese state.

similar and different – a combination that is especially useful for theorizing about religious-state interaction and generalizing across diverse authoritarian contexts.

COMPARING RELIGIONS, COMPARING CASES

The chapters that follow draw on twenty-eight months of fieldwork in Russia and China. A detailed discussion of the methodology, data collection, sources, and challenges of conducting research in authoritarian contexts is included in Appendix A. Because Russia and China are both large and plural author-itarian regimes, this study employs two additional levels of comparison: a within-country comparison of four cities – Nizhny Novgorod, Kazan, Shang-hai, and Changchun; and an interreligious comparison of Christianity, Islam, Buddhism, Taoism, Judaism, folk religions, and new religious movements. These additional layers of comparison provide four distinct advantages. One is to promote greater generalizabilty of the findings. A second is to control for country and regional variation. A third is to address in a more systematic way how and when political elites and religious groups cooperate and when and why cooperation breaks down. A final advantage is to evaluate which religious actors are most successful at establishing close relations with those in power and which religions are left behind.

The four cases in this study were selected because they vary on several dimen-sions, including the degree of political openness, local government autonomy, and religious composition.[34] In terms of the last factor, each locale has regis-tered religious communities that operate alongside a number of unregistered ones. These are religious communities that, for various reasons, refuse (or are denied) registration from the state and operate without legal protections. In this study, interviews with unregistered groups are included, but they are far less systematic for understandable reasons and therefore less amenable to draw-ing generalizations. Thus, the arguments and analysis of the book are based primarily on religious communities operating in the public sphere – that is, religious groups that are registered or seeking registration with the state.

Among the four cases, Nizhny Novgorod, Russia (formerly known as Gorky), is located approximately 250 miles east of Moscow on the Volga River and is the capital of the Volga Federal District.[35] Because of its defense indus-tries, Nizhny Novgorod was a "closed" city for both foreigners and citizens until the early 1990s. The city, however, remains an important industrial center with a focus on industrial fabrication, chemical production, and automobile manufacturing. The municipal government is elected but is largely dominated by the United Russia party (*Edinaja Rossija*) and maintains close ties to the

---

34 On subnational comparisons, see Hurst (2010).
35 The Volga Federal District is one of the eight federal districts of the Russian Federation estab-lished in 2000.

Kremlin. The religious landscape is diverse, including Orthodox Christianity (Russian Orthodox and Old Believers), Islam, Judaism, Buddhism, Catholicism, and a variety of Protestant denominations. The Orthodox Church represents the largest religious entity and claims roughly 60 to 70 percent of the local population.[36] The second largest religious community is the Tatar-Muslims, who make up less than 20 percent of the population.

Kazan, the capital city of the autonomous Republic of Tatarstan and the homeland of the Tartar minority, offers a second point of comparison in Russia. In contrast with Nizhny, Tatarstan has had a much more contentious relationship with Moscow. In the 1990s, a Tatar nationalist movement called for secession from Russia and successfully negotiated a power-sharing arrangement with the Center that granted the republic exceptional privileges, including lower tax remittances to Moscow, autonomy over Tatarstan's oil resources, greater protection of property, and exemptions from military service for Tatar men.[37] In Kazan, the religious profile is roughly balanced between Tatar Muslims, who make up more than 52 percent of the population, and Russian Orthodox Christians, who represent 40 percent. In addition to large Muslim and Orthodox populations, Kazan is also home to numerous Protestant denominations, Catholics, Old Believers, Baha'is, and Jews.

In China, the diversity and administrative autonomy of Shanghai makes it an ideal case for exploring religious and authoritarian relations. Religious practices draw from all five official religions (Buddhism, Taoism, Islam, Catholicism, and Protestantism), and there are also flourishing cultural and folk traditions as well as unregistered Protestants and Catholics. Shanghai has also been at the leading edge of local religious reforms in China; in 1996, the city implemented additional regulations for the management of growing religiosity and protection of religious activities.[38] Moreover, Shanghai has been at the forefront of economic reforms and political liberalization in China; this openness has translated into an influx of foreign investment and tourism, making the city of more than twenty million one of the most populous and arguably the most cosmopolitan in the country. Administratively, Shanghai is equivalent to a province in China, consisting of eighteen districts and one county. To facilitate comparison among the four cities, I follow the administrative divisions and focus on the relationship between religious and district-level (*diqu*) government actors.

Changchun, located in Jilin province in the northeast corner of China, offers a final comparison for this study. The religious landscape includes four of the

---

[36] In terms of the number of functioning Orthodox churches, Nizhny is third in the country after Moscow and St. Petersburg; see "O religioznyh konfessijah" (1997: 3).

[37] Solnick (1996).

[38] See, for example, "Regulations of Shanghai Municipality on Religious Affairs," adopted at the 23rd Session of the Standing Committee of the 10th Shanghai Municipal People's Congress on November 30, 1995, and amended April 21, 2005.

five official religions – Buddhism, Islam, Catholicism, and Protestantism – and
the religious revival is considerably more muted than in Shanghai. What makes
Changchun an interesting site of religious variation, however, is the significant presence of unregistered (and therefore illegal) religious groups. Falun
Gong, the quasi-spiritual movement mentioned at the start of this chapter,
originated in the province and, despite extensive repression, still maintains
a presence. Additionally, the unregistered Protestant community has built a
dense and thriving religious network with transnational linkages. Changchun
also provides an important economic and political contrast to Shanghai. With
a largely industrial and agricultural economy, the city has experienced a more
gradual approach to economic development, and political elites are much more
dependent on Beijing for support. To summarize: the political, economic, and
religious variation of these four locales make them ideal testing grounds for
a comparison of how local authorities manage religious groups and how religious entities engage the authoritarian state to become important political and
economic players.

PLAN OF THE BOOK

The plan of this book and summary of arguments are as follows. Chapter 2,
"Religion and State Games," presents an interests-based theory of religious-
state interaction in authoritarian regimes, showing how the relationship turns
on a combination of uncertainty, needs, and resources. Chapter 3, "Regulating the Religious Marketplace," traces the central laws and policies in Russia
and China pertaining to religion and religious freedom since the mid-1980s.
This chapter details how these policies create more space for religious freedom,
while at the same time empower local authorities to manage religious groups
according to different standards. The next two chapters draw on fieldwork
to flesh out the nature of religious-state interaction and the varying degrees
of cooperation, compliance, and control. The result is usually cooperation,
but conflict occurs as well. Chapter 4 "The Political Economy of Religious
Revival," expands on the bargaining games that revolve around money, and
Chapter 5, "The Politics of Faith, Power, and Prestige," considers cooperation over nonmaterial resources. Chapter 6, "Cooperation, Conflict, and the
Consequences," revisits the findings of the previous chapters and presents a
systematic comparison between the two countries and among the four case
studies. I conclude by identifying the implications of this study for research in
comparative and international politics.

2

Religion and State Games

Uncertainty is a fundamental condition of authoritarian politics.

– Andres Schedler[1]

The interaction between religion and politics at the local level is complex, given the interests of religious and political authorities to ensure their survival and expand influence amid the institutional fluidity and ambiguity – indeed, the sheer uncertainty – that characterizes many authoritarian regimes. This chapter analyzes the politics of religion in such contexts by laying out an interests-based theory of local government and religious interaction. This framework places mutual cooperation and interdependence at the center of religious and regime relations. I argue that at the local level – where the political management of religion takes place and the strength of religious associational life resides – a strategic process of exchange takes place in which innovative government officials and ambitious religious leaders barter resources and negotiate the rules of their relationship.[2] As with most bargaining processes, each side seeks to maximize its interests and discovers that such goals are frequently best met through collaboration. Although conflict can certainly occur, there is ample room for mutual empowerment.

The chapter begins by introducing the underlying motives behind religious-state bargaining, suggesting the give-and-take dynamic is driven by a combination of uncertainty, needs, and resources. The next section lays out some of the various forms collaborative arrangements can take. Here we find that

---

[1] Schedler (2013: 28).

[2] I use the terms "local government" and "local regime" to refer to government officials and bureaucrats in Nizhny Novgorod, Kazan, and Changchun. However, because Shanghai is administratively equivalent to a province in China, the local level refers to district governments in the larger Shanghai municipality.

religious-state interaction tends to center on the core issues of politics: money, power, and prestige. The chapter concludes by presenting a series of arguments suggesting when religious-state collaboration is likely and where its limitations lie.

RELIGION AND RATIONALITY

In constructing an interests-based theory of religious-state interaction, there is little doubt that autocratic elites are instrumental and take action to entrench their powers; however, it is not necessarily obvious why religious communities follow a similar decision-making calculus.[3] Religion after all is about faith, and religious actors are motivated by issues that are difficult for social scientists to observe and analyze, such as the desire for eternal salvation or achieving nirvana.[4] Nevertheless, a rational choice framework has gained currency in the study of religion and politics.[5]

This approach is guided by several key assumptions. One is that although religious communities are ideologically motivated by otherworldly concerns, they are also practically constrained by the real world – churches must be built, bureaucratic permits obtained, ministers paid, and charities staffed.[6] Therefore, a rabbi may pray for the construction of a new temple, but she must also seek donations and submit the necessary paperwork before breaking ground. A second assumption is that religious groups are as rational and goal-oriented as their secular peers. They have well-defined preferences, weigh the costs and benefits of potential action, and choose strategies that will allow them to pursue their goals with the fewest number of constraints.[7] Of course, the objectives of religious organizations may differ significantly from secular ones; they may be centered on growing the faith and fervor, sidelining their competition, or advancing society in a more sacred direction.[8] Finally, a rational-actor framework is appropriate particularly when studying religious entities in the political realm because they are generally seen as highly disciplined organizations; united by shared values and solidarities; often have clearly recognized and respected

---

[3] On the assumption of rationality and strategic calculations of authoritarian rulers, see Svolik (2012); Dobson (2012); Bueno de Mesquita and Smith (2011); Wintrobe (2007); Besley and Kudamatsu (2007); Bueno de Mesquita et al. (2003).

[4] Gill (2008: 27–30).

[5] Rational choice theory has become one of the dominant approaches in the study of religion, see, for example, F. Yang (2011, 2010, 2006); a special issue of *Religion* (2011) devoted to rational choice and religion in China; Berman (2009); Gill (2008, 1998); Lang, Chan, and Ragvald (2005); Finke and Stark (2005); Warner (2000); Stark and Finke (2000); Iannaccone (1997, 1995); Young (1997). More generally, on this approach, see Tsebelis (1990); Arrow (1951: 3). Rational choice has also been applied to explain the mobilization of other ideational groups, see Hardin (1995). On the concern of treating religious groups as rational actors, see, Alles (2009); Bruce (2008); Neitz and Mueser (1997); Chaves (1995); Mainwaring (1986); Olson (1965).

[6] See especially Gill (2008: 29–30; 1998: 55–6).

[7] Gill (2008: 201).

[8] Becker (1976).

leadership; and members tend to defer to religious leaders and allow them to speak on behalf of group interests. As a result, the assumption of a single actor is appropriate.

These guiding assumptions are a useful starting point for building a theory of religious-state interaction under autocracy. The arguments advanced here assume that religious groups and local political authorities are both rational and strategic in the pursuit of their interests and goals. Just as autocratic elites are concerned with staying in political power and neutralizing opposition, religious leaders are likewise concerned with survival and limiting intrusions. By this, I do not mean to suggest that issues of faith and theology are unimportant and do not influence a religious groups' behavior or that economic goals necessarily trump spiritual ones.[9] Rather, the point is that when politics is repressive and religious liberty limited, religious entities are *also* acutely concerned with securing the future of their community. An interests-based framework is instructive because it elevates the strategic interests and political behavior of religious actors, and in doing so focuses on the nature of their relationship with those in power. What comes to the forefront then is what religious and political authorities want and can get from the other; whether cooperation or conflict is the optimal form of interaction for meeting these concerns; and finally the purpose, processes, and consequences of their interaction. Addressing the theoretical reasoning behind this interaction is the focus of the next section.

THEORIZING RELIGION, THEORIZING AUTHORITARIANISM

In authoritarian regimes, the interaction between religious and local political authorities can take numerous forms, but it is essentially a strategic process of exchange.[10] This exchange is driven by a combination of uncertainty, needs, and resources. First, each side is faced with uncertainty and harbors suspicions of what the other side might do – for instance, a local government fears religious groups may encourage instability, incite rebellion, or invite foreign influence; and religious communities fear that those in power may seek to contain, co-opt, or simply crush their activities.

Second, religious groups and their authoritarian overseers have certain needs that must be met for their survival and prosperity. Local political authorities may be concerned with safeguarding political power, collecting revenue, and enlarging their base of support; whereas religious groups may be focused on attracting new members, expanding places of worship, and promoting their spiritual message. Here, it is important to note that these needs are not necessarily competing, but can be mutually supportive and symmetrical.

---

[9] In fact, the empirical chapters reveal how religious ideas can constrain religious-state interaction – for example, some Old Believers communities refuse government registration on spiritual grounds but nevertheless endorse politicians and even provide voting lists to members.

[10] On cooperation as strategic exchange, see Milner (1997); Parsons (1951).

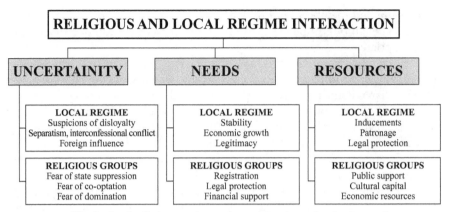

FIGURE 2.1. The logic of religious and state interaction in authoritarian regimes.

Finally, each side has a distinct set of resources at its disposal that can be offered to the other to help meet key needs. Local authorities may promise religious communities special subsidies in return for support of state policies, and religious leaders may "bless" political elites to secure protection and influence in political decision making.

As summarized in Figure 2.1, although the two sets of actors certainly have different interests and objectives, the nature of their relations can be cooperative because each side has the ability to provide resources needed by the other and can maximize its own interests through cooperative activities. To be clear, religious-state cooperation does not imply that political authorities have suddenly "found religion" or that religious communities have forsaken their faith. Rather, both parties make decisions to best navigate the authoritarian context. Cooperation, in short, is strategic.

The Logic of Collaboration: The Local Regime

What compels authoritarian political elites to seek alliances with religious actors? How does collaboration serve the interests of the regime? In authoritarian regimes, political actors are incentivized to collaborate with religious communities for the three concerns outlined above: uncertainty, needs, and resources. Here, it is important to recognize that the core interests of authoritarian politicians are not unlike those of their democratic counterparts. At the top of their list of concerns is the tenure of their office.[11] Holding on to power in an authoritarian regime, however, is far more complicated. As Andreas Schedler writes, "authoritarian rulers have a twin problem of uncertainty. They have a problem of *security*. They can never lean back and relax. They have to continually prevent, detect, and contain threats to their hold on

---

[11] Tullock (1987); Geddes (1999: 129).

power. And they have a problem of *opacity*. They can never know for sure how good they are at preventing, detecting, and containing threats to their survival in power."[12] This twin problem of uncertainty means authoritarian rulers are notoriously insecure.

Although it is hardly surprising that authoritarian leaders are anxious and apprehensive about their tenure, I argue that this same insecurity is present among local political elites. Not only must local officials be careful to satisfy authoritarian elites above, they must also accommodate their own local selectorate to maintain stability and promote economic growth.[13] This can be particularly difficult when political winds shift frequently, information is incomplete, institutions are absent or not well defined, and there are high stakes associated with political, economic, and social change. To navigate this uncertainty, local governments can draw on a number of familiar instruments from the authoritarian toolkit, such as coercion, containment, and co-optation. Many of these tools are well known to observers of contemporary authoritarianism; however, there is another instrument that also serves the interests of the regime but receives little attention: cooperation.

Cooperation seems like an unlikely tool for authoritarian overseers. Cooperation rarely makes the headlines, and there is a general assumption that authoritarian rulers rely on coercion to rule.[14] And yet cooperation provides several advantages for local political elites. One is that most government officials place a premium on stability and economic growth, which they take to be interdependent. Cooperation with religious entities allows local governments to draw on a religious groups' diverse resources to achieve these strategic goals. A benevolent official, for instance, may court religious communities to attract investment, which can then energize the local economy, create jobs, and enhance tax revenue. A more predatory official may view religious organizations as little more than opportunities for rent seeking. However, whether an autocrat is benign or malevolent, cooperation is a tactical decision. As Jennifer Gandhi writes, all authoritarian elites "must solicit the cooperation of those they rule. Even if their interests lie only in accumulating wealth and power, incumbents will have more to amass if their countries are affluent and orderly."[15] Thus, religious-state cooperation has obvious returns.

Another advantage is that cooperation may lighten the governing load of those in power. A mosque, for example, may take over some of the obligations of the local government such as providing charity programs or other public

[12] Schedler (2013: 21), *italics* in original. For important discussions of uncertainty within authoritarian regimes and the implications, see Bunce (2013); Schedler (2013); Stern and Hassid (2012); Kuran (1991); and O'Donnell and Schmitter (1986).

[13] See Bueno de Mesquita et al. (2003) on the selectorate and Landry (2008) on the importance of satisfying higher-ranking officials.

[14] But also see Gandhi (2008) on cooperation and Jowitt (1992: 88–120) on the strategy of inclusion in authoritarian regimes.

[15] Gandhi (2008: xvii–xviii).

services, which can be extremely beneficial when government capacity is limited and political elites are under budgetary constraints. Milton Esman and Norman Uphoff explain that government actors have powerful incentives to seek partnerships with associational groups "not necessarily to control them – though this may be either a motive or a consequence – but to enable the agency to perform its activities more effectively."[16] In fact, religious groups may be better equipped than the local government in operating social welfare programs because of their dense on-the-ground networks and organizational resources.[17] Moreover, when trust in government is low, religious actors may be particularly effective because their motives are seen as more altruistic and less corrupt than regime representatives.

Religious-state cooperation may also help local political elites protect themselves and their position. Local government officials may court religious communities to legitimate their rule, build trust among citizens, and define local identity. It is important to note that even in authoritarian settings, state actors are accountable to citizens.[18] Although competitive elections may not be in place, local authorities have powerful incentives to reach out to a diverse body of constituents to expand coalitions of support and maintain local stability.[19] Indeed, if local authorities are seen as partners to, or at least accommodating of, religious communities, they may indirectly enhance their basis of support by borrowing a religious group's "sacred resources."[20]

In the scenario in which local government authorities are suspicious of religion subverting the state, a strategy of direct engagement may have the additional benefit of keeping religious groups dependent (if not docile) through inducements. Local officials have a variety of resources they can offer religious groups to contain them and keep them supportive of those in political power, including bureaucratic stamps necessary for registration, subsidies for the reconstruction of religious buildings, interest-free loans, tax-exempt status, and tariff privileges. Other inducements more closely resemble special privileges, such as legal and political recognition, blessings of the state, ability to pressure the religious competition, and access to public schools and prisons. In these cases, patronage extends the reach of the local government into religious organizations and demands compliance in return. Patronage is particularly useful because local authorities are able to neutralize potential threats, ensure a stable distribution of local power, and establish the state as the source of a religious group's legitimacy. In subsidizing religious groups, the local government also advertises the fact that religious communities receive benefits from the state. Again, the very appearance of support can be important because

---

[16] Esman and Uphoff (1984: 39), quoted in Foster (2001: 92).
[17] On these points, see Foster (2001).
[18] Tsai (2007).
[19] See Wilkinson (2004); Horowitz (1991).
[20] Seul (1999); Stark and Bainbridge (1985).

local officials are wary of fostering conditions that may contribute to mobilization against the regime. Local governments do not want to "overstep bounds between what religious persons will tolerate and treatment or social conditions that will provoke believers into challenging secular authority."[21]

Finally, and as alluded to earlier, cooperative relations between religious and political authorities are preferred because the alternatives can be costly. Coercion is expensive, can invite unwanted scrutiny from above, and may sow the seeds for anti-regime mobilization and the politicization of religion.[22] Coercive mechanisms of the state also require local authorities to devote considerable financial and human resources to monitor and police religious communities, without resolving the question of the efficacy of repression or addressing the unintended consequences. After all, an "opiate of the people" approach did not eradicate religious beliefs in either Russia or China, but drove believers underground until the political space reopened in the 1980s.[23] It is striking to note that even after decade-long campaigns against religion, up to 80 percent of Russians identify with a religious tradition and that China is home to more than 300 million religious believers – meaning that people of faith outnumber communist party members over four to one.[24]

The Logic of Collaboration: Religious Communities

What compels religious communities to seek links with authoritarian political elites? How does cooperation help religious groups achieve their strategic goals and spiritual interests? Again, it is important to remember that even within authoritarian regimes, religious-state relations are interactive, not unidirectional. The same combination of uncertainty, needs, and resources shaping the interest of authoritarian political elites act as powerful motivators for religious groups. Like political elites, religious groups also face constraints,

---

[21] Brown (1996: 79).

[22] Svolik (2012); Gill (2008); Besley and Kudamatsu (2007); Philpott (2007); Haber (2006); Wintrobe (1990).

[23] Powell (1967: 367).

[24] In practice, Russia is home to more than 120 million Orthodox Christians, 14 million Muslims, 1.5 million Protestants, 900,000 Buddhists, 600,000 Catholics, 400,000 Lutherans, and 230,000 Jews. Lutherans are generally considered in a different category from other Protestant denominations because they are closely associated with the ethnic German population in the Saratov region; see Filatov and Lunkin (2005); Kääriäinen (1998); Burdo and Filatov (2005: 107–18). In China, a 2006 government-sponsored survey estimated 31.4 percent of citizens (aged 16 and older) are religious believers, marking a sharp increase in previous government reports that estimated 200 million adherents (in 2002) and 100 million adherents (in 1997); see J. Wu (2007). Although these figures are impressive, other surveys indicate these estimates are too low. The Pew Research Center (2012), for example, estimates at least 640 million people are religiously affiliated in China, with almost 300 million linked to folk religions. On the difficulty of estimating religious believers in China, see Madsen (2011); Bays (2003: 491–2); F. Yang (2006).

information deficits, and must navigate tight political spaces. As a result, they seek more predictable and supportive relations with those in power. In the extreme, this can mean that religious groups try to capture the state; however, the more common course is to pursue alliances and coalitions with those in power. Religious groups seek vertical ties; they strive for cooperative not combative relations; and they solicit neutral and stable relationships with the state. This does not mean that religious groups would not want greater autonomy or have abandoned their theological missions, but because politics is repressive and religious liberties are limited, they seek alliances to secure survival and spiritual prosperity.

For religious communities, friendly relations are important because local officials and bureaucrats determine the rules of the game. They are the gatekeepers of daily religious life; they set the parameters on legal religious expression; they control entry into the religious market; and they have the discretionary power to revoke religious freedoms by labeling groups as cults or threats to social stability. However, it is not simply that local authorities have the power to make life difficult for religious actors, but also that they control important resources that allow religious groups to meet and maintain their spiritual goals. For instance, regime elites can help grow the faith by erecting new houses of worship, put pressure on religious rivals, and even prop up a religious monopoly.[25] In regard to this last concern, Rodney Stark and William Bainbridge point out that regime alliances are necessary because "a religious monopoly can be achieved only by reliance on the coercive powers of the state."[26]

Here, it is also important to note that the argument that religious groups will seek alliances rather than distance from those in power is in fact a well-identified strategy of secular associational groups operating under similar constraints.[27] Kevin O'Brien writes of civil society groups openly embedding themselves with the powerful and resourceful, even if doing so means sacrificing autonomy: "[t]hey realize that independence at this point means irrelevance and that future development demands sensitivity to existing power relations."[28] Similarly, Ma Qiusha explains that "having close ties with governmental organizations or high officials helps NGOs obtain approval for registration, gain protection from all kinds of trouble, and often win access to state financial, personnel, and information resources."[29] Likewise, Amaney Jamal finds that in political

---

[25] Of course, not all faiths will have identical goals. Proselytizing religions, such as Christianity and Islam, may seek to increase their followers whereas nonproselytizing religions, such as Buddhism and Judaism, may attempt to maintain current numbers or prevent defection to other religions. For a more detailed discussion of this dynamic, see Gill (1998).

[26] Stark and Bainbridge (1985: 508); also Wood (1999).

[27] On the willing incorporation of Chinese associations, see also Foster (2001); Ma (2006); White et al. (1996).

[28] O'Brien (1994: 101).

[29] Ma (2006: 10).

contexts in which there is little room for civil society organizations to exist outside of government networks, associational groups must seek an insider position if they hope to produce change.[30] Thus, religious groups, like their secular peers, favor collaboration over conflict because local governments have the resources needed to ensure an interrelated set of goals, whether this means evangelizing, increasing the collective spiritual good, or minimizing state intrusion.[31] Therefore, it is wrong to assume that close religious-state relations are a sign of co-optation or manipulation by the authoritarian state over religious actors. Indeed, there is the possibility, albeit a small one, that religious groups are the ones doing the manipulating.[32]

It is finally important to recognize that religious communities that do opt out of the bargaining games (even when the motivations are spiritually based and benign) invite state scrutiny at best and at worst face open repression. Opting out of the public sphere also introduces two practical concerns for religious groups. One is that rival religions may quickly and gladly fill the vacuum. The other is that it may be more difficult to recruit new members. For example, unregistered religious groups cannot openly advertise their activities and must change the times and locations of their services to avoid detection; there can also be inflated costs for members to join a group not condoned by the state.[33] Opting out of the public sphere, in other words, raises a number of practical concerns for religious communities and their potential for growth.

DYNAMICS OF COLLABORATION: MONEY, POWER, AND PRESTIGE

The chapter thus far has argued that the relationship between religious groups and their authoritarian overseers is influenced by a combination of uncertainty, needs, and resources. Although the two sets of actors certainly have different interests and objectives, there is considerable room for cooperation because each side can provide resources needed by the other, and thus maximize their own strategic goals through collaborative activities. Again, I do not wish to suggest that conflict does not occur or that the two sides are equal players. Rather, the point is that religious groups are not necessarily under the thumb of authoritarian political elites nor are they passive actors in the bargaining games.

The introduction of bargaining games raises a number of questions about the actual dynamics of religious-state interaction. For instance: What do political and religious actors bring to the bargaining table and offer to one another? What are the short- and long-term consequences of the bargaining games? Do political elites risk or enhance their political futures through cooperation?

---

[30] Jamal (2007: 16–17).
[31] For a similar collaborative dynamic among black churches and local governments in the United States, see Owens (2007).
[32] Ma (2006: 10–11).
[33] Grim and Finke (2011: 7), but also see Wiktorowicz (2001).

Does cooperation weaken or strengthen the prophetic voice of religion? These questions serve as a guide for the remainder of the discussion, as well as fore-shadow the chapters to come. As we will discover, a wide range of resources may be exchanged between religious and political actors. However, the bargaining games tend to cluster around the core issues of politics – namely, the distribution of money, power, and prestige.

Money

Among the various points of contact between religious and local government actors, one central area of focus is around material concerns. Indeed, there is a cash nexus at the core of religious and local government relations where both sides use material resources as bargaining chips to achieve individual strategic goals.[34] Material resources, defined as the economic assets of an organization, are preferred because they tend to minimize confrontation and provide power-ful motivators to maintain cooperative and stable religious-state relations.

In practice, this means that local officials may offer a religious community government subsidies in return for public support of a government policy or law. Local bureaucrats may also reward religious communities with interest-free loans, access to land and real estate conveniently located near public transportation (which is important for religious growth), and building per-mits to enlarge places of worship. Although secular policies in authoritarian regimes (including Russia and China) generally prohibit government repre-sentatives from supporting and subsidizing religion directly, there are several ways to navigate around these restrictions. One strategy is to designate places of worship as a cultural relic in need of state protection. This designation is important because it allows, for instance, the local Ministry of Culture to legally subsidize a religious building under the auspices of preserving cultural artifacts and historical architecture. Another innovative strategy is to rename a religious building as a museum or cultural center. As a state-protected cul-tural relic or museum, a designated religious site is eligible for direct gov-ernment support by way of shifting rationales from the religious to the more desensitized secular – that is, cultural, municipal, and even national develop-ment.[35]

Although the pockets of religious communities are generally not as deep as those of the local governments, they do bring important material resources to the bargaining table that are sought after by those in power. Religious groups may host religious festivals and fairs that can attract thousands of visitors (both pilgrims and tourists) and bring significant revenue to their locales. At temple festivals, for example, local authorities not only collect taxes from vendors and receive a share of admission fees but also benefit in more informal ways such

---

[34] My thanks to Rob Culp for suggesting the expression "cash nexus."
[35] For a similar dynamic, see Oldmixon (2005).

as by receiving "free tickets, good food, cigarettes, and liquor."[36] A religious group may even offer to take over some of the welfare responsibilities of the state, such as providing charity programs and other social services. For the local regime, this can be an attractive arrangement because they are able to shift scarce resources elsewhere. Finally, religious communities may tap into the financial resources of their believers to encourage faith-based investment, which can be extremely lucrative in terms of generating tax revenues and providing informal rents for local officials.

Power and Prestige

There is also ample room for religious-state bargaining around issues of power and prestige. In the bargaining games, religious groups and their authoritarian overseers exchange a variety of nonmaterial resources, including access to organizational networks and the sharing of symbols and information. In practice, political elites may invite religious leaders into policy-making circles, actively participate in religious rituals, invoke religious symbolism, and even publically privilege some faiths over others. At the same time, religious leaders may endorse a politician for an upcoming election, speak in favor of a government policy to their followers, and bless the state and its earthly leaders. The rationale behind nonmaterial collaboration is straightforward: political elites collaborate with religious communities to maintain stability, increase legitimacy, and appease public demands; and religious groups build vertical alliances to secure their own pressing needs, such as ease in the registration process, promises of protection, or assistance advancing their religious mandate.

It is striking to note that religious groups are comparatively rich in nonmaterial resources and can offer a surprising amount of prestige, primarily in the form of cultural capital to local governments. For instance, endorsements of state policies by religious leaders can bolster local government legitimacy because religious leaders are often assumed to be trustworthy pillars of society and above politics. Close relations with faith-based communities may also broaden the base of support for secular political elites, particularly among those who hold religious values dear.

In nonmaterial bargaining games, the stakes of cooperation are considerably higher. In material exchanges there is a direct transaction of goods and services and the outcomes are clear: religious groups that pave roads are rewarded with registration. The exchange of power and prestige, by contrast, is far less transparent and may lead to unintended consequences. Not only is it illegal for local authorities to directly empower religious groups, but there is also the danger of local state capture by a religious tradition. Moreover, once religious leaders enter the political realm, they may also be difficult to remove. Therefore,

---

[36] Chau (2003: 44). Temple fairs are generally held at least three times each year, at the birth and death of the temple deity and during the Lunar New Year.

political elites must carefully calculate the opportunity costs of cooperation with religious leaders. Cooperation is a risk, but a calculated one.

Of course, religious organizations face risks of their own. Cooperation with authoritarian overseers may disillusion and divide followers and weaken the moral authority of religious leaders, particularly if they are seen as being puppets of the regime and abandoning their spiritual mission for a political one. Thus, there are risks for both religious and political actors, but the risks (and potential rewards) are considerably higher when power and prestige are the focus of their concern.

ARGUMENTS AND EXPECTATIONS

The interests-based theory I have outlined here suggests that religious and state actors exchange a combination of resources to achieve strategic needs and goals. For local governments, collaboration reduces uncertainty and may simplify the management of religious communities through a system of patronage or other mechanisms. Cooperation can soften the fear among political elites that religious groups will seek to challenge the legitimacy of the regime and incite instability. As a result of this softening, even more space may be available for religious expression. The bargaining games, moreover, can promote economic growth by enabling local authorities to harness the potential capital – monetary, cultural, and otherwise – of religious entities. For religious communities, collaboration is also preferred because the religious marketplace is tightly regulated and barriers to entry are high. Religious actors seek to develop close ties to the state not only for survival but also to secure resources to meet their spiritual goals and improve their position vis-à-vis other religious groups. Again, this is not to suggest that religious groups would not like greater autonomy, but within an authoritarian regime the options are often limited and religious groups are not locked in a fair fight.[37]

This interests-based framework also generates a number of hypotheses about when and where religious-state cooperation is likely to occur. The remainder of the chapter situates these expectations within the context of contemporary Russia and China – our laboratory for religious and authoritarian interaction – and discusses how the religious complexion of a region, resource endowments, restrictions on religion, and regime durability shape and constrain interests and actions.

Alliances for Support

As outlined in the foregoing sections, local authorities have powerful incentives to reach out to a diverse body of constituents to expand coalitions of support. Although competitive elections are not in place across most authoritarian regimes, the logic of political competition nevertheless applies. Therefore, we can expect the religious complexion of a region to influence religious-state

---

[37] Jamal (2007: 9).

interaction in several ways. When one religious community represents a large portion or majority of the population, controls a monopoly of belief in the region, or enjoys widespread popular legitimacy among the population, local elites will naturally turn to that majority for support.[38] The argument here is that religious monopolies tend to have the kinds of resources that local political elites seek: widespread support and resources to draw rents. As the religious complexion in a region shifts from homogeneous to plural, the incentives for local authorities to build coalitions among multiple religious communities, and especially among religious minorities, dissipate. Put simply, the willingness of local political elites to bargain with religious groups will depend on both the degree of religious pluralism and size of religious groups.

Resource Endowments: Material and Nonmaterial

A second important factor in the bargaining games is the resource endowments of religious communities, or what they bring to the bargaining table. Here, we assume that political authorities prefer to reach out to religious communities that will help them maximize profits and minimize costs. In the context of contemporary Russia and China, therefore, we would anticipate economic burdens to impact religious-state interaction. The recent decades of reform and restructuring have created more autonomous local governments in both countries, but often at the cost of greater financial responsibility for the provision of local public goods and services. However, given the limited capacity for taxation, low levels of bureaucratic development, and high levels of corruption, local governments can be severely constrained in their ability to provide these services.[39] Thus, we would expect local governments facing financial constraints to collaborate more with religious communities around material concerns.

At the same time, even when local governments are financially secure and not facing economic burdens, religious-state cooperation is preferable because it allows political elites to retain and redistribute resources elsewhere. Because poor and wealthy local governments both have incentives to cooperate with religious groups, attention should be placed on the specific resources religious actors bring to the bargaining table and their relative demand. Where religious groups are willing and able to fill in the gaps (for example, by opening a religious site for tourism, building roads, and staffing charities), they are tolerated and even courted by local officials because these commodities are in demand and can yield lucrative financial returns. More generally, religious communities

---

[38] A religious monopoly is present when one religious tradition dominates the local market and exercises influence over other religious communities with the help of the state.

[39] There are many systematic discussions of the challenges facing local governments in China and Russia. See, for example, Mertha (2009); Landry (2008); Tsai (2007); Pei (2006); Perry and Selden (2003); Steen and Gel'man (2003); Treisman (1999); Burawoy and Verdery (1999); Levy (1995); Jowitt (1992); Lieberthal (1992).

that are resource rich will be more sought after by local authorities than those that are resource poor, with the understanding that local regime sets both the market value and demand of any given resource.

In a similar vein, nonmaterial resources, such as the cultural and moral influence of religious groups, also have an impact on religious-state interaction. There is some evidence that post-Soviet and post-Mao leaders, like their predecessors, draw on forms of cultural capital to reformulate political legitimacy, strengthen national identity, and even encourage nationalism.[40] For instance, there is an increasing trend among China's leaders to speak of religious values helping to build a "harmonious society" and calls for the revival of "Holy Rus'" to resurrect national identity in Russia.[41] This turn to culture is not surprising in a context in which Marxist-Leninist and Maoist ideology have lost support and regime leaders are seeking alternative ways to legitimate their rule. To borrow from Ann Swidler, religion, unlike other repositories of meaning, has become part of the repertoire authoritarian leaders use for constructing new lines of action and building ideological legitimacy.[42]

In thinking about how nonmaterial cooperation plays out locally, we would expect religious-state cooperation to be more likely with religious groups that are considered to have deep reserves of cultural capital – that is religious organizations that are considered "insiders" rather than "outsiders." The distinction here is that religious insiders are groups that are indigenous or have deep, historic ties to a region, and religious outsiders are those that are seen as newcomers or groups with strong foreign connections. It follows, then, that religious insiders deeper cultural reserves lend themselves more easily to supporting nation-building projects. Religious insiders are also more likely to command loyalty among a larger portion of the population. In contrast, religious outsiders are disadvantaged because they do not have the same ties to national identity and may actually provoke suspicions of outside influence or manipulation from abroad. In the context of Russia, we would expect religious-state cooperation in Nizhny Novgorod to be dominated by the Orthodox Church because of its strong ties to national identity and the post-Soviet nation-building project, and religious-state cooperation in Tatarstan to be dominated by Muslims for similar reasons. In Changchun and Shanghai, none of the five official religious traditions are as closely linked to local (or national) identity-building narratives, and yet some religious traditions have more cultural capital than others. In the larger national context, Buddhism and Taoism are generally seen as being deeply engrained in Chinese culture, whereas Protestantism and Catholicism are portrayed as foreign faiths, a feature that hinders cooperation with the regime.

---

[40] See, for example, Shambaugh (2008) on cultural reimaginings of the Chinese Communist Party; Fagan (2013) on Russia.

[41] *Xinhua* (2013); Fagan (2013); Grove (2013).

[42] Swidler (1986).

The cultural capital of popular or local religions in China introduces an important nuance. Although these groups technically fall outside the five "normal" traditions identified by the state and tend to operate with ambiguous legal status, they are indigenous. Indeed, many popular religious groups possess greater cultural capital and popular legitimacy than the five official religions. Therefore, cooperation with popular and folk religions is possible and may be even preferable for local governments because of their insider status and rich reservoir of cultural capital they bring to the bargaining table.

Restricting Religion

The degree to which local governments regulate and restrict religious freedom is another important factor shaping the bargaining games. In authoritarian political systems, religious groups in the public sphere have incentives to seek alliances with the powerful and resourceful to achieve strategic goals and spiritual interests. When restrictions on associational life are high and religious liberty limited, religious groups are more likely to be dependent on the state for survival. Therefore, we would expect religious groups operating in the public sphere to seek linkages rather than distance from those in power because it allows them to secure the future and interests of their community. As regimes liberalize and restrictions are lessened – through new policies or other measures – religious groups will have fewer incentives to forge protective alliances and more opportunities for independence.

One caveat is in order: when a religious group establishes a monopoly, it is unlikely to walk away from such a privileged and powerful position even when the state is on a liberalizing trajectory.[43] In fact, one could imagine a religious monopoly actively working against greater religious liberty because it would lower the barriers to entry in the religious market and introduce unwanted competition.[44] It follows that because China is a more restrictive authoritarian system with greater constraints on religion and Russia a hybrid regime with fewer constraints, Chinese religious communities in the public sphere will more actively seek alliances for survival than religious groups in Russia. At the same time, we would also expect dominant religious communities, such as the Orthodox Church, to maintain linkages with those in power to preserve its hegemonic position.

Regime Durability, Regime Legitimacy

The prospects of religious-state bargaining must finally be understood within the context of the durability and legitimacy of the authoritarian regime. Here, I do not mean to suggest that religious groups have any special insights in

---

[43] Of course, it is an open question whether a liberalizing authoritarian regime would continue to support a religious monopoly.

[44] See, for example, Gill (2008: 44–6).

prophesying the collapse of authoritarian rule – such predictions are exceedingly rare even among students of authoritarian politics – simply that perceptions of regime durability and legitimacy influence religious-state interaction.[45] When religious communities see the regime as stable, the "only game in town," and likely to occupy this position for many years to come, we would expect religious leaders to seek alliances with those in power.[46] As regimes lose legitimacy – through internal splits, popular uprisings, excessive use of force against civilians, or by other means – religious groups will prefer greater distance from those in power. However, moving away from the authoritarian regime does not necessarily mean that religious groups will mobilize in opposition or push for more democratic outcomes. Rather, religious actors recognize the costs of cooperation and see their futures less tied to those in power. Again, the exception to this expectation rests with religious monopolies. A religious monopoly will be the last to defect from the regime because doing so will likely mean the end of their hegemonic status.

CONCLUSIONS

This chapter has sought to theorize the dynamics of religious and local regime relations in authoritarian regimes. The arguments advanced suggest that the nature of the contemporary authoritarian project generates uncertainty for religious and state actors, and the combination of symmetrical needs and transferable resources provides incentives for collaboration, rather than conflict. It is the desire to secure money, power, and prestige that informs local authorities' attitudes and behavior, and encourages cooperative innovation with religious communities. At the same time, it is religious groups' capability to attract and encourage capital, consolidate political power, and impart legitimacy to secular leaders that they leverage to their advantage. In this sense, religious groups and their autocratic overseers become strange bedfellows.

The underlying logic behind this argument – that mutual empowerment can be derived through unlikely alliances – is familiar to many students of politics. Scholars of American government may find patterns of religious-state cooperation similar to logrolling in democratic legislatures, in which elected officials from competing parties trade votes on separate issues for individual gain.[47] Like logrolling, religious-state interaction requires reciprocity, follows a quid pro quo logic, and allows for stability in political outcomes. Those more familiar with interest group politics and corporatism may also identify striking similarities.[48] Corporatist arrangements can parallel religious-state

---

[45] Kuran (1991).
[46] Linz and Stepan (1996: 5).
[47] Buchanan and Tullock (1974).
[48] The literature on corporatism is extensive, but it can be generally defined as "a pattern of interest group politics that is monopolistic, hierarchically ordered, and structured by the state"

bargaining games in that both are asymmetrical and the state is the dominant player exercising some degree of authority over organizational groups. However, rather than dominating organized labor (or religious communities), ruling elites instead prefer strategies of patronage to achieve desired outcomes, with the idea that state resources are granted to select, loyal constituents.[49] Moreover, like corporatist arrangements, religious groups in turn can learn from these exchanges, and apply the lessons of their interactions to future negotiations with local authorities. Here, it is also important to note that both parties can secure favorable outcomes through their interaction. Similar to the corporatist model, "the state and society relationship is based on achieving consensus and common goals, not a zero-sum struggle for power."[50] Finally, when tensions arise either in the process of corporatist or religious-state bargaining, the state tends to opt for a more quiet form of repression, such as excluding groups from subsidies rather than naked repression. As a result, excluded organizations – whether they be labor unions or Pentecostals – are informally marginalized and subsequently weakened because of reduced access to resources.

Religious-state relations in authoritarian regimes is also consistent with patterns of clientelism, in which interaction between patrons (autocrats) and clients (religious groups) are seen as durable and hierarchical but unequal.[51] Similar to patron-client relations, religious and political actors engage in a process of reciprocal exchange of goods and services. Where the bargaining games differ from clientelistic exchanges is in the underlying incentives for interaction that can be mutually empowering rather than exploitative. James C. Scott, for instance, writes of traditional patron-client relations as generally exploitative and "the patron is in a position to supply unilaterally goods and services which the potential client and his family need for their survival and well being."[52]

(Collier 1995: 135). On corporatist arrangements in the Soviet Union, see Bunce (1983). For discussions of corporatism in Latin America, see Schmitt (1984); Collier and Collier (1979); Schmitter (1974). On "democratic corporatism," see Katzenstein (1985). For a policy-centered approach, see Pontusson (1991); Schmitter (1990). On corporatism in China and the bargaining between local authorities and nonstate actors see, Dickson (2000); Walder (1994); Chan (1993); Oi (1992).

[49] Collier and Collier (1979).

[50] Dickson (2000: 532).

[51] There is a large and diverse literature on clientelism as a pattern of social interaction embedded in traditional societies; see especially Scott (1972); Lemarchand (1972). Recent scholarship has extended clientelistic frameworks to democratic politics; see Kitschelt and Wilkinson (2007); Piattoni (2001); Kitschelt (2000).

[52] Scott (1972: 125). Simona Piattoni's (2001) more nuanced conceptualization of clientelism as a political strategy is closer to religious-state interaction outlined here. She explains patron-client relations as "exchange relations whose terms depend on the relative power of the parties, in turn dependent on the contextual circumstances that affect both demand and supply. Some such relations are rather similar to exploitation – the negative end of the spectrum (negative reciprocity) – while others are rather close to gratuitous support – the positive end of the spectrum (generalized reciprocity). In between lies a whole range of relations in all similar

The assumption is that the client is entirely dependent on the patron, and the goods and services received are enough for survival but insufficient for empowerment. To be sure, the bargaining games between religious and local authorities are also unequal, but the nature of goods and services traded go far beyond those needed for survival. In fact, they have the potential to politically empower and even entrench some religious organizations.

The Breakdown of Cooperation

Religious-state interaction can be mutually empowering, but it is misleading to assume that the bargaining games are free from conflict or that cooperation will not become contentious overtime and breakdown. As the following chapters demonstrate, there is variation in types of collaborative exchanges ranging from mutually beneficial and consensual to selective and reluctant. These coalitions are formed depending on what is at stake, the religious groups involved, and the resources brought to the negotiating table. The chapters also reveal that even within positive-sum exchanges, there are clear winners. Often, but not always, the government gains more. Local bureaucrats may choose to collaborate selectively and even preclude some religious traditions altogether. Moreover, vertical ties will strengthen some religious groups, whereas others fear that the same interaction will undermine their prophetic voice over time.

Religious-state bargaining games may also breakdown when political opportunity structures expand and shift so that one group reevaluates the importance of an alliance.[53] The nature of religious-state interaction should be understood as fluid and not fixed. On the one hand, this elasticity is driven by the uncertainty of authoritarian politics, but also by the practical departure of local authorities from office. As political elites are promoted (or demoted), religious groups may be left scrambling to reestablish ties with a new cohort. On the other hand, the elasticity in religious-state relations can also come from religious actors themselves. As religious communities grow in number and popularity, new opportunities arise and they may find that vertical alliances are less important and may even become burdensome. Yet, disentangling from the authoritarian state is another story.

It is also important to remember that authoritarian regimes are tightly controlled political ecologies where the state has the upper hand. Religious groups rarely have the financial independence or cultural clout to challenge their authoritarian overseers; there is limited legal recourse for religious communities; and the state controls the purse strings and permissions to carry out public religious life. For these reasons, religious groups that choose not to engage the

---

to the morally neutral market exchanges (balanced reciprocity). If we interpret clientelism and patronage as strategies we will come to expect that both parties will try to alter the circumstances in which the exchange takes place so as to move the relation to the more favorable end" (Piattoni 2001: 12–13).

53 Tarrow (1994).

state or opt out of the bargaining games may face subtle and not-so-subtle forms of repression. Religious communities that have taken this path – including a number of Protestant house churches and Catholics in China and some evangelical Protestants in Russia – are vulnerable to government interference.[54] In 2007, for example, the Beijing Public Security Bureau passed a regulation prohibiting landlords from renting properties to persons with "irregular lifestyles," including those who conduct "illegal religious activities."[55] This new policy therefore indirectly interferes with unregistered religious groups by punishing the landlords who rent to them.

This suggests a final point. When religious-state collaboration collapses authoritarian officials may return to more coercive mechanisms of control, such as introducing new rules restricting religious freedoms, refusing the registration and accreditation of religious groups, and denouncing some faiths as threats to social stability. Control may also come in more informal and uncontestable forms, such as delaying building permits or propping up rival faiths, with the intention that the targeted community will slowly wither away. Although formal and informal instruments of repression remain firmly in the authoritarian toolkit, the following chapters will demonstrate that collaboration is surprisingly common. In the next chapter, the discussion turns to the national stage and how central laws and policies set the context for religious-state collaboration at the local level.

---

[54] To be clear, some Protestant house churches have sought direct registration with local authorities but refuse to affiliate under Three-Self Patriotic Movement churches, which is currently required.

[55] See the 2008 U.S. Department of State International Religious Freedom Report for China, available at: http://www.state.gov/g/drl/rls/irf/2008/108404.htm (last accessed August 14, 2013).

3

Regulating the Religious Marketplace

All politics is local.

– Tip O'Neill

In the previous chapter, I argued that the logic behind religious and state collaboration is based on a combination of uncertainty, needs, and resources:
uncertainty of what one side can do to harm the other, symmetrical needs that
are mutually supportive and reinforcing, and resources that each has at its
disposal and can be offered to the other to meet pressing needs. It is precisely
this tripartite framework that facilitates religious and local regime cooperation
in authoritarian settings. In this chapter, the discussion turns to *why* the management of religion is largely a local game. The chapter begins with a detailed
tracing of central laws and policies pertaining to religion and religious freedom in Russia and China since the mid-1980s. I demonstrate that over the
past several decades, central policies regulating religious expression and activities have created more space for religious freedom; however, these policies are
often ambiguous and contradictory. On the one hand, such ambiguity gives the
central government (the Center) the flexibility to adapt and amend religious
policies as needed to ensure that religion continues to serve the interests of
the authoritarian state. On the other hand, the same flexibility empowers local
officials to manage religious groups in innovative ways. Thus, what represents
a tactical advantage for the Center allows for considerable diversity in the
treatment of religious communities locally.

RELIGION, GORBACHEV, AND THE COLLAPSE OF THE SOVIET UNION

In the mid-1980s as the Soviet Union began to liberalize under the leadership of Mikhail Gorbachev, the Russian Orthodox Church was again recognized as a legitimate public institution. Gorbachev needed moral and material

support to implement *glasnost* and *perestroika*, and the rehabilitation of religious groups, particularly Orthodox Christians, provided him with valuable political capital.[1] In an effort to reconcile the regime's repressive treatment of religious communities and move beyond a policy of state-atheism, Gorbachev conceded:

> Not everything has been easy and simple in the sphere of church-state relations. Religious organizations have been affected by the tragic developments that occurred in the period of the cult of personality. Mistakes made in relation to the church and believers in the 1930s [the Stalinist era] and subsequently are being rectified. . . . Believers are Soviet people, workers, patriots, and they have the full right to express their convictions with dignity. Perestroika, democratization and glasnost concern them as well – in full measure and without any restrictions. This is especially true of ethics and morals, a domain where universal norms and customs are so helpful for our common cause.[2]

Two additional steps to improve religious-state relations followed this dramatic rhetorical shift. The first was symbolic: Gorbachev allowed the public celebration of the millennium baptism of medieval Rus' (*Kreschchenie Rusi*), the memorial date when Prince Vladimir converted to the Orthodox faith in 988.[3] As part of the state-sponsored festivities, church bells that had been silent for decades rang during the finale of the Bolshoi Theater's gala. What is important to recognize here is that not only did the Bolshoi audience hear the bells, but also every citizen tuned into state-controlled media because the millennium celebration was broadcast uncensored across the Soviet Union. In a strikingly symbolic way, the regime signaled greater tolerance for religion and the return of the Church.[4]

Gorbachev's second step at normalizing religious policy was institutional. During a trip to the United Nations, he pledged new religious policies of "the highest [international legal] standards" that would rid the regime of its antireligious aurora.[5] This new policy came into effect during the fall of 1990 and guaranteed religious liberty to all individuals, groups, and faiths.[6] The law

---

[1] Witte and Bourdeaux (1999).

[2] Quoted in Bourdeaux (1990: 44).

[3] Ancient Rus' or Kievan Rus' (880 to the mid-twelfth century) is considered the early predecessor of modern Russia, Ukraine, and Belarus.

[4] Bourdeaux (2000: 10).

[5] "The Gorbachev Visit, Excerpts from Speech to UN on Major Soviet Military Cuts" (1988). Here, one can speculate that Gorbachev was referring to Article 18 of the Universal Declaration of Human Rights that states: "Everyone has the right to freedom of thought, conscience and religion; this right includes freedom to change his religion or belief, and freedom, either alone or in community with others and in public or private, to manifest his religion or belief in teaching, practice, worship and observance."

[6] "O svobode sovesti i religioznykh organizatsiiakh" [On freedom of conscience and religious organizations], *Vedomosti SSSR* 41, item no. 813 (1990); hereafter the 1990 Law. A similar law on the freedom of worship was passed in the Russian Soviet Federative Soviet Republic (RSFSR) on October 25, 1990, "Zakon o svobode veroispovedenii" [Law on the freedom of religion],

declared that the "freedom of worship is an inalienable right of the citizens" guaranteed by the constitution, and that citizens all share "the right to select and hold religious beliefs and to freely change them"; moreover, "all religions and denominations shall be equal before the law."[7] At the same time, it was understood that religious groups were to stay out of politics and education, and in return the state would not interfere in their internal affairs.

Gorbachev's bold reforms transformed the political landscape across the Soviet Union and opened the window for greater religious freedom; yet at the same time, the communist party was rapidly losing its monopoly on power. Constituent republics began calling for popular referendums on national sovereignty as well as asserting their autonomy and independence. This "parade of sovereignties" continued until December 1991 when Russia also seceded, triggering the Soviet Union's collapse; thereupon, Gorbachev handed all powers over to Boris Yeltsin, the new president of Russia.[8]

Under Yeltsin, post-Soviet Russia's early years were far from stable as reformers tried to reconfigure the socialist machine into a democratic and capitalistic country. And yet there was strong support for democracy and a deep optimism for the future. This optimism boded well for religious liberty – religious groups were left largely alone and the spirit of 1990 Law endured. Across the country monestaries, churches, synagogues, and mosques began the long process of reopening and rebuilding, and church bells and calls to prayer could again be heard from Kaliningrad to Kamchatka.

This early period of liberalization was also reflected in Russia's new political institutions. The 1993 Constitution codified the separation of religion and state, protected religious freedom, and promoted equality among all faiths. Article 14 stresses the need for a separation between church and state, stating: "The Russian Federation is a secular state. No religion may be established as a state or obligatory one. Religious associations shall be separated from the state, and shall be equal before the law." Article 28 protects the freedom of belief proclaiming "Everyone shall be guaranteed the right to freedom of conscience, to freedom of religious worship, including the right to profess, individually or jointly with others, any religion or to profess no religion, to freely choose, possess and disseminate religious and other beliefs and to act in conformity with them." Indeed, the protection of religious beliefs is noted throughout the constitution: Articles 13 and 29 underscore the importance

---

Vedomosti RSFSR 21, item no. 267–1, 240 (1990). Hereafter the 1990 RSFSR Law. The laws replaced Stalin's 1929 Law on Religious Associations that forbade the opening of new religious buildings, religious training academies, the engagement in social work and philanthropy, the publishing and distribution of liturgical literature, or the general meeting for religious study. Stalin's law only permitted religious worship in registered religious buildings; however, this was difficult to achieve considering only a few hundred churches remained open; see Walters (1999: 42).

[7] 1990 RSFSR Law, note 10, Article 25.

[8] Beissinger (2003); Hale (2000).

of religious tolerance, while prohibiting associational groups that encourage national and religious strife; Article 19 guarantees equal rights and freedoms to all citizens regardless of religious beliefs; and Article 59 allows citizens to replace required military service by alternative civilian service when religious convictions contradict such activity. Thus, what these policies reveal is that in the early 1990s as Russia transitioned away from its communist past and toward a more democratic future, religious groups were largely ignored by the regime. All of this was about to change.

After Atheism: Regulating the Russian Religious Marketplace

The religious freedoms protected in the constitution, like many of the reforms of the late-Soviet era, did not necessarily accomplish what the designers planned. Instead, they created many challenges for the fledgling democracy. Two such challenges were the influx of foreign missionaries into the country and the growth of new religious movements. Foreign missionaries were diverse in beliefs and origins, ranging from the Unification Church, Mormons, Pentecostals, and Scientologists, to practioners of Aum Shinrikyo, Sunni Muslims, and Hare Krishnas. It would seem that many religious communities from both the East and West saw Russia as a large and open "market of souls" waiting to be converted, and as a result, competition grew fierce.

As more religious groups entered the country there was a noticeable shift in public opinion regarding religious freedom. The shift was not so much that religion should *not* be protected, but rather that *some* religious traditions should be protected more than others. Editorials began appearing in newspapers expressing alarm about the flood of foreign missionaries and their aggressive proselytizing tactics, both of which were labeled as an affront to traditional Russian culture and national identity.[9] Leading the charge against the influx was the Orthodox Church, which had only recently regained its footing and was attempting to recover its sacred place in a secularized society. Sergei Filatov suggests this was not any easy task: "the ROC [Russian Orthodox Church] did not have the necessary intellectual, organisational or missionary capacity to mount an effective mission to the people, especially a people who, though having some interest in religion, were deeply secularised and could hardly be expected to understand the content and practice of Christian faith."[10]

The Orthodox Church went on the offensive. In a speech presented at the World Conference of Churches in November 1996, Metropolitan Kirill (Gundyayev) of Smolensk and Kaliningrad warned of the dangers of foreign

---

[9] See, for example, "Obrashchenie svjashchennosluzhitelja k pravoslavnomu narodu Pravoslav-noe slovo" (1995: 7); Shterin and Richardson (2000: 257–62). But also see Richters (2013: 41) and Fagan (2013: 58–9), who note that the reports of a foreign deluge of missionaries and explosive spread of new religious movements were grossly exaggerated in the Russian media.

[10] Filatov (2008: 201).

proselytism and likened foreign missionaries to "spiritual colonizers" invading Russia. Acting as a spokesperson for the Church, Kirill charged:

> Missionaries from abroad came with dollars, buying people with so-called humanitarian aid and promises to send them abroad for study or rest. We expected that our fellow Christians would support us and help us in our own missionary service. In reality, however, they have started fighting with our church, like boxers in a fight with their pumped-up muscles, delivering blows. The annual budget of some of the invading missionary organizations amount to dozens of millions of dollars. They have bought time on radio and television and have used their financial resources to the utmost in order to buy people.... For many in Russia today, "non-Orthodox" means those who have come to destroy the spiritual unity of the people and the Orthodox faith – spiritual colonizers who by fair means or foul try to tear the people away from the Church.[11]

For the Church to compete in an increasingly crowded marketplace, hierarchs depicted foreign missionaries and faiths as "aggressors, occupiers, and money-spinning despots," and suggested that the spread of new religious movements were not only a threat to Russia's spiritual traditions, but also "a challenge of the country's integrity and geopolitical existence."[12] In short, the Church boldly stepped into the political arena as the protector and defender of Russian national identity.

As the Orthodox Church embraced a more political stance, domestic politics was consumed by a fierce struggle between "Westernizers" and "Slavophiles" – two groups competing to lead Russia's transition. For the most part, Church leaders sided with the Slavophiles, a coalition that was also deeply suspicious of the West and its growing influence in the country. A more politicized Church also grew increasingly proactive in defending its position. Church leaders devoted significant attention to publicizing the harmful activities of foreign "totalitarian sects" (*totalitarnye sekty*); formed alliances with candidates for the upcoming 1996 federal election campaign who promised to take measures against harmful (read: foreign) religious groups; and founded an unexpected coalition with communists and nationalists against the influx of foreign groups.[13] The Orthodox red-brown alliance converged around the shared idea that the liberal religious policies of the early 1990s were whimsically adopted "on a wave of democratic romanticism," which gave too much freedom to proselytizing Western missionaries and failed to protect traditional denominations such as Orthodox Christianity.[14] From the Church's perspective, the stakes were high and Russia was under attack: "Proselytism is the fact of invasion

---

[11] Quoted in Witte and Bourdeaux (1999: 74–5). Metropolitan Kirill became the patriarch of the Russian Orthodox Church in February 2009.

[12] Richters (2013: 40–1).

[13] Richters (2013: 38–43).

[14] Filatov (1999: 163).

by another culture.... This invasion is taking place after the old missionary patterns of colonial times. It is not merely a desire to reveal Christ to people – people have confessed Christianity for over a thousand years at that – but also to refashion their culture in the Western mode."[15]

The Backsliding

By the mid-1990s, Russia was a messy state, sometimes bordering on anarchy. There was an ongoing war in Chechnya, high-profile mob hits in the capital, and general lawlessness in the regions. The big bang privatization policies recommended by the West had resulted in the plundering of the state's most valuable assets and enriched a new class of oligarchs. Yeltsin's "shock therapy" produced astronomical inflation, rendering the average Russian's life savings worthless. This led to widespread disillusionment with Russia's democratic experiment, resentment toward Yeltsin and his liberal advisors, anger directed at the West, and nostalgia for the Soviet Union.[16] As the Slavophiles and the Orthodox Church prevailed over the Westernizers in shaping the domestic discussion on the appropriate trajectory for Russia's transition, control over religion was again tightened.[17] This was first felt at the local level, with more than one-third of regional legislatures passing ordinances restricting religious activity and limiting the proselytizing activities of foreigners.[18] At the federal level, a new law reminiscent of Soviet control over religious groups was introduced: the Law On Freedom of Conscience and on Religious Associations.[19] The 1997 federal law became the cornerstone of religious policy and marked the beginning of restrictions on non-Orthodox faiths. More important, the new law revealed the rekindling of relations between the Church and state – an alliance both saw as beneficial.[20]

The 1997 Law remains the principal legislation on regulating religious communities in Russia yet it is rife with contradictions. The preamble affirms "the Russian Federation is a secular state," but also recognizes the "special contribution of Orthodoxy to the history of Russia and to the establishment and development of Russia's spirituality and culture." The law goes on to ensure legal protection of "Christianity, Islam, Buddhism, Judaism and

---

[15] Kirill (2000: 74).

[16] Colton (2008), for instance, has compared this period in Russia to the Great Depression in the United States.

[17] Gradual restrictions include a 1993 attempt to amend the 1990 Law. Although this attempt was vetoed, several regions passed local laws in the spirit of the 1993 amendment to control the religious revival. Here, see especially Marsh and Froese (2004).

[18] Homer and Uzzel (1999); also see Shertin and Richarson (1998).

[19] "Federalnyi Zakon 'O svobode sovesti i o religioznykh ob'edineniiakh' [Federal law 'On freedom of conscience and religious associations, No. 135-FZ (September 26, 1997); hereafter the 1997 Law. This law passed by a 337 to 5 vote in the Duma.

[20] Marsh (2011: 127); Knox (2005).

other religions and creeds that constitute an inseparable part of the historical heritage of Russia's peoples."[21] However, the special attention given to Orthodox Christianity and the division between it and other historical religions (distinguishing Orthodoxy from Christianity) is somewhat curious considering the equality of all religions professed in the constitution and the multiconfessional reality of the country.[22]

The contradictions of the 1997 Law are even more striking in how religious entities are defined. Specifically, the law contradicts the equality of all religious traditions outlined in the constitution by creating a hierarchy among different types of religious associations. The law defines a *religious association* as a

> Voluntary association of citizens of the Russian Federation and other persons permanently and legally residing [therein] formed with the goals of joint confession and possessing features corresponding to that goal: a creed, the performance of worship service, religious rituals, and ceremonies; the teaching of religion and religious upbringing of its followers.[23]

Religious associations are then divided into two distinct categories with different corresponding rights and protections: *religious groups* and *religious organizations*.[24] Religious groups are situated at the bottom of the legal hierarchy and permitted to carry out worship services and rituals but have no access to state resources.[25] Religious organizations, by contrast, are formally registered with the state and eligible for greater protections and benefits. Some of the entitlements include the right to own property and land, permission to engage in

[21] Taken from the preamble of 1997 Law. Chapter 1 of the 1997 Law reiterates the themes of the preamble, including the right of citizens and foreign citizens the freedom of conscience and creed (Article 3.1), forbids discrimination based on religious beliefs (Article 3.3), and maintains the secular nature of the Russian Federation (Article 4.1) by stating that religious groups are not to take part in political affairs and that education in public schools must remain secular (Article 4.2).

[22] Here, one can speculate that Christianity is referring to Catholics and Protestants. Nevertheless, some have questioned the idea of singling out "traditional religions" and giving them special privileges because only paganism could be considered as a traditional and indigenous faith in Russia. See, for example, Mitrokhin (2003).

[23] 1997 Law, Article 6.1.

[24] A religious group is defined as "[a] voluntary association of citizens, formed for the goals of joint confession and dissemination of their faith, carrying out its activities without state registration and without obtaining the legal capabilities of a legal personality, is recognized as a religious group in this federal law. Premises, and property necessary for the activities of a religious group, are to be provided for the use of the group by its participants" (Chapter 2, Article 7.1). A religious organization is defined as "[a] free association of citizens, or other persons permanently and legally residing on the territory of the Russian Federation, formed with the goals of joint confession and dissemination of their faith, and registered as a legal personality in accordance with the practice established by law, is recognized as a religious organization" (Chapter 2, Article 8.1).

[25] Religious groups vary across Russia's regions, but the category generally includes those who refuse registration on spiritual grounds (some Old Believers and Baptist congregations) and new religious movements (groups that entered Russia after the collapse of the Soviet Union).

business, and exemptions from creditors seeking to reclaim real estate or other religious objects.[26] By law, religious organizations are also allowed to provide religious services to hospitals, orphanages, homes for the elderly or disabled, as well as prisons.[27] Religious organizations may also produce and distribute print or other media, carry out charitable activities, and develop institutions for the professional training of religious personnel.[28] Religious organizations further have the exclusive right to establish and maintain international contacts and invite foreign visitors for professional religious purposes.[29] Finally, religious organizations may be beneficiaries of direct financial support from the government. More specifically, the law affirms that the state may grant religious organizations "tax privileges and other privileges to religious organizations;... [and] provide financial, material, and other aid to religious organizations in the restoration, maintenance, and protection of buildings and objects that are monuments of history and culture."[30]

The 1997 Law further subdivides religious organizations into two additional categories, again with different corresponding privileges: *localized* and *centralized* religious organizations. Here, the main distinguishing factor between the two is the amount of time an organization has been "active" in the country. A localized religious organization must be active and registered for fifteen consecutive years in the territory of the Russian Federation, consist of ten or more citizens who are at least eighteen years old, and permanently reside in one locality.[31] Centralized religious organizations, by contrast, must encompass at least three local religious organizations and have "been active in the territory of the Russian Federation on a legal basis for no fewer than 50 years."[32] Therefore, when the 1997 Law went into effect, to be considered a centralized religious organization, a religious organization had to demonstrate consistent and legal registration in the country since 1947, and since 1982 for a localized religious organization.[33]

In determining whether a religious organization may be classified as centralized or localized, the 1997 Law reveals inherent biases. First, it is much easier for a religious organization with a hierarchical organizational structure, like the Orthodox Church, to meet the requirements of having three or more branches,

---

[26] 1997 Law, Articles, 21, 21.5, 23.

[27] 1997 Law, Article 16.

[28] 1997 Law, Articles 17, 18, 19.

[29] 1997 Law, Article 20.

[30] Here, the law is vague on the meaning of "other privileges," leaving the door open for religious groups to receive other types of state funding (1997 Law, Article 4.3).

[31] 1997 Law, Article 8.3.

[32] 1997 Law, Articles 8.4, 8.5.

[33] Other traditional religious communities of Russia, such as Muslims, Jews, and Buddhists, were illegal after 1917 and before 1905. Although these religious traditions were legal briefly between 1905 and 1917, they were not centralized and therefore are classified differently from the Orthodox Church.

and more difficult for Protestants or more decentralized religious communities, such as Jews and Muslims, to meet the same requirement. However, even clearly hierarchical religious organizations, such as the Catholic Church, are still at a disatvantage because in 1947 only one religious organization was both active and legally registered in the Soviet Union: the Orthodox Church.[34]

Second, the fifteen-year threshold to be classified as localized limits eligible organizations to the traditional religions designated in the preamble of the law – Islam, Buddhism, Judaism, and some Christian denominations. All other newcomers are excluded. Moreover, the fifteen-year rule can be a significant challenge for some traditional religions. In 1982, for example, only a handful of Baptist congregations and two of the 160 Roman Catholic parishes were registered and fully functioning under the communist regime.[35] This is not to say that religious groups did not exist or were not active across the Soviet Union. Indeed, many mosques, synagogues, and churches were open but functioning without state approval and largely in secret. Therefore, the fifteen-year requirement presents a sizeable hurdle because few religious organizations were legally open for business during Soviet times.

The classification as a centralized or local religious organization is meaningful because it carries different rights and privileges for religious communities, particularly in terms of state oversight and access to resources. According to the law, localized religious organizations must individually register annually with the state, whereas centralized religious organizations may submit one registration application on behalf of all their parishes.[36] Here, the implication is that the Orthodox Church registers once, while Muslims might be required to register annually. This registration process is generally straightforward but can be cumbersome and invasive for some groups. Registration requires the following: (1) a complete list of members (indicating their citizenship, home addresses, and dates of birth), which must include at least ten Russian citizens;[37] (2) a religious charter;[38] (3) minutes from the founding meeting; (4) documentation from the local government confirming that the religious organization has

---

[34] In the postwar period, Stalin relaxed some of the pressure on Orthodox Christians and allowed several churches to reopen. There were limits to Stalin's tolerance, however, religious activities were confined to designated worship services, Church hierarchs were expected to remain loyal to the regime, and the KGB openly interfered in the internal workings of the Church. Indeed, some argue that by the time Gorbachev came to power, more than half of all Orthodox priests were on the KGB payroll; see Armes (1994). More generally on the Orthodox Church under communism, see Ware (1997: 155–7).

[35] Witte (1999: 14–15); Uzzell (1998).

[36] Chapter 2, Article 11.2.

[37] The emphasis on Russian Federation citizenship as imperative in forming a religious organization or religious group marks a shift from the 1990 Law that allowed foreigners to form religious associations.

[38] A charter includes the name and type of religious organization, address, creed, aims and goals, structure of the organization (i.e., its administrative organs and internal measure of competence), and source of finances and property (1997 Law, Chapter 2, Article 10.2).

existed for no less than fifteen years in the relevant territory; (5) a history of the religion and its practices; and (6) documentation confirming the legal address of the religious organization and place of worship.[39] Religious associations that refuse to register with government authorities (for political, financial, or spiritual reasons) are then classified as religious groups, which places them at the bottom of the legal hierarchy with limited rights and protections.

Another difference is that only centralized religions may use the word "Russian" (in any of its forms) in the title of their religious organization.[40] This generally means that only the Orthodox Church is eligible for such a national honor.[41] However, the privileges of the Church extend far beyond the inclusion of Russian in its title. For example, the preamble of the law notes Orthodoxy's special role in Russian culture and history, and later goes on to promise subsidies for the "restoration, maintenance, and protection of buildings and objects which are monuments of history and culture."[42] On the one hand, open support for the Orthodox Church within the 1997 Law should not come as a complete surprise because the Church was on the receiving end of intense state repression in the past. On the other hand, all religious traditions were targeted under communism, but these communities are not afforded the same special privileges as the Orthodox Church.[43] Thus, the implication is that the Orthodox Church is the favored beneficiary of state subsidies for the restoration of cultural monuments and buildings, while other religious groups are overlooked.

Russian Religious Policy in Perspective

Since the Gorbachev period, Russia's religious policy has come full circle. The liberalizing reforms of perestroika and glasnost moved beyond state atheism and allowed greater religious freedom. Yet, as Russia transitioned toward democracy, there was a noticeable backsliding of religious liberty. The 1997 Law On Freedom of Conscience and on Religious Associations ended an era of religious pluralism and introduced a formal hierarchy of religions with clear winners and losers. Orthodox Christianity enjoys a privileged status at the top as a centralized religious organization similar to its prerevolutionary position as the center of Russian religious life.[44] This position grants the Orthodox Church full legal protection and special state benefits not available to other religious traditions. The second tier encompasses localized religious

---

[39] See 1997 Law, Articles 9.1, 10.2, 11.5. Here, it is interesting to note that 1997 Law has served as a template to control and monitor other associational groups, including the 2006 law to regulate non-governmental organizations; see Marsh (2011: 127).

[40] Witte (1999: 14).

[41] One interesting exception is the Russian Union of Evangelical Christians (Pentecostals) [ROSXVE; *Rossijskij ob"edinennyj Sojuz hristian very evangel'skoj (pjatidesjatnikov)*], which is also permitted to use "Russian" in its name; see Fagan (2013: 72).

[42] 1997 Law, Articles 4.3, 22.1.

[43] Gunn (1999: 246).

[44] Ramet (1998: 241–2).

organizations, including Islam, Buddhism, Judaism, and some Christian denominations that also are considered to have traditional status in Russia. These religions also have full legal protection but receive limited state benefits. However, because of the fifteen-year rule to qualify as a localized religious organization, there is room for unequal implementation of the law, and the regulation of religious communities according to different standards. The third and bottom tier covers all other religious groups with no traditional or historic ties in Russia. These groups "receive only a pro forma guarantee of freedom of worship and liberty of conscience" and face the greatest obstacles when attempting to register with local governments.[45] This religious hierarchy not only challenges notions of secularism and the equality of all confessions guaranteed in the constitution, it also has important implications on the local level.

Local bureaucrats and officials become the arbitrators of religious freedom because they are supposed to implement the religious policies from above by determining whether a group has authentic historical roots in the region or is part of foreign missionary activity. It is local officials who decide whether the liturgical texts are genuine, if leaders are competent, or if a religious group is really a totalitarian sect masquerading as a benign religion. This can be highly problematic, because "many regional administrations conclude that they can act arbitrarily and with impunity in dealing with religious minorities and newer religious organizations."[46] An ill-trained bureaucrat may liquidate a religious organization based on her biased understanding of religion and interpretation of the law. At the same time, there is also room for her to informally prop up one religious community over another or adopt other quiet forms of discrimination. Although the Russian central state has set guidelines for religious expression and activities, religion and ritual are regulated locally. In the next section, the discussion turns to how a similar pattern of ambiguous central policies also creates a localized game in China.

AFTER ATHEISM: CHINESE RELIGIOUS REFORM IN THE 1980S

Chinese religious policy during the post-Mao period has followed a trajectory similar to that of Russia with central reforms that depend on local implementation. Much like Gorbachev's push toward liberalization in the 1980s, Deng Xiaoping's policies of Opening and Reform (*gaigekaifeng*) provided the institutional groundwork for greater religious expression. Again, like Gorbachev, these policies allowed the Chinese government to appear more liberalizing to international audiences as well as build domestic coalitions to implement controversial reforms. The liberalization of religious polices formally began with the 1982 Constitution, which marked a major shift in religious

---

[45] Witte (1999: 12); also Marsh (2011: 128).

[46] Homer and Uzzel (1999: 285); Knox (2005); also see Fagan (2013: 84) on the "telephone law" implementation of religious policies.

policies from the Cultural Revolution (1966–76) and the total ban on religious activities. The constitution safeguards religious beliefs (and the freedom not to believe), and guarantees legal protection for "normal" religious organizations and activities.[47] The constituion states:

> Citizens of the People's Republic of China enjoy freedom of religious belief.
>
> No state organ, public organization or individual may compel citizens to believe in, or not to believe in, any religion; nor may they discriminate against citizens who believe in, or do not believe in, any religion.
>
> The state protects normal religious activities. No one may make use of religion to engage in activities that disrupt public order, impair the health of citizens or interfere with the educational system of the state.
>
> Religious bodies and religious affairs are not subject to any foreign domination.[48]

The second crucial document outlining religious freedom was introduced in 1982, Document 19: The Basic Viewpoint and Policy on the Religious Question During Our Country's Socialist Period.[49] Document 19 functions less as a law detailing definitive policies (in fact, there is no "religious law" in China) and more as an internal circular for the revised philosophy of state-religious relations. The document begins much like Gorbachev's religious policy, recognizing the tenuous relationship between religion and state and the need for reconciliation. It is worthwhile here to quote the document at length.

> Since the founding of the People's Republic of China, there have been many twists and turns in the party's work with regard to the religious question.... [T]he antirevolutionary Lin Biao–Jiang Qing clique... forcibly forbade normal religious activities by the mass of religious believers. They treated patriotic religious personages, as well as the mass of ordinary religious believers, as "targets for dictatorship," and fabricated a host of wrongs and injustices which they pinned upon these religious personages. They even misinterpreted some customs and practices of the ethnic minorities religious superstitions, which they forcibly prohibited. In some places, they even repressed the mass of religious believers, and destroyed ethnic unity. They used violent measures against religion which forced religious movements underground.[50]

---

[47] As discussed later in the chapter, the constitution does not elaborate what constitutes a "normal" (*zhengchang*) religious organization or "normal" religious activity. Ostensibly, normal means under state management.

[48] The protection of religious beliefs was also in the 1954 and 1957 Constitutions, however, these protections were largely ignored and religious adherents were commonly branded as anti-revolutionary, rightists, or puppets of imperialism and subsequently sent for re-education.

[49] "Zhonggong zhongyang guanyu woguo shehui zhuyi shiqi zongjiao wenti de jiben guandian he jiben zhengce (wenjian no. 19)" [Document 19: The basic viewpoint and policy on the religious question during our country's socialist period], hereafter Document 19.

[50] Document 19, section 3.

To be sure, Document 19 represents a new approach toward religion but is careful to imply that Marxism is correct and religion will eventually die out. At the same time, the document suggests when religious groups are driven underground (as during the Cultural Revolution), they grow stronger, create martyrs, and become more difficult to control.[51] Thus, one major theme of the new policy is to bring religion out of the shadows to serve the interests of the authoritarian state.[52] To achieve this end, Document 19 states:

> In this new historical period, the party's and government's basic task in its religious work will be to firmly implement and carry out its policy of freedom of religious belief; to consolidate and expand the patriotic political alliance in each ethnic religious group; to strengthen education in patriotism and socialism among them, and to bring into play position elements among them in order to build a modern and powerful socialist state and complete the great task of unifying the country.... [O]ur policy and freedom of religious belief lies in our desire to unite the mass of believers and nonbelievers and enable them to center all of their will and strength on the common goal of building a modernized, powerful socialist state.[53]

To harness religion for the development of the state, Document 19 borrows the language used in the constitution and identifies "normal" religious activity as involving only the five major religions in China: Buddhism, Taoism, Islam, Protestantism, and Catholicism.[54] The continuation of this language is important because it reinforces the idea that the state sets the legal boundaries of religious orthodoxy and orthopraxy, and those operating outside of these faiths do so at great risk and have no legal protection.[55]

A second theme in the religious policy is the importance of national unity. Document 19 encourages the cultivation of religious leaders who "love their motherland" and "support the socialist path."[56] Indeed, patriotism is particularly stressed in the training of all religious personnel, advising seminaries to admit only "young religious personnel, who, in terms of politics, fervently love their homeland and support the party's leadership and the socialist system,

[51] On the mistakes of managing religious groups in communist countries around the world, see Zhong (1998).

[52] Liu (1996).

[53] Document 19, section 3, 4.

[54] Document 19, section 3 identifies the following religious histories in China, Buddhism (dating over 2,000 years), Taoism (a 1,700-year history), Islam (1,300 years), and Catholicism and Protestantism (arriving following the Opium Wars 1834–43 and 1856–60). Here, it is important to note that legitimate or normal Catholicism is considered autonomous from the Vatican. On the history and conflict of the Catholic Church in China, see Madsen (2004, 1998); Wiest (2004); Lozada (2001); Leung (1992).

[55] F. Yang (2004: 105).

[56] According to Document 19, section 5, "We must foster a large group of model figures, who love their motherland, accept the leadership of the party and the government, firmly support the socialist path, and safeguard national and ethnic unity; are knowledgeable about religion and capable of working with the religion-practicing mass."

and who possess sufficient religious knowledge."[57] The emphasis on ardent patriotism above religious knowledge (the latter need only be "sufficient") is revealing because it reflects the regime's inherent misgivings of religious actors and their questionable loyalty.

Document 19 further suggests that patriotism and national unity may be nurtured through direct government support of religion. Specifically, patriotism can be cultivated through the state-sponsored restoration of churches, temples and other religious sites of "cultural and historic value." The policy notes that priority should be given to "major temples and churches famous for their scenic beauty . . . [and] important historic value" but only in locations where there are still active believers.[58] At the same time, the document cautions local authorities against the "indiscriminate building and repairing of temples in rural villages" and instead stresses the importance of restoring temples in midsize cities; presumably where state organs can more readily monitor religious activities.[59]

Finally, to ensure state control over religious institutions, Document 19 asserts that all funding for the restoration and maintenance of religious sites be limited to domestic donations and income derived from house and property rentals of religious buildings. Here the policy is quite clear: religious organizations may not solicit or receive funds from abroad, once again revealing an inherent fear of foreign influence.[60]

Religious Patriotic Associations

Document 19 also takes an important institutional step toward the management of religious actors. The policy announces the reinstatement of state-sponsored religious patriotic organizations. Religious Patriotic Associations (RPA) that had been disbanded since the Cultural Revolution were redeployed for each of the five religions to ensure that religious leaders worked for the larger goals of the regime.[61] It is important to note that these associations are not independent from the government but are considered branches of it. For instance, the Three-Self Patriotic Movement in China (TSPM) was founded in the 1950s

---

[57] Document 19, section 9.

[58] Document 19, section 6.

[59] Ibid.

[60] According to Document 19, sections 7 and 11 clarify that foreign believers in China may personally give donations or offerings; however, large contributions must not come from foreign churches. If a foreigner wishes to donate a sizable private contribution, "permission must be sought from the provincial, urban, or autonomous-area governments from the central government responsible for these matters before any religious body can accept them on its own, even though it can be established that the donor acts purely out of religious fervor with no strings attached."

[61] RPAs were originally established in the 1950s to assist the government in implementing religious policy. They are organized on the national, provincial, municipal, and prefectural level to manage various religious organizations within the regions.

and is the legal Protestant church of China. The TSPM is a nondenominational church organized around three principles: self-governance, self-support (i.e., financial independence from foreigners), and self-propagation (i.e., domestic missionary work). Likewise, state-sponsored patriotic associations exist for the other recognized faiths, such as the Buddhist Association of China that oversees Buddhists, and the Catholic Patriotic Association that oversees Catholics.[62] The patriotic associations serve as central bureaucratic structures that reach down to the village level and have the task of keeping their respective religious groups in line: they are designed to serve as conduits between religious groups, the party, and the government.

The RPAs are hierarchically organized, and the party must approve its leaders. It is not compulsory for the head of the RPA to be religious and may be a communist party member (i.e., a mandatory atheist). However, in terms of general staffing, the RPAs are managed by a combination of believers and atheists. For the most part, this management is procedural because there is little question about where ultimate loyalty lies. The founder and first president of the TSPM, Wu Yaozong, reinforced this point stating:

> Without the communist party there would not have been the Three-Self Movement of the Christian church, nor the new life of the church, and we Christians would not have received education in socialism and the opportunity to change our political standpoint and become one with the people as we march happily on the road to socialism.... I love the communist party.... For over a hundred years imperialism had been using the Christian church to advance its aggressive designs.... And so for now the Three-Self Movement has carried on this work of cleansing the church, but this was a work which could not have been carried on without the support and direction of the party.[63]

The central charge of religious patriotic organizations is to implement the party's religious policy, organize normal religious activity, and act as a compass to direct every element of the Chinese church. Specifically, Document 19 notes that RPA's should assist the party and government "to implement the policy of freedom of religious belief, to help the broad mass of religious believers and persons in religious circles to continually raise their patriotic and socialist consciousness, to represent the lawful rights and interests of religious circles, to organize normal religious activities, and to manage religious affairs well."[64]

[62] Document 19 permits the reorganization of eight national patriotic organizations: the Chinese Buddhist Association (*Zhongguo Fojiao xiehui*), the Chinese Taoist Association (*Zhongguo Daojiao xiehui*), the Chinese Islamic Association (*Zhongguo Yisilanjiao xiehui*), the Chinese Catholic Patriotic Association (*Zhongguo Tianzhujiao aiguohui*), the Chinese Catholic Religious Affairs Committee (*Zhongguo Tianzhujiao jiaowu weiyuanhui*), the Chinese Catholic Bishops' Conference (*Zhongguo Tianjujiao zhujiaotuan*), the Chinese Protestant "Three-Self" Patriotic Movement (*Zhongguo Jidujiao 'sanzi' aiguo yundong weiyuanhui*), and the Chinese Christian Council (*Zhongguo Jidujiao xiehui*).

[63] Wu (1958).

[64] Document 19, section 7.

Again, there is little ambiguity in where actual power lies: "all patriotic religious organizations should follow the party's and government's leadership."[65]

In terms of managing daily religious life, the patriotic associations control the allocation of resources and personnel and are responsible for interreligious relations. For instance, it is the patriotic association that has the authority to open a new religious building and appoint religious personnel across the country based on the TSPM's projected needs. Recent seminary graduates may be sent to a rural church and posted in various capacities, including ministers, preachers (who have limited capabilities in the church), or teachers (in charge of Bible studies), or even as local bureaucrats for the TSPM.[66] Finally, it is the patriotic associations that are tasked with protecting domestic religious groups from foreign intrusions. On this point, the policy is emphatic that patriotic associations should "resolutely resist the designs of all reactionary religious forces from abroad who desire to once again gain control over religions in our country. They [RPAs] must determinedly refuse any meddling or interfering in Chinese religious affairs by foreign churches or religious personages, nor must they permit any foreign religious organization to use any means to enter our country for missionary work or to secretly introduce and distribute religious literature on a large scale."[67] As such, RPAs function as both the watchdogs and gatekeepers of their religious communities, ensuring that religion continues to serve the interest of the state.

Institutionalized Ambiguity

As outlined in the previous section, Document 19 presents a new framework for religious policy in post-Mao China, but the document should be read more as a philosophical approach toward religion than as a clear guideline for reform. At best, it is a policy in broad strokes aimed at rehabilitating religious professionals, restoring places of worship, and permitting bounded religious activities across the country. At worst, it is a document that institutionalizes ambiguity and raises a number of questions in the implementation of religious policy. One area that is particularly problematic is the continued classification of only five so-called normal faiths. China's religious landscape is far more diverse than five religious groups. Indeed, even a recent government-sponsored survey estimated that the most significant religious revival has been among popular religious communities, and external estimates suggest that more than 20 percent of the Chinese population is affiliated with folk religions.[68] However,

---

[65] Ibid.

[66] Interview with former TSPM employee F, May 2007, Shanghai.

[67] Document 19, section 11.

[68] The Chinese government supported survey finds that 40 percent of all religious adherents practice some form of popular religion; see J. Wu (2007), but also see the Pew Research Center's (2012) report on global religious landscapes. To manage folk and popular religious, one government official explained that in the early 2000s, an unofficial government department at the SARA; however, I have been unable to confirm whether this branch is being replicated

Document 19 makes no mention of these communities and their practices. With the parameters of religious activity so limited, the question emerges as to how local authorities should treat religious groups that do not neatly fit into the fivefold category.

Another area of concern is the process of registration. To operate in the public sphere, all religious groups must register with the proper authorities, but the details of how to do so are noticeably absent. For instance, several organs of the state manage and monitor religious groups, such as the Religious Affairs Bureau (RAB), the United Front Work Department (UFWD), and the Public Security Bureau (PSB).[69] This raises a nearly endless series of questions: Should religious groups register with each one? If registration is denied by one organ of the state, can a religious group appeal to another? How should local authorities respond to religious groups that refuse registration on spiritual grounds, such as some Protestant house churches?

A final area of ambiguity relates to the return of religious property. Document 19 provides few guidelines for the return of religious property, compensation for religious buildings that were destroyed, or the rules of fair exchange for properties that were converted for other uses after 1949. It is unclear, for instance, whether functioning hospitals and schools established by foreign missionaries should be returned to their contemporary religious equivalents or remain under the control of their current work units. Additionally, the fate of religious relics that wound up in museums, or temple lakes and gardens that were "collectivized" into fishponds and farms, is equally uncertain. Local officials also have no guidelines for addressing religious buildings that house military and other government personnel. The stakes for these contested properties are especially high given the soaring prices of real estate in China compounded by the relatively sought-after locations where historic religious landmarks usually reside.

Where the religious policy is most lucid is in the policing of religious activities. Document 19 states that authorities must "crackdown on all criminal and antirevolutionary activities that hide behind the façade of religion, which includes all superstitious practices that fall outside the scope of religion," and that religious activities involving secret societies, sorcerers, witches, phrenology, fortune telling, and geomancy (*feng shui*) will be "severely punished according to the law."[70] Once again, the omission of criteria determining whether a group qualifies as a recognized religion or not means the practice of defining what is religiously licit or illicit falls to local authorities. Thus, given the lack of practical articulation in Document 19, it is hardly surprising that

locally. Interview with bureaucrat O from the State Administration for Religious Activities, June 2007, Beijing.

[69] The central RAB has been renamed as the State Administration for Religious Activities (SARA), whereas the provincial offices remain the RAB.

[70] Document 19, section 10.

the religious reforms were haphazardly implemented and led to considerable confusion and conflict at the local level.

New Religious Regulations

Shortly following the introduction of Document 19, Beijing began looking for ways to clarify the management of religion on the local level. Within three years, a new report was released by the Standing Committee of the National People's Congress clarifying some of the confusion caused by Document 19.[71] The new report identifies several areas of contention in the management of growing religiosity. One is that "some local authorities show very little conscientiousness where the returning of building properties is concerned, and use various pretexts to withhold some of this property for long-term use by their employees and family members."[72] A related concern is that local authorities are often vying for influence over newly opened religious sites. Document 19 fails to define the duties and responsibilities of different local government departments, which means that RPAs, bureaucrats in charge of the management of cultural relics, bureaucrats who manage parks and gardens, as well as local officials in charge of tourism all compete for influence over the reconstruction of religious sites.[73] The report notes that intergovernmental competition was particularly fierce because religious groups sought to restore sites for ritual use, whereas other departments had designs on using religious buildings to develop the local economy. Interestingly, the report calls for mutual respect between religious and commercial interests while at the same time mentioning religious groups "must actively support and assist tourist departments in their work and promote the development of the tourist industry."[74]

The government report identifies a final challenge facing local authorities in their management of religion: a "paucity and poor quality of monks and priests."[75] Considering the nationwide closure of schools during the Cultural Revolution, the decade-long campaigns targeting religious activity, and thus the few qualified religious personnel who were willing and able to step in and manage temples and churches in the 1980s, the concern over the limited training of religious personnel is not unfounded. Yet, the remedy suggested in the report is informative of the regime's low opinion of religion. The report recommends all religious communities should attract "fewer but better" young people who "politically love their country and support the party's leadership

---

[71] "Zhongyang bangongting diaocha zu guanyu luoshi dang de zongjiao zhengce ji youguan wenti de diaocha baogao" [Survey report concerning the implementation of the party's policies and religion and relevant issues], issued by the Standing Committee of the National People's Congress, December 10, 1985.

[72] "Zhongyang bangongting diaocha zu guanyu luoshi dang de zongjiao zhengce ji youguan wenti de diaocha baogao" (1985: 37).

[73] Ibid., 42.

[74] Ibid., 43.

[75] Ibid., 39.

and the socialist system and who are at the same time well-versed in religious learning and knowledge."[76] Put differently: patriotism is seen as the panacea for curing the religious quality problem.

In the same year as the Standing Committee's report, the PSB also released a short monograph alerting local government authorities to the rise of reactionary sects and secret societies across China.[77] Much like Russia's experience of a plural religious revival in the early 1990s, the PSB manuscript details the return of reactionary sects and secret societies masquerading as legitimate religious groups.[78] It warns local authorities that greater religious freedoms have led to the development of quasi-religious groups who "flaunt the banner of freedom of religious belief" and are "falsely proclaiming themselves to be adherents of the 'Buddhist religion,' or of the 'Confucius religion.'"[79]

The PSB mongraph is equally striking in its portrayal of religious groups, their potential for rebellion, and future challenges to the authority of the CCP. In one case, the manuscript claims entire villages are reverting to their pre-1949 syncretic loyalties. In another example, it tells of quasi-religious groups attempting to "fabricate rumors, attack the party and the socialist system, and proclaim themselves to be gods in the vain hope of bringing about a change of dynasty."[80] In Jilin province, for instance, it notes that the leader of one secret society declared himself emperor and then swindled followers out of ¥8,500 RMB (roughly $1,000), six watches, and one bicycle on the pretext that he was planning to overthrow the regime.[81] At other points the monograph details how followers of the sect *Da Dao Hui* (Big Sword Society) in Sichuan took to the streets shouting: "First we'll kill the party, then we'll kill the Youth League, and then we'll kill every single cadre in the brigade and in the commune!"[82] In Yunnan, it notes that the Taoist sect *Yi Guan Dao* (Way of Unity) has extensive networks extending to "over six different regions, prefectures, and municipalities – embracing in all 78 communes and 6 labor reform units, and encompassing a total of 1,045 active members," warning local cadres that they might soon be irrelevant.[83] The underlying message is one of caution – the religious revival is unpredictable and potentially dangerous.

The 1980s–90s: Tightening Religious Policies

By the late 1980s, a whirlwind of documents had been circulated from various goverment ministries with the common purpose of better managing the growing

---

[76] Ibid., 40. On the relationship between Protestantism and patriotism in China, see also Dunch (2008); Vala (2009).

[77] *Fandong Hui-Dao-Men jianjie* [An introduction to the reactionary sects and societies] (1985).

[78] On the danger of folk religions transforming into cults, see Luo (1997).

[79] *Fandong Hui-Dao-Men jianjie* [An introduction to the reactionary sects and societies] (1985: 56).

[80] Ibid., 61.

[81] Ibid., 63.

[82] Ibid.

[83] Ibid., 56.

religiosity on the ground. It was increasingly clear that local cadres did not know quite what to make of the central directives or how religion should be used to serve the state.[84] At the same time, regime leaders were watching events unfold across the communist neighborhood and increasingly nervous of their potential diffusion. Of particular concern was the Solidarity movement in Poland, which united workers, teachers, and intellectuals with the Catholic Church and ultimately led to a democratic Poland.[85] To be sure, images of the protestors marching behind pictures of Pope John Paul II were not lost on China's top leaders. To contain these threats, a circular was released calling for greater control over the Catholic Church in China.[86] The policy brief claimed that the Vatican was trying to gain control over the independent Chinese Catholic Church and had "made use of its international status and the faith that the clergy show toward the Pope to send agents into China."[87] The circular argued that the Vatican "has also used other clandestine means to appoint bishops secretly and has conspired to stir up underground groups"; therefore, the party must firmly implement the policy of independence and autonomy of the Chinese Catholic Church and intensify the ideological education of the clergy.[88]

The fears of foreign influence and the potential role for religion in challenging the authority of the party were not alleviated. In the aftermath of the 1989 Tiananmen student uprising, central party documents reflected the leadership's escalating concern of associational groups, and of religion in particular, as a potential force to split the nation. This shift is not surprising considering the recent collapse of the Soviet Union, the perception that communist countries in Eastern Europe had failed to control religion, and the fear of contagion. Although the Chinese student movement had no overt ties to religion, many religious leaders were openly supportive of the students and the protests. This suggested to regime leaders the need for greater supervision over all forms of associational life.[89] To reflect these concerns, new policies were released re-emphasizing that religion should not be used by "hostile forces from abroad" to infiltrate and divide the nation.[90]

---

[84] Some of these documents include the following: Document 16, which details how religion should be treated in schools in minority areas; Document 60, which contains information concerning Buddhist and Taoist monasteries and their reconstruction; and Document 68, a combined document from eight ministries distinguishing between religion and feudal superstition. For a detailed discussion of these and other directives, see Seymour and Wehrli (1994), also see W. Yu (1994) on how to manage religious groups and interpret central policies.

[85] See Sarotte (2012); Ramet (1992); Nielsen (1991).

[86] Document 3: Circular on Stepping Up Control over the Catholic Church to Meet the New Situation.

[87] Document 3, 50.

[88] Document 3, 50–1.

[89] Marsh (2011: 219–20).

[90] Document 6: A Circular on Some Problems Concerning the Further Improvement of Work on Religion. In January 1994 the State Council released Order 144: Regulations on the Supervision of the Religious Activities of Foreigners in China.

Over the next several years, reports continued to reach Beijing of local governments' inconsistent registration or ad hoc suppression of religious communities. Again, this reinforced the opinion that offical policies needed revision. To address these concerns, additional documents seeking to standardize the management and registration of religious venues were handed down.[91] These documents clarified (and repeated) that only the five official religions may register with local authorities, all religions must have a fixed place of worship, a state-approved professional clergy, a management committee for religious adherents, proof that citizens are believers and regularly participate, and a legal (domestic) source of income.[92] Religious groups that do not satisfy all of these criteria are denied registration and are therefore illegal. Like Russia, the registration process for religious groups is renewed annually and is fairly straightforward; however, the Chinese addendums indicate that an additional "opinion" may be submitted by the village (or township) government or from the city neighborhood committee to a religious groups' application.[93] Although the document does not explain what the opinion should contain, it is likely that some actual sense of the local situation might inform the legality of the religious venue and patriotic nature of the religious personnel.

In 1996, the State Administration of Religious Affairs (SARA) circulated yet another layer of oversight over religious actors.[94] This addendum explains that the local departments responsible for religious groups' registration must also conduct annual inspections. Inspections are evaluated on a pass or fail basis, and the main criteria for a passing grade include demonstrating obedience to national policies, no connections with foreign religious groups, and transparent financial practices.[95] Religious venues that fail an inspection are given a grace period to rectify any errors; however, if a religious group is unable to rectify the errors or refuses any aspect of the inspection, it will be ordered to immediately cease all religious activities.[96]

The Anticult Campaign

Despite the ambiguities in religious policy, or perhaps because of them, the religious revival continued throughout the 1990s. In addition to the five official religions, traditional *qigong* groups became increasingly popular across the country.[97] In Chinese, *qi* literally means energy or cosmic breath and *gong*

---

[91] Order 145: Regulation Regarding the Management of Place of Religious Activities (1994) and Registration Procedures for Venues for Religious Activities (Released by the State Council May 1, 1994); Spiegel (1997).
[92] Registration Procedures for Venues for Religious Activities, Article 2.
[93] Ibid., Article 3.
[94] Method for the Annual Inspection of Places of Religious Activity, released by the RAB of the State Council, July 29, 1996.
[95] Method for the Annual Inspection of Places of Religious Activity, Articles 8–10.
[96] Ibid., Article 14.
[97] The qigong movement has a long history in China, dating back to medical texts in the Jin dynasty (265–317 CE). In modern history its importance can be traced to the 1950s when

translates to skill. Although, there is no Western equivalent to qigong, it most closely resembles New Age movements in which practitioners combine breathing exercises, meditation, and mysticism to improve spiritual and physical well-being.[98] In the 1990s, "qigong fever" (*qigong re*) infected a diverse stratum of society with the promise of healing powers and an ethical code linked to traditional Chinese valuses. Some estimates suggests that at the height of the qigong fad, the number of practitioners ranged between sixty and two hundred million, which would make them one of the largest associational communities in China.[99] Other scholars maintain that the popularity of qigong reached even to the highest levels of the party and that qigong benefited from indirect government encouragement.[100] In 1986, for example, the government openly supported the establishment of the nationwide Qigong Chinese Research Association, with the hope that mass practice of qigong would lessen the demands on an already overburdened health care system.[101]

Qigong fever, however, was not universally welcome in all locales. Reports of local officials criticizing and cracking down on different qigong groups and their charismatic masters began to appear in the Chinese media. At the center of many of these controversies was the popular qigong group Falun Gong.[102] Falun Gong is a quasi-religious qigong movement that began in the early 1990s in northeast China and combines breathing exercises, daily meditation, and shadowboxing routines with the syncretized teachings of Buddhism and Taoism.[103] The teachings of Falun Gong explain that meditation cultivates truth, benevolence, and forbearance among followers, and with great discipline believers can cultivate supernatural powers and "reach very high realms, enlightening to the true meanings of life, and finding the path of return to their origins and true selves."[104]

---

qigong was championed by the CCP as a more holistic and Chinese alternative to Western medicine, see Leung (2002: 767). For a discussion of the origins, rise, and fall of the qigong movements in China, see Palmer (2007); Chen (2003b; 1995). On Falun Gong, see Ownby (2008); Leung (2002); Tong (2002, 2009).

[98] An increasingly popular form of qigong in the West is taichi.

[99] See statement made to the Congressional-Executive Commission on China by Dr. David Ownby, "Unofficial Religions in China," May 23, 2005, available at: http://www.cecc.gov/sites/chinacommission.house.gov/files/documents/roundtables/2005/CECC%20Roundtable%20Testimony%20-%20David%20Ownby%20-%205.23.05.pdf (last accessed August 13, 2013).

[100] Leung (2002: 772); Ownby (2003: 306).

[101] Ownby (2003: 304). It is worth mentioning that Falun Gong was a member of the national association in 1992.

[102] Falun Gong, also called *Falun xiulian dafa*, literally means "Practice of the Wheel of Law," and *Falun Dafa* translates as the "Great Way of the Wheel of Law." These names are used interchangeably.

[103] The *Zhuan Falun* is the primary text of the Falun Gong movement and is available in ten languages at: http://www.falundafa.org/eng/books.html (last accessed August 13, 2013).

[104] Quoted from the Falun Gong official website. Available at: http://www.falundafa.org/eng/intro.html (last accessed August 13, 2013).

The teachings of Falun Gong, its path to enlightenment, and the authenticity of its claims of supernatural healing were questioned in various media outlets across the country. In response to these criticisms, supporters of Falun Gong took to the streets in protest.[105] In 1998 more than one thousand practitioners gathered outside of a Beijing television station following a critical report about Falun Gong. In Shandong, Falun Gong adherents staged a sit-in in front of the *Shandong Qiliu Evening News Daily* office demanding an apology for an inflammatory report about the group's leader. The protests escalated after an editorial warned that Falun Gong adherents were being swindled by "deceitful lies" and the parlor tricks of its leader. Indeed, this polemical article piqued the Falun Gong community who mobilized more than six thousand followers to march on government offices in Tianjin. Unsatisfied by the response of the local authorities, and perhaps even a bit emboldened by the lack of sanctions, Falun Gong practitioners escalated their tactics. In April 1999, approximately ten thousand Falun Gong enthusiasts sat in silence from sunrise to sunset outside of *Zhongnanhai* – the offices and residential compound of top-ranking party officials in Beijing. The demonstration called for an end to harassment of Falun Gong by local media outlets and the freedom to practice their form of qigong without government interference or discrimination. This time the government took notice.

The Zhongnanhai demonstrations shifted the political opportunities for Falun Gong and more generally for all religious groups in China. First and most important, it signaled to Chinese leadership that Falun Gong was an organized and efficient group willing to take political risks to achieve its aims.[106] Whether or not this was Falun Gong's intention, the mobilization in front of Zhongnanhai seemed to take the government and public security forces by surprise, fueling fears that Falun Gong was more than a qigong group, but perhaps also a secret society seeking to subvert the regime.[107] Second, the propaganda machine of the CCP unveiled a swift media campaign against Falun Gong labeling it as an "evil cult" (*xiejiao*) with a nefarious agenda.[108] A warning was printed on the front page of the *People's Daily* forbidding citizens, especially party members, to take part in the beliefs and practices of the cult; news reports showed images of Falun Gong books and videos being burned and bulldozed; a government documentary about the evils of the cult and how it had disrupted social order, spread fallacies, and deluded people was repeatedly broadcast on national television; and, finally an order for the arrest of Li Hongzhi, the founder and spiritual leader of Falun Gong, was released to all

[105] Before the April 1999 protests, criticisms of Falun Gong spawned more than 300 protests, including uprisings in Guanxi, Henan, Gansu, and Shenzhen; see Leung (2002); Xiao (2001); Eckholm (2001).

[106] Tong (2009: 660).

[107] On the government's failure to anticipate the Falun Gong protests, see Tong (2009); Hu (2003); N. Chen (2003b); Kipnis (2001); Shue (2001).

[108] On the framing of the anticult campaign, see Tong (2009).

internal public security organs and Interpol.[109] Even top party leaders spoke out against the dangers of the cult as a profound threat to social stability and challenge for the CCP. Party Secretary General Jiang Zemin, for instance, drew parallels with the Solidarity movement that challenged communism in Poland, and the head of the United Front Work Department (UFWD) asserted that "[t]he Falun Gong incident is the most important political incident since the 'June 4' [Tiananmen Square] political disturbance in 1989. The generation and spread of Falun Gong is a political struggle launched by hostile forces both in and outside the country to contend with our party."[110]

Third, the propaganda campaign was also followed with legislation banning Falun Gong and legalizing the punishment of associational groups that promoted "cultlike" activities.[111] New legislation was introduced criminalizing such followers, directing that "those who organize superstitious sects and secret societies or use superstition to violate laws or administrative regulations" are subject to three to seven years impriosonment.[112] The Ministry of Public Security also released a notice to all local public security offices and religious bureaus regarding the identification and banning of cults. Any organization with the following characteristics should be identified as a cult:

1. Groups that set up illegal organizations in the name of religion or qigong;
2. Groups that deify their leaders;
3. Groups that initiate and spread superstitious and heterodox beliefs;
4. Groups that utilize various means to fabricate and spread superstitions and heterodox beliefs to excite doubts and deceive the people, recruit and control its members by force; and
5. Groups that engage in disturbing social order in an organized manner that brings injury to the lives and properties of the citizens.[113]

Even at the height of the anticult campaign, the Chinese government stressed the respect and protection of legal religious activities, but the effects of the crackdown reverberated across the larger religious community.[114] Religious leaders from the five official religions released statements against Falun Gong, calling it a cult and its members "hoodwinked by the malicious fallacies of

---

[109] See, for example, "Circular of the Central Committee of the Chinese Communist (CCP) Party on Forbidding Communist Party Members from Practicing Falun Dafa" (1999); "Ministry of Personnel Issues Notice Stipulating that State Functionaries May Not Practice Falun Dafa" (1999); "Regarding the Wanted Order Issued for the Suspect of Li Hongzhi" (1999); N. Chen (2003b: 514–16); Leung (2002: 778–80).

[110] Z. Wang (1999).

[111] See especially Xia and Hua (1999a); Tong (2009) for a discussion of the laws, ordinances, and polices involved in the suppression of Falun Gong.

[112] Article 300: The Criminal Law of the People's Republic of China, Section 1 (1999).

[113] Notice on Various Issues Regarding Identifying and Banning of Cultic Organizations (2000).

[114] "Freedom for Religion, No Room for Evil Cults" (2001).

Li Hongzhi," the leader of Falun Gong.[115] The vice-chairman of the TSPM described Li Hongzhi as "a vulture covered with beautiful feathers, whose ugly body will be exposed to the public if shaken slightly," and the head of the Taoist Association called on all Chinese Taoists "to strongly fight against the cult and try to help more victims of Falun Gong return to the right track."[116] The RPAs also took a strong stance against the group. Publications from the five patriotic associations all ran anti–Falun Gong editorials denouncing it as a cult and distancing their religious practices from Falun Gong. Many Buddhist and Taoist temples and monestaries even organized additional public forums to educate their followers on how their faiths differed from the practice of Falun Gong.[117] Finally, the anticult campaign even spilled over into secular associational groups. Recall from the introductory chapter that ballroom dancers in Changchun (Li Hongzhi's hometown) also cancelled their morning activities for fear of being associated with Falun Gong, thus rendering public parks almost empty.[118]

New Regulations on Religious Affairs

As the anticult campaign wound down, Beijing released a new round of policies aimed at solidifying control over religious affairs. The lengthy Regulations on Religious Affairs (forty-eight articles and seven chapters) was designed as a handbook for local cadres to manage religious life.[119] This new document did not mark a dramatic shift from previous policies in either spirit or content but instead attempted to eliminate some of the arbitrariness of earlier central directives. For example, the new regulations limited the five legal religions' activities to fixed places of worship, such as registered Buddhist monasteries, Taoist temples, mosques, churches and other "fixed premises for religious activities." By focusing on "fixed locations" for religious activities, the handbook emphasizes that the state has the right to confiscate any property used for religious activity without prior approval.[120] The implication here is that the policy implicitly targets unregistered Catholics and Protestant churches, which meet in private apartments.

The 2005 document further details the requirements for erecting new places of worship. More specifically, the plans for new religious buildings (for worship and training) must be unanimously approved by three levels of bureaucracy: the county or municipal Religious Affairs Bureau where the religious site is planned, the Religious Affairs Bureau at the provincial or autonomous region level, and finally at the national level by the SARA. In this process,

---

[115] "Chinese Religious Leaders Indignant over Falun Gong" (2001).
[116] Li and Di (2001).
[117] Zhao and Yu (2002); see also Ji (2012–13).
[118] Also see F. Yang (2006: 113).
[119] "Regulations on Religious Affairs," March 1, 2005.
[120] Ibid., Article 43.

registration begins at the lowest level and must be vetted at each subsequent level. For a proposal to advance, there must be evidence of (1) sufficient demand among local citizens, (2) qualified religious personal, (3) domestic funding for construction and maintenance, and (4) the guarantee that the intended place of worship will not interfere in the normal production and livelihood of the neighboring units and residents.[121]

The new regulations additionally clarify that "qualified" religious personnel must be approved by the Religious Affairs Bureau at the county level, and all religious leaders must demonstrate their religious training to both their patriotic associations and the SARA, thereby ensuring that all religious personnel are vetted by the state. In fact, the new regulations go so far as to single out two religious leaders that must be approved at the national level: the secession of the living Buddha in Tibetan Buddhism and the appointment of Catholic bishops.[122] Again, these details evoke the suspicions of religious groups and fear of outside influence.

The new regulations further clarify the responsibility of the management of religious sites that function as places of worship and tourist attractions. Although earlier documents suggest that task is shared among the three separate departments of religion, tourism, and parks and gardens, the new regulations place the local government in charge.[123] This shift is revealing of the expanding control over religion because a preponderance of religious sites are playing the dual role of places of worship and tourist attractions. For instance, of the roughly 350 religious sites in Shanghai, a sizable number are also considered tourist attractions. Thus, the implication is that a majority of religious sites are under the authority of nonreligious bodies.

Finally, it is important to note that one section of the new policy increases the rights of religious actors. Article 48 states that "[a]ny state functionary, in administration of religious affairs, abuses his power, neglects his duty or commits illegalities for personal gain or by fraudulent means, and a crime is thus constituted, he shall be investigated for criminal liability according to law."[124] To be sure, this is a positive step for the protection of religious actors by addressing state abuses of power, but such a step is small in the face of the many other long-standing concerns.

Chinese Religious Policy in Perspective

Among the remaining ambiguities in Chinese religious policy, three are of particular concern. The first is the artificial categorization of only five religions, which perpetuates the oligopoly of Buddhism, Taoism, Islam, Protestantism, and Catholicism in China. Religious groups that fall outside these five faiths

---

[121] Ibid., Articles 12–14.
[122] Ibid., Articles 27–9.
[123] Ibid., Article 26.
[124] Ibid., Article 38.

or blend elements of more than one are offered no legal protection or right to engage in religious activities. A second concern is the continued use of "normal" (*zhengchang*) to describe religious activities and groups.[125] Such language reaffirms the role of the state in defining the parameters of normalcy. However, none of the religious policies explain precisely what qualifies as "normal" or "abnormal" behavior, or how to distinguish between the two. Thus, local authorities have considerable room for interpretation of religious policies, which can lead to uneven implementation. Moreover, religious groups are in the uncertain position of not knowing whether their activities fall inside or outside the boundaries of the law and whether these boundaries are fixed or fluid.

A final concern is the absence of rights and protections for religious communities. Imagine the plausible scenario of conflict erupting between a predatory local cadre and a religious community. What are the avenues of redress for religious actors? If the patriotic association is unable to come to the aid of the religious community, can religious leaders appeal higher up the bureaucratic ladder, and if so, to whom and how? Thus, despite more than three decades of reforms and a succession of religious policies that have been written and revised, many important questions remain unanswered in both the management of religion and the boundaries of religious freedom.[126]

CONCLUSIONS

From this survey of religious reforms in Russia and China, we can draw several lessons. The first is that despite the very different economic and political restructuring taking place during the 1980s and 1990s, both Moscow and Beijing embarked on remarkably similar paths of creating a more hospitable environment for religious expression while simultaneously maintaining control over religious actors. In the 1980s, both countries sought to reconcile their regimes' repressive histories with religion, usher in a period of greater religious freedom, and bring religious polices more inline with international standards. A brief honeymoon period of liberalizing reforms and an unregulated religious market followed. However, as the religious revival grew in size and diversity, it became clear to a still evolving and nervous regime that its policies on religious groups would need to retighten. Fear of foreign influence and religious communities subverting the state loomed large, and increasing state control of the religious marketplace was reflected in new policies. In Russia, a hierarchy of religions was established with clear winners and losers; and in China, a flurry of policies were introduced to monitor and manage religious groups.

Underlying reforms in both countries is the idea that religion should continue to serve the state. This meant that the Russian Orthodox Church would

---

[125] *Zhengchang* is often translated as "normal" but may also be understood as orthodox.
[126] Spiegel (1997); Seymour and Wehrli (1994).

regain its position of privilege and help underwrite the nation-building projects of the Kremlin. In China, religious groups from the five religions were strongly encouraged to develop patriotic believers and promote national unity, and religious groups operating outside of the state's parameters would not be tolerated. Therefore, through either direct or indirect channels, the return of religiosity purportedly served the interests of the state.

A second lesson is that the central laws and directives on religion are often vague and contradictory. Religious policies follow a familiar pattern of implementation, reform and then yet another round of policies. The need for constant revisions, however, is more than simply a product of carelessly written polices – it also suggests a tactical approach by Moscow and Beijing to manage religious associational life. Both regimes seek flexibility to amend religious policies based on changes in political climates and political opportunity structures. As the Center's priorities become better informed – based on internal surveys, pressure from religious communities, or reports filtering up from the regions – vaguely written policies give the Center the elasticity to refine its approach toward religion, while ensuring religious groups continue to serve the interests of the regime. For Moscow and Beijing, then, the creation of ambiguous policies is a strategy that allows the Center the flexibility to adapt and amend preferences over time. This is not entirely surprising, considering that authoritarian elites do not want to be constrained and often have a pragmatic approach toward policy making.[127] However, it is also reasonable to suggest that a second rationale is to allow local governments a certain amount of leeway in regulating religion. Here, we can assume that the Russian and Chinese leadership recognize that local officials tend to have a more nuanced grasp of the situation "on the ground" and are more capable of managing local issues identified by the Center. To this extent, then, delegation from the Center to the local takes advantage of the decentralized systems already in place.

At the same time, the ambiguity and open contradictions in religious policies empowers local authorities to manage groups according to different standards and may in turn encourage some bureaucrats to view ambiguous central policies as the equivalent of having no policies at all.[128] As Tu Weiming writes more generally of Center-local relations, "the regions themselves have clearly benefited from the accommodating policies of the Center. They seem to know well how to exploit Beijing's lack of self-confidence and the ambiguity of the central directives, without totally undermining the system and thus risking the danger of anarchism or, perhaps worse, warlordism."[129] This suggests that

---

[127] Here, it is also important to note that the differences in types of authoritarianism reveals the rinse and repeat strategy is more noticeable in China, where the party is less constrained by democratic institutions and can introduce new policies without going through the appearance of legislative debate.

[128] Manion (1992); also Grim and Finke (2011: 136).

[129] Tu (1993: xii).

the ambiguity on paper can run counter to the Center's intended goal, and what may represent a tactical advantage for the Center can foster noncompliance or considerable discrepancy in the treatment of religious communities at the local level. It also raises the more general question: will wiggle room in the religious arena spill over into other policy areas?

The final lesson from this chapter is that the practical implementation of religious policies lies in the hands of local governments and bureaucracies. It is up to local elites to decide whether religious activities and rituals in their region are illegal, whether they fall under the definition of feudal superstitions and should be suppressed, or whether they can be officially registered and protected. Religious policies that are lacking in content or unclear on paper leave local authorities to their own devises in their implementation. As the next two chapters reveal, this has led to innovative management of religion resulting in greater religious freedom in some areas to the harassment of religious actors in others. In China, several local goverments have issued additional religious regulations to help clarify the ambiguity from above and accomindate the local religious landscape.[130] Zhejiang's and Hunan's religious policies, for example, delete reference to the five official religions, presumably to allow for the legal practice and registration of folk religions; Heilongjiang and Inner Mongolia added sections recognizing the Russian Orthodox Church as a traditional religion; and Zhejiang, Hunan, and Chongqing's policies permit religious services to be held in private homes, so long as these activities do not negatively influence the lives of participants and neighbors.

Other regions did not go as far as implementing new religious policies but are equally pioneering in their management of religious groups that fall outside of the five religions. In Fujian, for example, the popular Mazu cult, which falls within the Center's definition of feudal superstition, has flourished with the help of the local government. Local cadres have found ways around central policies and permit greater popular religious freedom by reinventing Mazu as a cultural relic and tourist attraction. Correspondingly, on the island of Putuoshan in Zhejiang, local authorities harnessed the healing powers of the Buddhist Goddess of Mercy *Guanyin* to attract tourism.[131]

Similar patterns of uneven and selective implementation of religious policies have emerged in Russia. Following the 1997 Law on religion, local bureaucrats became the arbitrators of religious freedom with the power to determine whether a group has historic roots in the region, whether its liturgical texts are authentic, and whether its leaders are competent. This proved to be highly problematic because of the seemingly arbitrary characteristics of political decision making and the fact that the regime was not holding up its own constitutional

---

[130] Including, Shanghai, Henan, Shanxi, Zhejiang, Anhui, Beijing, Hunan, Chongqing, Heilongjiang, and Inner Mongolia.

[131] For the reinventing of religious activities as culture, see also Savadove (2012); Szyoni (2005); M. Yang (2004a); Lyons (2000); Yeung (2000); M. Wang (1993).

protection of religious freedom.[132] For instance, in Tula, the local government initiated intimidation campaigns against evangelical Baptists, including shutting off power and water to their church and hiring local laborers to break up a tent revival.[133] In Khakassia, local authorities announced plans to demolish a Pentecostal church, maintaining that it was an illegal construction and threatening the health of neighbors.[134] In Moscow, a district court banned all organized activity of Jehovah's Witnesses on the grounds that they posed a threat to society and revoked the nongovernmental organization registration of the Salvation Army as a "paramilitary foreign organization."[135]

These examples remind us that religion is political and that all politics, even in strong authoritarian regimes, is local. It also compels us to focus our analysis on the microlevel and to systematically rethink what factors shape political authorities' attitudes and behavior toward competing religious communities, and which strategies are employed by religious actors to pursue their own strategic and spiritual interests. These issues serve as the focus of the next two chapters.

---

[132] Fagan (2013).

[133] Since the closing of the tent revival, there have been 10 arson attacks on Baptist churches in Tula. Pastor Nikolai Dudenkov of the Tulan Baptist Church told International Religious Freedom Watch that the local police are the key suspects; see "U.S. Commission on Security and Cooperation in Europe (Helsinki Commission) on Hearing of Unregistered Religious Groups in Russia" (2005). See also Elliott and Corrado (1999) for an itemization of 69 instances of state harassment, restriction or threat of restriction against non-Orthodox religious communities in the 15 months following the implementation of the 1997 Law.

[134] "V Sajanogorske pod ugrozoj snosa okazalsja zhiloj dom pastora Cerkvi hristian very evangel'skoj 'Proslavlenie'" [The house of the pastor of the evangeical Christian Church in Sayanogorsk is under the threat of demolition] (2010).

[135] In October 2006, the European Court of Human Rights issued a judgment against the Russian government and the liquidation of the Salvation Army; see http://sclj.org/press_releases/ 06-1009-Religious_Freedom_Protected.htm (last accessed August 13, 2013).

4

The Political Economy of Religious Revival

When it's a question of money, everybody is of the same religion.

– Voltaire

The previous chapter concluded that it is at the local level where the political management of religion largely takes place and, consequently, where the relationship between the autocratic state and religious life is defined. The purpose of this chapter, therefore, is to explore the dynamics of religious and local regime relations to illustrate the varying degrees of cooperation, compliance, and control. This chapter demonstrates that the key points of contact between religious groups and their authoritarian overseers are often based on material, rather than spiritual, concerns. Indeed, what frequently brings the two sides together is a common preoccupation with money.

Transition politics across Russia and China have left local governments and religious communities facing varying degrees of uncertainty. Some of the most pressing concerns are economic, and as a result political elites seek creative solutions that will not only maintain stability and assist in governance, but will also grow the economy. Religious communities also face financial concerns of their own. Since the 1980s, religious groups in Russia and China have been slowly reclaiming property that was confiscated or destroyed by the state. With the return of property, comes the daunting task of rebuilding after decades of neglect. The reality is that much of the property is in a serious state of disrepair or simply too small to accommodate the growing number of worshipers. What is more, religious organizations rarely have the financial means for such large-scale restoration projects. In addition to these financial burdens, religious communities must also navigate bureaucratic red tape to legally reopen places for worship. After all, these are authoritarian political systems where religious freedoms are vaguely defined and selectively protected, and there are no guarantees that religious groups will be able to secure the required permits. These conditions, in short, provide powerful incentives for government officials and religious leaders to trade favors, offer promises of reciprocal support, and above all exchange resources to meet pressing needs.

This chapter begins by introducing the material resources each side brings to the bargaining table and shows that these resources are often highly idiosyncratic. The next section analyzes the range of bargains struck between religious groups and their authoritarian overseers, suggesting that material-based cooperation can evolve from single-issue games to more lasting and strategic partnerships. Here, I highlight two arenas of collaboration: property politics and faith-based tourism. The conclusion of the chapter revisits several of the arguments guiding this study, compares religious-state bargaining in the two countries, and identifies who is gaining the most from these exchanges and why.

THE CURRENCY OF EXCHANGE

Material resources are bargaining chips used to secure interests and goals. They are the assets of an organization – tangible and quantifiable resources that are easily identifiable and divisible, and that can be reduced to their monetary value. This does not mean, however, that the vast majority of material resources exchanged between religious and autocratic actors are limited to simple transfers of hard currency. On the contrary, both local governments and religious communities are creative in identifying and ascertaining their own assets and the needs of the other side. Moreover, religious-state bargaining around material concerns does not mean that nonmaterial assets, such as cultural capital and political power, do not enter into the complex negotiations between the two sides (this is the focus of the next chapter) but rather that economic concerns tend to be at the center of their interaction. Indeed, there is a cash nexus at the core of religious and local regime relations, where material resources flow between the two sides, facilitate their interactions, and promote smooth and efficient relations so that both stand to profit. It is much easier for religious and political authority to find a middle ground on issues of money, rather than on the more risky and less divisible areas of power and prestige.

The Material Resources of Local Governments

The material resources that local governments bring to the table are diverse but can generally be divided into two types: (1) bureaucratic stamps and (2) subsidies. Both of these resources have monetary value and are given selectively to reward and maintain stable relations with religious organizations. In authoritarian regimes like Russia and China, bureaucratic stamps are a necessary condition for religious communities to operate and grow legally in the public sphere.[1] Local officials and bureaucrats must sign off on permits to build and expand places of worship or centers for religious training; they determine whether a religious group qualifies for state support or should be suppressed; they decide whether religious leaders are competent to conduct services; and they evaluate whether religious bodies are allowed to publish and distribute liturgical literature. Local governments are the gatekeepers of all legal religious activity and have considerable influence over daily religious life. As a result, bureaucratic stamps are sought after resources that reduce uncertainty for religious communities and help ensure their survival.

At the same time, local governments also have access to a wide range of subsidies that have tangible returns for religious groups. More specifically, local governments may offer tax privileges, energy subsidies, free land, rent reductions, and interest-free loans to help lighten the financial burdens of religious organizations. The combination of these two sets of resources forms a powerful and comprehensive set of bargaining chips that local governments use to manage religious communities and solidify religious-state relations.

Red Stamps

In consolidated democracies bureaucracies are relatively rule-bound organizations. When a Baptist church in the United States applies for tax-exempt status or permission to expand their gymnasium, the process is generally straightforward, so long as the paperwork is in order. The bureaucratic organs and institutional structures in authoritarian regimes function quite differently and often with little transparency. When a Protestant church attempts to register in Russia or China, there is the real possibility that their application will be denied or, by accident or decision, lost for decades.[2] As one charismatic church pastor in Russia remarked: "the government never says no, but drowns us in paperwork."[3] Another suggested that "it is easier to register a nightclub than an evangelical church [in Russia]."[4] Technically, the registration of religious groups is a basic right and should be available to all eligible groups, but these statements indicate that under autocracy there is often a sharp disconnect between laws and practice.

The most basic and essential bureaucratic stamp sought by a religious group operating in the public square is registration. This stamp determines a group's ability to function legally, and nearly every other form of sanction or subsidy

---

[1] Of course, religious communities operating without red stamps are also able to grow and establish popular legitimacy, see Wiktorowitz (2001). However, they tend to face heightened risks of state suppression because they lack legal protections.

[2] Interview with former bureaucrat C, March 2006, Nizhny Novgorod; interview with Religious Affairs Bureau bureaucrat S, August 2007, Shanghai.

[3] Interview with charismatic Pastor V, July 2012, Nizhny Novgorod.

[4] Interview with charismatic church leader A, July 2012, Nizhny Novgorod.

depends on successful registration. However, as the previous chapter detailed, the process of registration is legally and practically complex.

In addition to registration, local authorities have other stamps within their toolkit that are beneficial and desirable to religious organizations. Of these, the option of designating a place of worship or a religious monument as a cultural relic is notable. Such an appellation can be a valuable resource for religious communities because it signifies the regime's long-term commitment to the preservation of religious property. As a cultural relic, moreover, government institutions can legally support a religious organization under the auspices of historical preservation, something that would otherwise be prohibited in Russia and China.[5]

The status as a cultural relic is advantageous for religious communities in other ways. Religious organizations may gain a certain amount of public recognition and prestige as a cultural relic by demonstrating their continuity with the past and position in society. The appellation lengthens the shadow of the future by memorializing part of the religious group into the official state archive. Practically speaking, such an appointment also provides a religious community with some protection from real estate developers and even government elites who might otherwise try to edge them off their land for commercial developments.[6]

At the same time, the appointment of a cultural relic is a resource that regime elites may only offer selectively. At a minimum, a religious group must have a defensible historical claim, which usually means prerevolutionary roots. However, even when prerevolutionary histories are present, there are limits to what local officials are prepared to protect. In Nizhny Novgorod, for example, the Evangelical Baptist Church is one of the oldest Baptist congregations in Russia, dating back more than 130 years. After the revolution, the Baptist church was one of the first to be razed, and the two-hundred-member congregation was forced to rent various spaces for services, including the philharmonic, a school auditorium, and finally a Lutheran church. By the 1930s, the Soviet state began

---

[5] In Russia and China, the laws and directives managing religion allow state preservation of religious property of historical significance. Article 4.3 of the Russian 1997 Law permits the state to "aid religious organizations in the restoration, maintenance, and protection of buildings and other objects which are monuments of history and culture." In China, a 1985 National People's Congress report stresses the importance of preserving religious sites for both their historic and tourist value; see "Zhongyang bangongting diaocha zu guanyu luoshi dang de zongjiao zhengce ji youguan wenti de diaocha baogao" [Report concerning the implementation of the party's religious policies and related issues] (1985).

[6] During 2005–6, there was concern about real estate developers in Nizhny and Kazan destroying property or attempting to push residents off of their land to make way for commercial developments. Local governments have also been involved in these efforts. In the mid-1990s, the Shaimiev administration in Tatarstan announced the "President's Housing Project," which involved clearing large swaths of Kazan to make way for luxury apartments. Following the announcement, there were a series of unexplained arsons in the targeted areas of dilapidated houses and prerevolutionary buildings where the residents refused to sell or relocate. On the President's Housing Plan, see Graney (2007: 19).

to intensely restrict religious activity, and it became impossible for the Baptists to find legal places of worship. At that point, the only option for the Baptists (as well as other Protestants) was to hold services in the basement of one of the few open Orthodox churches. Thus, from 1931 to 1935, the Baptists worshiped in the basement of an Orthodox church adjacent to the Nizhny Kremlin, which had maintained good relations with local authorities. Not surprisingly, this close proximity to power also allowed the regime to monitor their activities.[7]

By the mid-1930s, the window for any public forms of religious expression was quickly closing. During Stalin's purges, one Baptist pastor in Nizhny was imprisoned for refusing to cease preaching, and the remaining congregation was dissolved.[8] It was not until the beginning of the Second World War – when Stalin allowed for more open religious expression to increase support for the regime – that the fragmented Baptist congregation began to reorganize. Somewhat unexpectedly, at least to church leaders (and likely to regime elites as well), church membership had grown.[9]

When the window for religious expression widened under Gorbachev, the fragmented Baptist congregation had doubled in size. Plans to build a new church began immediately, and with the support of American Baptists, the congregation purchased land.[10] Because of an interest in preserving the history of the church, the new plans followed the blueprints of the church built in 1912. When church leaders approached the local government for the necessary permits, they realized they were also eligible to apply for status as a cultural relic because they were reconstructing a prerevolutionary building following original blueprints. Yet, despite the strength of the Baptist's historical claim, their application was repeatedly denied. One church leader explained that a bureaucrat from the Office of the State Cultural Heritage Protection for the Nizhny Novgorod Region (*Upravlenija gosudarstvennoj ohrany ob"ektov kul'turnogo nasledija Nizhegorodskoj oblasti*) commented that the only religious sites worthy of state protection are those connected to the Russian Orthodox Church.[11] This comment would seem consistent with the trend of state protected sites – in

---

[7] During the 1930s, religious communities were closely monitored and some suggest infiltrated by regime representatives; see, for example, Ware (1997); Armes (1994). According to Pastor Runov, in the 1930s, Baptist church leaders were aware that their services were monitored and their congregations were being watched, but the alternative would mean disbanding their church. Pastor Runov's grandfather was one of the Baptist pastors in the 1930s. Interview with Pastor Runov, February 2006, Nizhny Novgorod.

[8] After 1935, all religious services across the country were considered illegal.

[9] The church had fifty new members; interview with Pastor Runov, February 2006, Nizhny Novgorod. On the limited toleration of the Orthodox Church under Stalin, see Ware (1997: 155–6).

[10] There are numerous restrictions on foreign organizations financially supporting Russian churches; however, these restrictions did not come into place until 1997, long after the Nizhny Baptists had received financial support from abroad.

[11] Interview with Baptist church leader F, February 2006, Nizhny Novgorod.

the larger Nizhny Novgorod region more than 95 percent of the designated "cultural-heritage objects" (*ob'ekta kul'turnogo naslledija*) are linked to the Orthodox Church.[12] This pro-Orthodox pattern is also prevalent across the Russian Federation, where roughly 97 percent of all religious- and cultural-heritage sites are affiliated with the Orthodox Church.[13]

State Subsidies

Local governments may bring other kinds of financial assistance to the bargaining table as a way to influence religious-state interaction. A good example of this occurred in the early 1990s when the Russian Orthodox Church of Nizhny Novgorod struck an unusual bargain with local authorities. At this time, the local government was encouraged from above to help rebuild numerous Orthodox cathedrals that had been closed, destroyed, or converted to other uses during the Soviet period.[14] One government official even went so far as to suggest that it was the "patriotic duty" of the state to restore the Orthodox Church.[15] However, the Nizhny government as well as many other local goverments across the country were short on funds.[16] Therefore, Nizhny officials "overlooked" the Orthodox Church's duty-free importation of cigarettes for domestic resale, and its exportation of vodka – both highly lucrative commodities. Here, the intent was that the profits would be funneled into restoring and rebuilding dilapidated Orthodox churches across the Volga region. By the mid-1990s, this practice was gradually phased out after the much of the construction was finished and other religious groups became aware of the Orthodox Church's special privileges.[17] Yet this did not mean that subsidies for the Orthodox Church ended – cigarettes and vodka were replaced by free heating and electricity for cathedrals in the region. When considering the age,

[12] See "V Nizhegorodskoj oblasti, 850 religioznyh kul'turno-istoricheskih ob"ektov" [In Nizhny Novgorod region, 850 religious sites of cultural-historical importance] (2006).

[13] Specifically, there are 6,584 objects of cultural heritage for religious purposes. Of these, 6,402 are Orthodox, 79 Muslim, 68 Roman Catholic, 13 Evangelical Lutheran, 21 Buddhist, and 1 Judaic; see "Kul't i kul'tura delit imushchestvo" [Cult and culture to divide property] (2010).

[14] In 1996-1997, local authorities in Nizhny developed a program, "The Revival of Churches in Nizhny Novgorod." As part of this initative, fifty-five Orthodox churches, four Orthodox monasteries, three Old Believers churches, and eight mosques were scheduled to be restored; see "Obsuzhdaetsja programma vozrozhdenija" [The discussion of the revival program] (1995: 1).

[15] "Cerkov' i vlast': my vmeste sluzhim otechestvu" [Church and state: together we serve the fatherland] (2000).

[16] "Samoe dushevnoe stroitel'stvo" [Most spiritual construction] (1999: 3).

[17] One Orthodox priest remarked that this practice was quite widespread in other regions as well; interview with Orthodox Father Alexander, February 2006, Nizhny Novgorod. Fagan (2013: 42) reports similar import-export activities, including the Church's request to import chicken legs under the auspices of "humanitarian aid."

size, and draftiness of a typical Orthodox cathedral and the long, sub-arctic winters in the Volga region, heating subsidies are extremely valuable resources. Again, as in the case with cigarettes and vodka, when other faiths learned of the energy subsidies, they demanded equal treatment, and the program was discontinued.[18]

Subsidies for religious organizations can also be funneled via interest-free loans and tax waivers.[19] This "free money" confers a significant opportunity to the receiving religious organization in a practical sense, and offers a concomitantly strong legitimizing aspect by directly monetizing state support. Although it would seem the loans might come at the cost of autonomy or influence, it must be remembered that such interest rates are far better than any religious organization would be able to secure independently. Consider the following example. At a large Buddhist temple located in a commercial district of Shanghai, the abbot was able to negotiate a unique loan with the district government. In this case, the temple property was returned in 1980 and was badly in need of repair, having been vandalized during the Cultural Revolution. The remaining monks, like most religious communities across China, were unable to afford the renovation needed to reopen the temple. The local government stepped in to offer an interest-free loan with the understanding that 80 percent of all temple admission fees would go directly to the local government until the loan was repaid.[20] A second stipulation was that local officials would have a hand in the scale of the renovation, and they planned to make the temple one of the largest and most impressive in the city. In short, the temple would transform into a landmark tourist attraction.

Finally, and perhaps most revealing of the district government's motivations was the condition that the refurbished temple would set aside part of its property for commercial development. To comply with this arrangement, two of the temple's outer walls were converted into small upscale shops whose rents go directly to local authorities for twenty years. At the end of this term, the temple will be allowed to decide what to do with this commercial space – either retrofit it for worship or continue the current commercial arrangement and collect the rents for themselves.[21]

[18] Interview with former bureaucrat C, March 2006, Nizhny Novgorod; interview with Orthodox Father Alexander, February 2006, Nizhny Novgorod.

[19] For example, local authorities in Jinshan gave one halal restaurant linked to a mosque discounted rent and tax waivers; see Jinshan nianjian bianzuan weiyuanhui (1996: 230); Gu and Zhu (2001: 208).

[20] Interview with accountant A for the temple, May 2007, Shanghai. As a point of reference, in 2007, admission to the temple on the first and fifteenth of each month was ¥30 RMB ($4.73); on all other days, admission is ¥8 RMB ($1.26). In 2010, after a majority of the renovations were complete, ticket prices increased to ¥100 RMB ($15.77) and ¥50 RMB ($7.88), respectively.

[21] As of 2007, some monks were quite excited about the moneymaking potential and how the future profits would be directed. Interview with Buddhist monk A, May 2007 and July 2007, Shanghai; interview with accountant A for the temple, May 2007, Shanghai; interview with Buddhist monk B, July 2007, Shanghai; interview with Buddhist monk C, July 2007, Shanghai.

ILLUSTRATIONS 4.1 AND 4.2. Buddhist temple and attached commercial development in 2007. Photos by author.

ILLUSTRATION 4.3. Buddhist temple expansion in 2010. Photo by author.

Interviews revealed that not all monks welcomed collaboration with the local government but found themselves in such an arrangement because of insufficient funds to renovate the temple. In other words, the interest-free loan was the best option available to them at the time. Some monks quietly disapproved of the government's investments in their temple, because it runs counter to Buddhist principles – the temple should be a place of learning and not commerce.[22] Others had a more positive outlook and admitted that the five thousand additional visitors each month (among which about half are tourists) have significantly increased temple revenues as well as the prestige of Buddhism in this area of the city. For these reasons, Buddhist-state collaboration may not be all that negative in the long-run.[23]

Beyond interest-free loans for the reconstruction of religious buildings, local governments may offer other material resources to entice cooperation with religious organizations. In the case of the Buddhist temple just discussed, when the local officials faced resistance from monks at the idea of their temple turning into a tourist attraction, they offered to sweeten the deal by paying the tuition of the temple abbot to study for his MBA at a local university.[24] In fact, educational subsidies are fairly common. Several monks in the city have received tuition waivers for their MBA degrees with the understanding that the degree will improve the fiscal responsibility of Buddhist temples, many of which have become major tourist attractions, and district governments receive a percentage of the profits.[25] Other district governments across Shanghai have followed suit and invested in the continuing education of religious leaders under their jurisdiction. As one bureaucrat explained, these programs have the added advantage of improving the "religious quality" (*zongjiao zhiliang*) and the general level of education among religious professionals, something local authorities believe they are lacking.[26] There is some merit to these concerns. In the early 1980s, for example, over 55 percent of all Buddhist monks and nuns in Jilin province had not finished elementary school.[27]

The investment in education is largely welcomed among religious communities. In Shanghai, several Muslim leaders have attended private English classes at local universities at the expense of their district-level Religious Affairs Bureaus (RAB). Local government officials suggest that language classes will encourage "harmonious" relations among Muslims, minorities, and the state.[28] However, the participants in the courses also insist that this is an excellent opportunity on several counts. According to one imam, the government pays the tuition that his salary could not afford, and he is able to attend classes without going through the normal, rigorous application process.[29] For instance,

---

[22] However, temples have historically been at the center of commercial activity in China.

[23] Focused discussion group with Buddhist monks L, A, O, May 2007, Shanghai.

[24] Interview with accountant A for the temple, May 2007, Shanghai.

[25] Interview with Buddhist monk L, May 2007, Shanghai; interview with Buddhist monk D, May 2007, Shanghai; interview with Buddhist monk B, May 2007, Shanghai.

[26] Interview with Religious Affairs Bureau bureaucrat J, June 2007, Shanghai. On the importance of improving the quality of religious leaders in China, also see M. Yang (2008: 28).

[27] H. Jin et al. (2000: 106). One significant contributing factor of the low education levels among religious personnel was that closure of schools during the Cultural Revolution.

[28] Interview with Imam Y, August 2007, Shanghai.

[29] Ibid.

religious leaders do not have to take college entrance exams or even have graduated from secondary school to enroll. And, on a more personal level, many religious leaders are eager to attend university courses because their educational opportunities were cut short in the past precisely because of their faith.[30] As a point of comparision, the Russian government has also provided additional educational training for select religious leaders. In 2005, for example, the Russian Civil Service Academy offered a ten-day private course for Orthodox Church leaders on law, finance, and taxation, presumably to help facilitate Orthodox-state cooperation.[31]

The Material Resources of Religious Communities

Although the revenue of religious groups tends to pale in comparison to that of local political authorities, they too can bring important material resources to the bargaining exchange that are attractive to those in power and help solidify the relations between religious and state actors. The material resources of religious groups can be divided into two categories: (1) public goods and services and (2) faith-based revenue. The provision of social welfare programs is often a natural extension for many religious communities and one that local governments welcome. Religious groups are able to pave roads, organize volunteers, collect money for victims of natural disaster, or open drug rehabilitation centers – and tend to engage in these activities over the long-run – which allows governments to focus scare resources elsewhere. Religious communities may also tap into the material resources of their members to attract foreign and domestic investment or other types of faith-based business to their communities. Such promises of plenty are highly sought after by political elites whose own legitimacy and prospects for promotion are tied to delivering economic prosperity to their locale.

Public Goods and Services

Public goods and services are one of the most important material resources that religious communities can offer local governments. Religious communities possess dense networks that provide a solid base of volunteer recruitment; they are organized and meet on a regular basis, which facilitates coordination; and they include highly motivated members driven by altruism.[32] However, the advantages in providing public goods extend far beyond fulfilling normative committments and religious doctrine. Religious communities can strengthen solidarity among members who volunteer, may promote their religious brand in society, or even growth their faith. For instance, by opening a soup kitchen,

---

[30] Interview with Imam Z, July 2007, Shanghai; interview with Imam Y, August 2007, Shanghai.
[31] "Arhierei seli za party" [Archbishops at their desks] (2005: 2).
[32] On the resources of religious groups, see Smith (1996).

a church may attract and even convert new members who seek to follow their example. It may also energize the religious base, which sees its values in practice. Moreover, acts of charity can improve a religious group's image in the larger community, which ties back into the expansion and survival of the religious group. As one Pentecostal minister remarked, "A Pentecostal church needs three things [to survive]: good education, good lawyers, and good P.R."[33] Offering public goods and services, therefore, can be especially helpful for religious communities on the margins to diminish the suspicions of local governments, demonstrate their civic and patriotic potential, and present a more favorable image of their faith to the larger community.

In terms of improving religious-state relations, offering public goods and services is also an important strategy to curry favor with the state, especially for religious groups who have strained relations with those in power. Indeed, some leaders of the unregistered Catholic Church in China have adopted a strategy of providing welfare services to secure greater autonomy from local authorities. In China there are two Catholic Churches: the Chinese Catholic Patriotic Church (often called the open Church), which is managed by the Chinese Catholic Patriotic Association (*Zhongguo Tianzhujiao aiguo hui*; CCPA), and the unregistered Roman Catholic Church, which only recognizes the authority of the Vatican.[34] The underground Catholic Church is illegal and without formal places of worship or state protection. Clergy are trained abroad or in hidden seminaries and can live quite itinerant existences moving from city to city to remain below the radar.[35] Despite these challenges, the unregistered Catholic Church has managed to establish a presence in some districts of Shanghai with little government interference. Members of the Church credit their success in part to the provision of much-needed welfare services. In one district, the underground laity established a home for the disabled. The facility is more than a decade old and houses 15 to 20 men with severe disabilities. Most of these men were abandoned in state orphanages as infants and never adopted. When they came of age, they were no longer

---

[33] Interview with Pentecostal Pastor I, July 2012, Nizhny Novgorod.

[34] On the history and conflict between the Catholic Church and Chinese state, see, Madsen (2004, 1998); Wiest (2004); Leung (1992). In the 1950s, the Religious Affairs Bureau established the Chinese Catholic Patriotic Association (CCPA) to manage the Catholic population and to rid the church of (the foreign cum political) Vatican influence. The staunchly anticommunist Pope Pius XII, however, did not recognize the authority of the patriotic association over Chinese Catholics and declared that church leaders who participated in the activities of the CCPA, especially in the consecration of CCP appointed bishops, would face excommunication. The church was split into two groups: those who agreed to management by the state-sponsored patriotic association and those who refused; see Pius XII (1958). Since 1989, the Chinese government has allowed for greater Sino-Vatican relations and the recognition of the pope as the spiritual leader of the Church; see, for example, "Document 3" (1989), which allows Chinese Catholics to "maintain purely religious relationships with the Holy See." This means that Catholics can acknowledge the pope as the head of the church, publicly pray for him, and hang his picture in their church.

[35] Interview with Catholic priest A, April 2007, Shanghai.

considered wards of the state and had few options. The facility does not hide its religious underpinnings – there are pictures of the pope on the walls, and the outside placard suggests strong religious overtones. Laypersons who run the home explained that the district government is well aware of their presence and have even "unofficially" inspected the premises.[36] They are also aware that members of the so-called illegal Catholic Church staff the home; yet because they do not have the resources, facilities, or perhaps the desire to care for these men, they keep "one eye open, and the other closed" (*zheng yizhi yan, bi yizhi yan*).[37] In this sense, the underground Church has been able to partially emerge from the shadows and establish a presence in the community.

In Russia, religious communities on the political margins have also turned to philanthropy as a way of improving their standing with local authorities and the larger community. In 1995, Pastors Paul and Vera founded the charismatic Evangelical Bible Church "Pagit'" (Pasture) in the city of Bor, which sits on the opposite bank of the Volga from Nizhny Novgorod. Pastor Paul, who was trained as a linguist and interpreter, wanted to establish a ministry that reached out to what is considered the "lowest common denominator of society: drug addicts and alcoholics."[38] The larger Nizhny region, Pastor Paul explained, is home to more than fifty thousand addicts, and freeing Russians from addiction is one of the most pressing social issues for his church.[39] The Pagit church began as an unregistered itinerant ministry with an unusual method of evangelization. On a weekly basis, it would rent meeting halls – from movie theaters to hotel ballrooms – and church leaders would walk the streets inviting homeless and addicts to their services. The services would often come with a warm meal, clean changes of clothes, information about drug rehabilitation, and a heavy dose of charismatic evangelizing.[40]

In a few years, the Pagit church grew to more than 150 members and reha-bilitated dozens of addicts. In fact, one of their first success stories – a homeless HIV-positive addict – later joined the ministry.[41] Yet as membership grew, it became increasingly difficult for the church to rent meeting space. The unique ministry developed a negative image in the city, and landlords were reluctant to let their halls to an unregistered Protestant church that would turn around and use the space as a refuge for vagabonds and addicts. Moreover, the worship services (which were charismatic in nature) were considered "too aggressive"

---

[36] Interview with Catholic layperson G, May 2007, Shanghai.

[37] Interview with Catholic layperson M, May 2007, Shanghai.

[38] Interview with Pastor Paul, March 2006, Nizhny Novgorod.

[39] Interview with Pastor Paul, June 2012, Nizhny Novgorod. Among residents of Nizhny, Bor has a seedy reputation as being controlled by the mafia and a river port for trafficking heroin from Central Asia.

[40] Interview with Pastor Paul, March 2006, Nizhny Novgorod.

[41] In 2001, at least fifteen people were freed from addiction, eleven of whom joined the ministry; interview with Pastor Paul, June 2012, Nizhny Novgorod.

and "too loud"; rumors began to emerge that the Pagit church was a cover for drug smuggling.[42] Again, it is important to situate these challenges within the larger political context of the 1990s. As noted in the previous chapter, it was during this same time when the Orthodox Church was becoming politically engaged; the newly passed 1997 Law on Freedom of Conscience and Associations had limited religious freedoms and placed mounting social and political pressures on newcomers to the religious market; Orthodox Church hierarchs were warning of the invasion of foreign missionaries and labeling Protestants as "cults" and "totalitarian sects"; and, the media was taking an active role in portraying Pentecostals and charismatic Christians as "foreign spies" who "sacrifice children" and "drink blood."[43]

In light of these larger political dynamics, it is hardly surprising that similar dynamics played out locally. Both the media in Bor and leaders of the Orthodox Church targeted the Pagit Church. Pagit and its members were described as an "invading" and "dangerous sect" that targeted young people in the city. Orthodox Church leaders even suggested that the charismatic ministry "denies the very basics of traditional Russian culture" and is a threat to "Orthodox beliefs."[44] Following these public condemnations, some members of the congregation lost their jobs, and local police frequently harassed church leaders. "At one point," Pastor Paul explained, "I was told [by police] that I could just 'disappear!'"[45] Eventually, Pastor Paul turned over the Bor church to his second pastor and moved across the river to Nizhny to continue his ministry, with the hope that a change in leadership of the church would lessen tensions with local authorities.[46]

In 2003, Pastor Paul planted another church in Nizhny Novgorod, the Jesus Embassy Charismatic Christian Church (*Posol'stvo Iisusa*). The Jesus Embassy followed a familiar pathway of development as the Bor ministry. Because the church was not registered, they held worship services in rented spaces, church leaders evangelized on the streets, and most importantly they focused on rehabilitating addicts. The second time around, however, Pastor Paul was more transparent about his evangelizing efforts and directly contacted local authorities to inform them of his church's mission. This was a potentially risky move because Jesus Embassy was still not registered, the Orthodox Church had

---

[42] Interview with Pastor Paul, March 2006, Nizhny Novgorod.

[43] Interview with Pastor Igor Voronin, Bishop of RC XVE (Rossijskaja cerkov' hristian very evangel'skoj) [The Russian church of Christian evangelical Faith for Nizhny Novgorod region], July 2012, Nizhny Novgorod. Also see Marsh (201: 101–3).

[44] Markeev (2002: 4).

[45] Interview with Pastor Paul, March 2006, Nizhny Novgorod.

[46] The Pagit church remains active in Bor. In 2012, the church had approximately 200 members and continues to minister to homeless youth, addicts, and their families. Their activities are detailed on The Jesus Embassy church's webpage available at: http://ru.jesusembassy.org/?id=47 (last accessed August 15, 2013).

a monopoly in the city, charismatic Christians continued to be depicted as "destructive" and "totalitarian sects" in the media, and local politicians had been sponsoring a series of roundtables warning residents to not rent buildings or rooms to "aggressive sects."[47]

The Jesus Embassy church leaders wagered that the local officials would eventually find out about their ministry, so it was better to be open from the start about church activities and mission. It also did not hurt that the church was focusing its efforts on addiction rehabilitation, a project that neither the local government nor the Orthodox Church had yet to address.[48] The gamble paid off, and despite difficulties in finding space to rent, raucous services that occasionally drew noise complaints, and lingering mistrust toward Pentecostalized forms of Christianity, the Jesus Embassy encountered less government interference and police harassment. By 2006, the congregation had well over six hundred members with two hundred cell groups linked to the church and had founded new churches in three cities. Given their new size and resources, church leaders formally pursued registration. Figuring prominently in their successful application was a discussion of the welfare services of the ministry, including testimonies from rehabilitated addicts who were now productive members of society.[49] The church continues to grow, and as of the summer 2012, it had planted at least fourteen churches in the region, and grown to include more than 1,500 members.[50]

Other religious outsiders have also turned to charity projects to improve their image within society and odds of local registration. In Kazan, in the early 1990s, Pastor Pavel founded the Nazareth Church of Kazan (*Nazaret*).[51] At that time the registration process was straightforward and required little more than filing the necessary paperwork. However, this changed dramatically with the passing of 1997 Law, when nontraditional religions (like evangelical Protestants) were

---

[47] Devicyn (2004: 6); Gamzin (2004: 3); "Kruglyj stol s ostrymi uglami" [Roundtable with sharp corners] (2004: 4); "Totalitarnye sekty – ugroza bezopasnosti Rossii" [Totalitarian sects: a threat to Russian security] (2004: 4–5). It is interesting to note that leaders from the traditional religions attended the roundtables (Orthodox Christians, Muslims, and Jews), but no members from the Protestant community were invited; see "A sud'i kto?" [Who are the judges?] (2004: 4).

[48] Interview with Pastor Paul, March 2006, Nizhny Novgorod.

[49] Interview with Pastor Paul, March 2006, Nizhny Novgorod. However, what church leaders did not mention is that Jesus Embassy joined a union of churches to facilitate their registration process, the ROSXBE (*Rossijskij ob"edinennyj Sojuz hristian very evangel'skoj (pjatidesjatnikov)*) [The Russian Union of Evangelical Christians (Pentecostals)]. There are two large evangelical unions operating in Russia, and most independent Pentecostal and charismatic churches join one to facilitate registration. As part of the union, the registration process is much easier than it would be independently.

[50] The Jesus Embassy webpage: http://ru.jesusembassy.org/?id=47 (last accessed August 15, 2013).

[51] Nazareth church was also founded with the support of Baptist missionaries from Ukraine. Under Stalin, Pastor Pavel's family was relocated to Central Asia and denounced as "enemies of the state" for refusing to renounce their Protestant beliefs. Interview with Pastor Pavel, June 2006, Kazan.

required to document their history in the community. This documentation was important because the new law distinguished between localized religious organizations and religious groups, with the former given significantly more privileges.[52]

After the passing of the 1997 Law, all religious organizations across Russia were required to re-register with local bureaucracies. For the Church of Nazareth in Kazan, this meant that they were in danger of being classified as a "religious group," which would severely limit their activities. They were a new church and had only been in operation since 1991. Although there had always been a small Protestant community in Tatarstan, the Church of Nazareth had no official ties to any of these groups. Therefore, a strict interpretation of the 1997 Law would classifiy their church as a religious group. Yet they were able to negotiate a better registration status as a local religious organization because of their strong record of philanthropy. "Philanthropy," explained Pastor Pavel, "is an active part of church life and they [the government] noticed. They now even encourage the homeless to come to our church for help."[53]

Religious communities in China have also turned to providing much-needed welfare services to gain legitimacy and diminish suspicions toward their religious community. In fact, this has been a particularly frequent strategy among religious organizations that are seen as outsiders or operate between the public and private spheres. One Protestant minister explained that in his previous posting at a rural church the local cadres were extremely hostile toward Christians and treated them as though they were a cult (*xiejiao*) – worship services were often interrupted, and members of the congregation were accused of promoting feudal superstition (*fengjian mixin*). To improve the image of local Christians, the minister used donations and labor from the congregation to pave a road leading into the village. Apparently, local authorities had been trying for years to raise funds for this project. After the road was paved, the local cadres posted a banner leading into the village as a gesture of appreciation reading: "Christians will always be welcome in this village!" and harassment of the congregation ceased.[54]

Similarly, faith-based nongovernmental organizations (NGOs), such as the Amity Foundation (*aide jijin hui*), have also turned to providing public goods and services to court Chinese authorities at both the central and local levels. The Amity Foundation is a Chinese Protestant organization established in 1985

---

[52] To recall from Chapter 3, for a religious organization to be considered a "traditional religion," it must demonstrate at least a fifteen-year history in a region. This status grants them full legal protection for conducting religious services and some state benefits. Religious groups, on the other hand, are those with a less than fifteen-year presence and are granted minimal legal protection and no state benefits.

[53] Interview with Pastor Pavel, June 2006, Kazan; also see K. Chan (2009: 65–73) for local authorities seeking the assistance of Christians to combat opium addiction in contemporary rural China.

[54] Interview with Protestant Pastor D, April 2007, Shanghai.

that seeks to contribute to China's social development and openness to the outside world, promote awareness of Christian involvement and participation in meeting the needs of society, and serve as a channel for face-to-face contact and the ecumenical sharing of resources.[55] Amity's activities are wide ranging, from education and environmental protection to public health and gender equality. In addition to providing a variety of social and welfare services, Amity is also active in other faith-focused projects, including support for Christian artists, and the printing of Bibles, hymnals, and other religious materials.[56] In fact, the Amity Printing Company is the only licensed, legal printer of Bibles in China and has printed more than 80 million copies.[57]

According to Dr. Theresa Carino, the coordinator of the Amity Foundation's Hong Kong Office, relations with the Chinese government have warmed over the years. When Amity was founded in 1985 it consisted of three staff members and two tables in the corner of a Nanjing warehouse. The only reason they were allowed into China was with the help of liberal (and Christian) allies in the Chinese Academy of Social Sciences, a powerful domestic think tank, who vouched for the good intentions of the NGO.[58] Amity was allowed two trial projects: the invitation of foreign English teachers, and a small printing press to publish Bibles in Chinese. Seeking to build a long-term presence in the country, Amity took several precautions, including vetting and training its teachers to ensure that they would not use their position in the classroom as a cover for evangelizing, working only with state-sanctioned religious communities, and seeking ways to provide public welfare that were desperately needed in rural areas.

In the first few years following Amity's presence in the mainland, local cadres remained skeptical of the NGOs activities and generally refused access to communities under their jurisdiction. The common excuse was that "no Christians lived in their locale" so they did not need Christian help.[59] However, there are two additional reasons to explain local authorities' reluctance. One is the uncertain political implication of faith-based NGOs operating in their region: would Amity's presence spark interreligious tensions or fuel the religious revival? The other is the aversion to relying on a Christian organization for social services and the negative message it might send to higher-ups with regard to dependence on foreign religious actors.[60] In fact, it took almost

---

55 See Amity Foundation's guiding principles, available at: http://www.amityfoundation.org/eng/ (last accessed April 15, 2013).

56 Zhang (2006).

57 Interview with Peter McInnis, Amity Printing Press general manager 1988–93, June 2007, Shanghai.

58 Bishop Ding of the Nanjing Protestant Seminary and his son vouched for the nonthreatening role of the Amity Foundation. Interview with Dr. Theresa Carino, coordinator of the Amity Foundation Hong Kong Office, June 2007, Hong Kong.

59 Interview with Dr. Theresa Carino, coordinator of the Amity Foundation Hong Kong Office, June 2007, Hong Kong.

60 Ibid.

a decade before Amity's service projects attracted enough national praise to dispel the concerns of local cadres and gain their confidence.

When religious groups do not have the resources or organizational capacity to develop their charitable projects like the Amity Foundation, religious groups on the margins – including the underground Catholics or evangelical Protestants mentioned earlier – might still improve their standing with local authorities and larger society by donating to state-sponsored charities. For example, religious groups can organize volunteers to work in state-run orphanages and homes for the elderly, sponsor state-appointed families in need, or contribute to national disaster relief. It is worth mentioning that donations of this type are generally part of the public record – governments publish donors and amounts in local newspapers, religious communities publish the amounts collected in bulletins, and all sides are acutely aware of how much their competition is donating.[61] Here, it is striking to note that competition is not only present among different faiths but also among government officials. District-level officials keep a close eye on how much is being raised in neighboring districts, municipal-level officials are aware of how much is raised in nearby cities, and the trend continues up the ladder of officialdom. It goes without saying that government officials have strong incentives to bring in large donations, especially when the cause receives widespread publicity, such as a natural disaster that has captured national (and international) attention. For the most part, religious groups willingly and enthusiastically participate. As one Chinese minister explained, "We know that the government is under pressure to support these projects, but has no money. We are happy to help and show that Protestants are also patriotic."[62]

At the same time, not all religious communities are comfortable with such a direct relationship with the government and their overtures are not always welcomed by those in power. One minister of an unregistered house church in China explained that his congregation engages in numerous local charity projects; however, because of their illegal status and more general regime biases, they are hesitant to identify themselves as part of a house church. The minister explained that local officials are particularly suspicious of Christians, and especially house churches, and labeling themselves as such may jeopardize their church and mission. For now, church members participating in service projects wish only to be recognized as good citizens, and perhaps in the future when restrictions on religious communities subside, they will reveal their beliefs

---

[61] Interview with Protestant minister G, October 2006, Changchun; interview with Protestant minister H, October 2006, Changchun; interview with Protestant deacon A, October 2010, Shanghai.

[62] Interview with Protestant minister D, August 2007, Shanghai. Indeed, patriotism was a theme introduced by many respondents as a motivation for philanthropic activities; interview with Protestant deacon A, October 2010, Shanghai; interview with Protestant minister L, September 2007, Shanghai; interview with Protestant minister A, June 2007, Shanghai; interview Protestant minister H, October 2006, Changchun.

and local cadres will associate their history of good deeds with their religious organization.[63]

Similarly, religious groups on the margins in Russia may also be overtly excluded from state-sponsored philanthropy projects because public perception of the group is negative. A pastor from one Pentecostal church in Nizhny Novgorod remarked that although his church has a number of social projects, it can be difficult for congregants to volunteer at state-run institutions. In one incident, church members began volunteering at a state-run orphanage and were initially warmly welcomed by the director. Shortly thereafter, however, local authorities contacted the pastor informing him that "their kind of assistance," which he interpreted to mean as "Pentecostal" was not wanted and church volunteers should not return to the orphanage.[64]

These kinds of rebuffs do not necessarily mean that religious outsiders have become less active, but rather that they have become more creative in how they approach charity projects that involve the state. For example, during the summer of 2010, multiple wildfires encircled Nizhny Novgorod leaving thousands homeless. Members of one Seventh Day Adventist church collected food, new clothing, and other necessities for the families that had been displaced by the fires. Church volunteers packed three buses with the donations and set out to deliver them to the disaster areas. To reach the hardest hit regions, the buses had to pass through various checkpoints. At one checkpoint, a police officer noticed posters for the Adventist Church pasted to the side of the buses and turned them away, claiming that donations from "sects" were not needed. The following day, however, the buses returned to the checkpoint with the posters removed. When asked about the origins of their donations, church members suggested they were coming from abroad, and they were quickly waived through.[65]

There can also be a darker side to providing public goods and social services or supporting state-run charities. Local officials' desire to collect donations for disaster relief can put religious communities in an awkward position. Religious leaders in Changchun and Shanghai – where the marketplace is more restricted and religious groups are more vulnerable to state pressures – find their organizations frequently courted to support various state-sponsored charities, from flood and earthquake relief to minority development projects in Tibet and Yunnan. Most religious practitioners strongly support the government's fundraising efforts; however, religious personnel privately worry about the growing burdens on their members. One religious leader remarked: "It seems like every

---

[63] Interview with house church Pastor K September 2010, Shanghai; similar sentiments were expressed among TSPM ministers; interview with Protestant minister M, August 2007, Shanghai.

[64] Interview with Pentecostal Pastor S, July 2012, Nizhny Novgorod.

[65] Interview with F. Dorofeev, professor at the State Lobachevsky University, June 2012, Nizhny Novgorod.

month we were told of a new charity to support. The government asks us to give, give, give, and they will take all of our Sunday offering...sometimes cadres even suggest an amount!"[66] This indicates there can be an element of rent seeking.

Faith-based Revenue

Religious groups may also bring additional revenue streams to the bargaining table, which is attractive to local officials whose own legitimacy is tied to delivering economic prosperity and growth. Religious organizations are able to enhance local economic development in three key ways. First, they can go into business for themselves. Such business tends to be shops and restaurants attached to temples and are designed to support the religious organization. Although they are relatively small-scale endeavors, they nonetheless represent taxable income for the local government. Indeed, in both Russia and China many religious communities try their hand at business, and some have become quite profitable. These businesses tend to aim at providing faith-based goods for their members. The mosques in Nizhny Novgorod opened butcher shops to provide halal meat for local Muslims.[67] Religious communities in Changchun have engaged in more diverse entrepreneurial activities to support their organizations – Catholics opened a rice refinery, a chicken farm, and clothing stores to support the Church; Protestants built a small hotel and opened an electronics repair shop; and Muslims built a tofu factory and slaughter house to support their mosque.[68] In Shanghai, several Buddhist and Taoist temples invested in teahouses and vegetarian restaurants to accommodate monks and pilgrims, and to attract tourists. Other religious organizations have invested in the local economy on a larger scale. The Orthodox Church, for example, was one of the first confessions to engage in business by converting part of the Danilov Monastery (the official residence of the patriarch) into the four-star hotel Danilovskaya, complete with conference center and spa. The hotel capitalizes on its reputation to attract customers and advertises the monastery as a place "to conduct business conferences, assemblies, and also to welcome guests with traditional Russian hospitality," and reflect on the "the elevated simplicity and purity of the Russian Orthodox faith."[69] The conference center has also become a popular retreat for political elites. In 2009, the hotel hosted a conference for United Russia's State-Patriotic Club and the Russian Entrepreneurs'

---

[66] Interview with Protestant minister M, August 2007, Shanghai.
[67] Interview with Umar-khazrat Idrisov, Chairman of the Religious Board of Muslims for the Nizhny Novgorod Region (*Duhovnoe upravlenie musul'man Nizhegorodskoj oblasti; DUMNO*), March 2006, Nizhny Novgorod.
[68] H. Jin et al. (2000: 38).
[69] See website for the Hotel Danilovskaya, available at: http://www.allrussiahotels.com/russia/moscow/hotel/danilovskaya.html (last accessed April 5, 2013).

Foundation around the themes of morality and how the Ten Commandments inform the platform of power.[70]

Second, religious activities themselves, such as Chinese temple fairs (*miaohui*) and other religious festivals, can attract thousands of visitors and bring significant revenue to the local economy.[71] Although the actual religious ceremonies are not a source of revenue, the associated event services are: they can be extravagant, span several days, and attract thousands of participants. The Buddhist Wisdom Temple (*Boresi*) in Changchun attracted more than sixty thousand visitors during the three-day temple festival in 1984.[72] In 1998, the same temple attracted even larger crowds and earned more than ¥7,000 RMB from ticket sales, ¥51,100 RMB from donations, and sold more than 8,644 books about Buddhism.[73] Temple fairs and festivals are also occasions for commerce for the local government, where the state collects fees and taxes from the hundreds of vendors and local police are paid for providing security.[74] As Illustrations 4.4 and 4.5 show, temple festivals are highly commercial events drawing tourists and pilgrims alike to the food stalls, carnival rides, and performances of local operas and acrobatic troops.

Finally, religious organizations are able to tap into the resources of their more entrepreneurial members to encourage religiously affiliated local investment, including new factories, foreign investment, and other commercial ventures. The economic reforms in both Russia and China have created an elite business class – the so-called New Russians (*novyj russkij*) or nouveau riche (*baofa hu*), were some of the first to get rich and benefit from privatization. Within this class are some with strong religious ties who want to use their wealth as a platform to promote their belief system.[75] In Russia, these individuals are commonly called "Orthodox oligarchs" (*Pravoslavnye oligarhi*) and in China "Christian bosses" (*laoban Jidutu*).[76]

---

[70] Samarina (2009).

[71] Temple fairs are generally held at least three times each year, at the birth and death of the deity of the temple and during the Lunar New Year. For a discussion of the commercial side of temple festivals, see Borchert (2005); Chau (2005b).

[72] H. Jin et al. (2000: 65).

[73] Ibid.

[74] Also see Chau (2003).

[75] Local government authorities are often aware of the role of Christian bosses play in the economy; see, for example, "Vstrecha v kremle" [Meeting in the Kremlin] (1999: 1).

[76] On Christian bosses, see especially C. Chen and Huang (2004); C. Chen (2005); Cao (2011, 2008). The phenomenon of Christian bosses is not limited only to Protestants in China; all religions have "bosses" who are merging their business practices with their belief system. For a profile of a former People's Liberation Army general who retired, converted to Buddhism, and is now a "Buddhist boss," see Webster (2008). On Orthodox oligarchs in Russia, see "Chubajs zamalivaet grehi v Nizhegorodskoj oblasti?" [Chubias atones for sins in Nizhny Novgorod oblast?] (2004: 8). There is also small but growing cohort of "Pentecostal bosses" in the Nizhny Novgorod region; interview with Pentecostal Pastor Z, July 2012, Nizhny Novgorod.

ILLUSTRATION 4.4. Food stalls at a temple fair in Shanghai, Lunar New Year 2007. Photo by author.

Christian bosses tend to be wealthy Christians, usually of ethnic Chinese origin, who made their fortunes at home or abroad and then sought to reinvest in the mainland. What distinguishes Christian bosses from other newly rich entrepreneurs is that they believe their businesses and subsequent economic success are a blessing from God.[77] As such, they use their wealth, influence, and business operations to promote their own brand of faith. Christian bosses tend to be quite open about their dual identities as Christians and entrepreneurs and do not hide their proselytizing activities from the government. Likewise, local governments have been surprisingly tolerant of the illegal evangelizing by Christian bosses and have embraced their model of mixing business and religion.

The Semiconductor Manufacturing International Corporation (SMIC) is a world-leading semiconductor foundry that manufactures custom computer chips. The founder and CEO of the company, Dr. Richard Ru-Gin Chang, was born in China, raised in Taiwan, educated in Texas at Southern Methodist

---

[77] Interview with Christian boss J, June 2007, Shanghai; interview with Christian boss B, August 2007, Shanghai.

ILLUSTRATION 4.5. Bumper cars at a temple fair in Shanghai, Lunar New Year 2007. Photo by author.

University, and worked for more than twenty years at Texas Instruments.[78] With the opening of China's borders to foreign investment, Chang founded SMIC in the Zhangjiang Hi-tech Park in Pudong, Shanghai. What distinguishes

---

[78] Chang stepped down as CEO in 2009.

ILLUSTRATION 4.6. Thanksgiving Church in Shanghai, 2010. Photo by author.

Chang from other Chinese entrepreneurs is that he is also a Christian boss, conjoining his strong religious beliefs with his business practices. In fact, the guiding motto of SMIC is: "We are called to China to share God's love!"[79]

Because of the investment potential of SMIC, local governments across China have welcomed Chang's model of mixing business with Christianity.[80] At SMIC's factories located in Shanghai, Beijing, Chengdu, and Tianjin, local authorities have outfitted each of his four plants with a TSPM church, provided land, and helped smooth the way for religious activities. In fact, when SMIC was deciding where to build its factories, one executive explained that during the negotiations competing municipal governments were extremely accommodating of Chang's faith and offered to build churches next to the facilities – they "dangled churches in front of us in hopes of attracting our factories."[81] This suggests that when financial stakes are high, local officials are quite flexible in their interpretation of central religious policies and support of religious groups. Illustration 4.6 shows the Thanksgiving Church next to SMIC headquarters in

---

[79] Interview with B.L., SMIC management, August 2007, Shanghai; also see Iritani (2002).

[80] In 2001, SMIC spent $100 million on building its facility in Shanghai and employs more than 6,400 people. Interview with B.L., SMIC management, August 2007, Shanghai.

[81] Interview with B.L., SMIC management, August 2007, Shanghai.

Shanghai; the main hall holds four thousand worshipers and offers multiple Sunday services that are generally at capacity.[82]

Not far from SMIC headquarters, other Christian bosses have opened unregistered churches with little government interference. These are Christian bosses who belong to the Protestant house church movement and quietly view the state-approved TSPM churches as illegitimate. Like Chang, these Christian bosses are dedicated to integrating their religious beliefs with business; however, they choose to do so without working through the official government churches. Rather, they spread their faith in more entrepreneurial ways. For example, when opening up a new factory, a Christian boss will file the paperwork, secure the land and labor permits, pass the building-code inspections, and, once all of these hurdles are cleared, they make one slightly surreptitious addition before the ribbon-cutting ceremony: a cross on top of the factory.

These factory-churches serve dual purposes; during the day they manufacture goods, and in the evening and on weekends they hold religious services. These unregistered churches often function with the full knowledge of the local government authorities, yet their activities are normally ignored for at least two reasons. One is that the factory-churches tend to follow the socialist, planned economy model of economic production. Factories are isolated microcosms of daily life, complete with dormitories, cafeterias, convenience stores, clinics, and bathhouses. Christian bosses add churches to these microcosms to fulfill the spiritual needs of their employees, giving them little reason to venture beyond the factory compound.[83] The insulated nature of factory life, including the evangelizing and worship that takes places within factory walls, allows the local government to ignore these indiscretions. The second and more important reason is that the factories are valuable investments in the local economy – paying taxes, providing jobs, and investing in infrastructure. A crackdown on factory-churches would jeopardize this investment, slow down economic growth, and thus invite greater scrutiny from above. Here, it is striking that two Christian bosses revealed similar stories of how local authorities view their activities. In both cases, they explained that the local governments are fully aware of their factory-churches, but only intervened to encourage them to "manage" (*guanli*) their religious activities around important political events. They explained that leading up to important domestic

---

[82] Interview with B.L., SMIC management, August 2007, Shanghai. I visited this church in 2007 and again in 2010, both times the main hall was full, and many worshipers said they planned to stay for multiple services.

[83] To be clear, not all workers at SMIC factories or other church-factories are Christian. Interviews revealed that many employees are Buddhist or atheist, and the management does little to pressure them into conversion. Moreover, so long as there are no religious conflicts with the factory, being of a different faith will not result in termination. However, several Christian bosses made it a point to emphasize that many employees do indeed convert after a few short weeks in the factory.

events, such as the Beijing 2008 Olympics and 2010 Shanghai World EXPO, they generally face additional pressures.[84] During these times, one Christian boss commented he usually takes down the factory cross for a few months until the political situation normalizes or, in the case of the Olympics, until the closing ceremonies.[85]

VARIETIES OF FINANCIAL COLLABORATION

Thus far, this chapter has examined the diverse material resources religious and political authorities bring to the bargaining table and what they hope to gain from the exchange. In this process, material resources are the currency of exchange transferred between the two sides to help achieve strategic needs. Local officials offer bureaucratic stamps, which are necessary for the legal practice of religious activities; they also provide helpful subsidies, which allow select religious groups to rebuild and expand. I have also shown that religious organizations are not only on the receiving end of this exchange, but also have important resources of their own to offer their authoritarian overseers. They provide public goods and services, which relieve the local government of responsibility and enable officials to direct resources elsewhere; they encourage faith-based investment, which enhances economic development and frequently provides lucrative revenue for the government. In return, religious communities may improve their standing with those in power and increase opportunities for greater religious expression. The remainder of the chapter analyzes the range of bargains struck between religious and local governments across Russia and China. Here, I introduce two common arenas of interaction: (1) property politics and (2) faith-based tourism. These arenas demonstrate that religious-state bargaining can range from single-issue contentious exchanges to more lasting partnerships that are mutually beneficial and reinforcing for both sides.

Property Politics

In Russia and China, one of the most contentious issues for religious groups is the return of and compensation for prerevolutionary religious property. According to central policies in both countries, if a religious building is still intact, the state must take efforts to return the structure to its rightful owners. If a religious building has been destroyed – as many were during the 1920s and 1930s in the Soviet Union, and the 1960s and 1970s in China – religious groups may petition for compensation for the lost land and property. The types of religious property under dispute generally fall into three categories: places of worship, such as monasteries, temples, mosques, and churches; religious

---

[84] Interview with Christian boss Q, June 2007, Shanghai; interview with Christian boss B, August 2007, Shanghai.
[85] Interview with Christian boss Q, June 2007, Shanghai.

buildings that provided social and welfare services, such a hospitals, schools, and homes for the elderly; and investment property of religious groups that was not used for religious purposes, such as estates or land that had been willed to religious organizations.

The petitioning process for lost property is long and arduous and can take decades before an application is approved. The process is so time-consuming in part because religious groups must compile detailed dossiers of confiscated property, complete with deeds, maps, and blueprints of religious buildings. For many religious communities, such documentation was lost or destroyed after the revolution, and what remains is scattered among different domestic and foreign archives – the former also often in various states of neglect and disrepair or under restricted access. For example, when the Catholic Church of Nizhny Novgorod began to compile its dossier for the return of religious property, the priest had to make a special trip to the Vatican archives in search of documents to establish the Church's prerevolutionary presence in the community because there were no documents to be found locally.[86] Another challenge facing religious groups, especially in China, is the limited access to government archives (which is yet one more institution tightly controlled by the regime) that hold the blueprints and maps of pre-1949 religious buildings. Because of the sensitive nature of religion, many archives have tagged documents with religious references as closed or "internal" documents (*neibu*), which require special government permissions to view or copy. Without access to these critical materials, religious organizations are often unable to successfully document their case.

Even when religious communities are able to compile complete dossiers, it is only the beginning of the arduous process. Petitioning can be further complicated if the property in question was converted to a school or hospital. In these cases, local governments will not return management or ownership of the property, because this violates important principles of secularism; and in these cases, fair compensation is the normal outcome. If the religious property in question has been converted for residential or commercial purposes, the government must make a concerted effort to relocate the current residents and businesses or work out an agreement in which the deeds will be transferred and the religious group will be able to collect rents on the property. If neither option is viable, the state may alternatively offer religious organizations a comparable parcel of land. During this process of negotiation, it is important to note that religious groups retain the right to refuse land that the state offers. This suggests that religious groups have some power in assuring that they will not be relocated beyond the communities they serve or far from public transportation.

Property politics in Russia and China has become increasingly contentious and expensive. When religious freedoms increased in the mid-1980s and early 1990s, local officials returned keys to religious buildings without question,

---

[86] Interview with Catholic Father Mario, March 2006, Nizhny Novgorod.

TABLE 4.1. *Changchun Government Expenses for the Return of Religious Property, 1985 (amount in RMB)*[87]

	Catholics	Protestants	Buddhists	Muslims	Total
Repair of religious sites	290,000	60,000	360,000	498,100	1,208,100
Moving expenses	95,000	300,000	524,000	0	919,000
Reimbursement for rents of confiscated property or compensation for destroyed property	489,845.08	159,649.88	137,885.04	8,166.12	795,546.12
Compensation for confiscated religious relics	100	1,051.63	7,560.68	450	9,162.31
Total	874,945.08	520,701.51	1,029,445.72	506,716.12	2,931,808.43

frequently holding grand ceremonies celebrating the return of religious property.[88] Overtime, the return of religious property became more complicated. This is because after the most obvious and highly visible cases were solved, local bureaucrats were left to sort through the thousands of petitions for less conspicuous religious buildings and relics that had been destroyed and converted to other uses – that is, petitions that would either involve monetary compensation, an alternative parcel of land, or the relocation of existing residents and businesses. Often, the return of religious property involves significant costs for local governments, and they have strong incentives to delay these petitions. In one telling example from 1985, the Changchun government spent more than ¥2.9 million RMB (more than $646,000) on the return, repair, and compensation for destroyed religious property. The amounts are detailed in Table 4.1.

Therefore, when considering the financial side of property politics, it is not surprising that petitions for disputed property are selectively approved, some are lost, and others are quickly shepherded through. For instance, between 1992 and 1998 in the Nizhny Novgorod oblast, 136 religious buildings were returned to various religious bodies. Among these buildings, close to 95 percent were handed over to the Orthodox Church.[89] Even when religious groups have solid

---

[87] H. Jin et al. (2000: 28).

[88] For some religious communities, official ceremonies celebrating the return of religious property have continued. In 2010, Putin returned Orthodox property to Patriarch Kirill on his name day (May 25), presenting him with flowers and icons and declaring that he "signed several orders to transfer a whole real estate package to the Church free of charge"; see "Putin congratulates Patriarch Kirill on his name day with the order on real estate transfer to Church" (2010).

[89] "Vopros reshaetsja mgnovenno" [The problem is solved immediately] (1998: 4).

legal claims to property, local bureaucrats are prone to stall applications for decades, honor only part of the petition, or tack on extraneous conditions. This is because it is much easier to stall religious communities (especially minority ones) than face protesting residents and powerful members of the business community who would require fair compensation and relocation and may be able to threaten their political futures.

Russian Property Politics: Three Cases

One example of the contentious nature of religious property and the lengthy petitioning process occurs in Nizhny Novgorod. In the late 1990s, the Religious Board of Muslims of Nizhny Novgorod (*Duhovnoe upravlenie musul'man Nizhegorodskoj oblasti; DUMNO*) began petitioning for the return of the land where a mosque once stood. The Yarmarka Mosque or the Fair Trade Mosque (*Jarmarochnaja mechet'*) was razed in the 1930s to make way for the construction of Lenin Square.

Much earlier during the eighteenth century, Nizhny emerged as a prosperous inland port on the Volga River and important trading city that attracted travelers along the Silk Road. To accommodate the spiritual demands of the merchants who settled in the region, in 1822 the local government permitted the construction of Yarmarka Mosque in the heart of the commercial district, opposite Makariev Fair (*Makarievskaja Jamarka*).[90] The mosque was well attended by the Volga Tatars, the resident Muslims of the area, as well as merchants from China, Iran, Azerbaijan, and the Crimea who had settled in the region.[91] Thus, the Yarmarka Mosque is both historically and symbolically significant for the Tatar-Muslims in the city. It is not only the first mosque in the area but also stands as a testament to the religious freedom in eighteenth century Russia – a time when Orthodox Christianity was the state religion and Muslims were persecuted in other parts of the country. The mosque is also an important cultural relic because it became the tsarist government's approved architectural model for mosques built across the Russian Empire.[92] Despite Yarmarka Mosque's historical and cultural significance, the petition for the return of the land was left pending for more than a decade.[93] In fact, only in September 2011 did local authorities finally agree to establish a working group with the DUMNO to discuss the rebuilding of the mosque.[94]

---

[90] Senjutkina (2005a).
[91] Muhetdinov (2005).
[92] Senjutkina (2005a).
[93] Interview with O. Senjutkina, Historian and advisor to the Religious Board of Muslims in the Nizhny Novgorod Region (*Duhovnoe upravlenie musul'man Nizhegorodskoj oblasti; DUMNO*) and leading the collection of materials on the Yarmarka Mosque, February 2006, Nizhny Novgorod.
[94] "V Nizhnem Novgorode vosstanovjat Jarmarochnuju mechet'" [Yarmarka Mosque to be restored in Nizhny Novgorod] (2011).

The Catholic Church in Nizhny Novgorod has also had difficulties getting their petitions approved for the return of church property. In 1991, church leaders began to compile a dossier for the return of three Catholic churches and a nunnery that had operated on the outskirts of the city before the revolution.[95] The buildings in question had long since been destroyed and local bureaucrats were reluctant to view the petition, maintaining that the Catholics did not have proper documentation.[96] After considerable negotiations, the local government agreed to return a portion of the land. The Catholics were given a small piece of land adjacent to one of the three historic churches. According to one bureaucrat from the Ministry of Religious Affairs, it was much easier (and more cost-effective) to offer an adjacent property, which at that time was a closed factory and storage shed, rather than relocate the businesses that stood on the original land of the church.[97] The local Catholic priest expressed satisfaction with the settlement even though it was considerably less than he had hoped. Although the Catholic Church had a strong case for the return of all of their prerevolutionary property, the priest decided not to pursue further legal channels.[98] He explained that as a minority religion in the city and in the country a legal claim would "damage the image of local Catholics and complicate matters with the government."[99] Moreover, the restoration of the Catholic Church in the city, and especially the nearby nunnery, had been deeply politicized in the local media. A group of Orthodox intellectuals had published a series of editorials denouncing Catholicism and reminding residents that Russia was the home of Orthodox Christianity and should be free from Vatican influence.[100] Indeed, even the local Orthodox Diocese protested the rebuilding of the Catholic nunnery, suggesting that it is an "unfriendly move by the Vatican" and a direct challenge to the Russian Orthodox Church.[101]

In Kazan, the return of the Russian Orthodox Cathedral of the Epiphany of Our Lord provides another example of the give-and-take between religious groups and their authoritarian overseers. The Orthodox cathedral sits on the corner of Bauman Street in the heart of the historic and cultural center of the city and dates back to the sixteenth century. Before the Russian Revolution,

---

[95] Only two of the three churches were registered with the Nizhny government.

[96] "Karmelitkam ne razreshili zhit v kottedzhom poselke" [Carmelites are not allowed to live in the cottage settlement] (2004: 16).

[97] Interview with former bureaucrat C, March 2006, Nizhny Novgorod.

[98] See also, "Komu meshajut nizhegorodskie katoliki?" [Who is bothered by the Nizhny Novgorod Catholics?] (2001: 11).

[99] Interview with Catholic Father Mario, March 2006, Nizhny Novgorod.

[100] "Zachem Nizhnemu katolicheskij monastyr'?" [Why does Nizhny need a Catholic monastery?] (2004: 15); see also "Byt' li Rossii pravoslavnoj?" [Will Russia be Orthodox?] (2004: 9); Makarskov (2004: 3).

[101] "Nizhegorodskoe katoliki podveli pravoslavnyh" [Nizhny Novgorod Catholics let the Orthodox down] (2004: 16); Makarskov (2004: 3).

the cathedral was one of the largest in Kazan, known for its seventy-four meter Baroque-style bell tower, which would ring to call the congregation of nobles, merchants, and peasants to services. The cathedral remained open and functioning until 1939, when it was confiscated by the state. Under state ownership the property was divided up among various institutions. The main cathedral was given to Kazan State University (Lenin's alma mater), whereupon its five domes were torn down, the icons painted over, and the main hall converted into a gymnasium. The bell tower became a government storage shed, and the cathedral's bell was transferred to a nearby theatre to be used in productions.

After the Soviet collapse, the Orthodox Dioceses of Kazan began petitioning for the return of its confiscated property, with the plan of rebuilding the entire cathedral to its prerevolutionary magnitude. The petition, however, met some opposition from select circles of the new government. The 1990s was a particularly turbulent period within Tatarstan. In late August 1990, the republic declared its independence, and its future as part of the Russian Federation was uncertain. A nationalist movement called for Tatarstan to follow the path of independence taken by other Soviet republics. As the movement gained popular momentum, their demands grew to include calls for the revival of Tatar identity with appeals for linguistic and religious revitalization, greater political autonomy from Moscow, and more control over Tatarstan's natural (oil) resources.

In the midst of the political turmoil, a referendum was held to gauge public support for an independent state. The referendum passed with a solid majority and emboldened the separatist-leaning leaders of the nationalist movement.[102] With a strong public mandate, the more radical flank of the movement captured power and refused to recognize the Russian constitution. Calls for secession intensified. It looked as if Tatarstan would be the next republic to join the "parade of sovereignties," and that violent conflict with Moscow was unavoidable.[103] However, the fate of Tatarstan was not yet sealed. Although Russian troops amassed on Tatarstan's borders, President Yeltsin initiated negotiations with leaders of the nationalist movement and brokered a deal with Tatarstan's president, Mintimer Shaimiev.[104] In February 1994, a formal power-sharing agreement was signed by Yeltsin and Shaimiev, which affirmed Tatarstan's place within the Russia Federation, quieted calls for secession, and

---

[102] The 1992 referendum passed with a 62 percent majority.

[103] In the span of 33 months, 41 former federal units of the Soviet Union declared themselves sovereign; see Kahn (2000); Solnick (1996); interview with Damir Iskhaov, Chairman of the Political Council of the Tatar Public Center and former leader of the Tatar nationalist movement, June 2006, Kazan.

[104] Interview with Damir Iskhaov, Chairman of the Political Council of the Tatar Public Center and leader in the Tatar nationalist movement, June 2006, Kazan; interview with Rashit Akhmetov, Leader of the Tatarstan Branch of the Democratic Party of Russia and former leader of the Tatarstan nationalist movement, June 2006, Kazan.

granted the republic exceptional privileges.[105] Bloodshed and further disintegration was avoided, but Tatar politics was forever changed.

It was in the midst of this political turmoil and growing Tatar nationalism that the Russian Orthodox Dioceses in Kazan began the petitioning process for the return of destroyed and confiscated religious property. In 1995, a portion of the Church's petition for the Cathedral of the Epiphany of Our Lord was approved. One of the four standing church buildings and the bell tower were returned. Father Oleg, the archpriest and rector of the cathedral, explained that Church hierarchs were not surprised when only one of four buildings was returned because the cathedral is located in the most expensive part of Kazan and the costs involved in the subsequent relocation of businesses was significant. What caught Father Oleg and other church leaders by surprise, however, was the refusal to return the accompanying bell for the cathedral's tower, stating that it was still "in use" at the nearby F.I. Shalyapin Theatre and could not be moved.[106] Although the Church had a legal claim to the bell, Father Oleg mused that the rejection reflected the hidden discrimination in the local government and minority status of the Russian Orthodox Church in Tatarstan. Father Oleg indicated that the nationalist movement still had considerable influence in local politics and "the [Tatar] nationalists did not want Orthodox churches in the center, and especially not our [Orthodox] bells ringing."[107]

Chinese Property Politics: Three Cases

The elasticity given to local officials in approving petitions for the return of religious property and the bargaining between religious and authoritarian actors is similarly present in China. The Catholic Church in Shanghai has a long history dating back to the Ming dynasty. In 1608, Xu Gangqi, a practicing Catholic and government official, resigned his post in Beijing and was traveling home to mourn the death of his father.[108] En route he stopped in Nanjing where he met Father Lazarus Cattaneo S.J. and invited him to accompany him to Shanghai. Less than two years after Father Lazarus' arrival, more than two hundred people had converted to Catholicism. Catholicism continued to grow with the assistance and good reputation of the Xu family, who actively supported the

---

[105] The treaty allows Tatarstan to independently exploit its natural resources, including gas and oil, exempt male citizens from military service in the Russian army, create a national bank, and have greater autonomy in foreign trade. See especially Kirkow (1998); Debardeleben (1997); Solnick (1996).

[106] F.I. Shalyapin (1873–1938) was a famous Russian opera singer of the twentieth century. Ironically, Shalyapin was baptized in the original Cathedral of Epiphany.

[107] Interview with Orthodox Father Oleg, Rector of the Cathedral of Epiphany of Our Lord, May 2006, Kazan.

[108] During the Ming dynasty when the parent of a government official passed away, he resigned his post and returned home for three years of filial mourning (*dingyou*).

expansion of Christianity and built churches in the surrounding area. By the eighteenth century, thousands of Catholics, both Chinese and foreign, resided in Shanghai. In fact, before 1949 there were more than three hundred Catholic churches, and the Shanghai Diocese had ownership of more than one-third of all of the land in the city.[109] After the communists came to power, the new regime confiscated much of this property.

During the Cultural Revolution, all religious buildings were closed, with many of them destroyed or used for other purposes. In the 1980s, the Shanghai Diocese began the petitioning process for the return of lost property. Many of the buildings were rendered un-returnable, having been converted to schools and hospitals; but the district-level governments across the city made considerable efforts to return the properties. As one priest explained, close to one-third of all confiscated churches and cathedrals were returned to the Church. Yet the returns are often accompanied with extraneous conditions.[110]

In Huangpu district, Church leaders have been negotiating the return of the Jun Yi chapel located in the Old City. The chapel was originally part of the Pan family estate, one of the most prominent families in Shanghai and builders of the famous Yu Yuan Garden. The chapel was built in 1640 by a granddaughter of the Catholic pioneer Xu Gangqi, who married into the Pan clan and wanted a chapel where she and her children could worship without having to travel. She converted a small, unused temple (*shichun tang*) into the Catholic chapel. After her death the chapel was given to the Shanghai Dioceses and briefly served as the headquarters of the Catholic Church and a small school.

Over the years, the Pan family fell on misfortune. Their seventy-acre estate in the heart of the Old Town was the center of violent conflict in the late Qing dynasty. Their residence housed imperial troops fighting the rebels of the Taiping Rebellion, the British occupied their gardens during the Opium Wars, and the Japanese bombed their remaining estate in 1937. During this period, the chapel also passed through various hands. It was converted into a temple to honor Guandi, the Taoist god of war, and then later returned to a school.[111] After 1949, the communists confiscated the Pan family estate, and the municipal government spent almost a decade turning the gardens into a public park, which opened in 1956. In 1982, the central government declared this area of the city a national historic treasure, and it has since become a center of tourism in Shanghai.

---

[109] Several Shanghai Catholic priests quoted that more than one-third of all the land in Shanghai was linked to the Church; however, I was not able to confirm this number with government sources. The priests explained that before 1949 several large districts in Shanghai were under the authority of the Church, including a majority of Xujiahui and large portions of Luwan and Huangpu. Interview with Catholic priest W, April 2007, Shanghai. On the number of pre-1949 Catholic churches, see L. Jin (2000).

[110] Interview with Catholic priest Z, May 2007, Shanghai.

[111] See B. Jin (2008).

The Shanghai Diocese has been in negotiations with the Huangpu government for the return of the chapel for almost two decades. The return of the chapel is complicated on several accounts. First, the Old Town area has been converted into a tourist center with the Yu Yuan Gardens and the Taoist City God Temple (*chenghuang miao*) as two of the main attractions. According to one Catholic priest, to introduce a Catholic chapel to this area changes the existing religious dynamic. Catholicism, after all, is viewed as a foreign religion, whereas the Taoist temple is seen as an indigenous Chinese faith.[112] Moreover, the temple honors a very local god – the City God and the protector of Shanghai. Second, the history of the chapel is layered. The chapel was originally built over an old temple (*shichun tang*) and later was converted to a Taoist temple. This raises the question as to which religious community is the rightful owner: Taoists or Catholics. Finally, there are significant financial concerns. The location of the chapel is in a high-rent commercial and tourist district, which means the costs for relocation and compensation are extremely sensitive.

In the autumn of 2007, an agreement was reached. The Church would regain possession on the condition that the property would not be used as a formal place of worship but instead turned into a museum for the history of Catholicism in Shanghai. The local government's rationale was that the district is already home to two Catholic churches so there was limited demand; the chapel space is too small to accommodate many worshipers; and a museum would fit better within the historic Old Town development.[113]

Other religious communities' petitions have met with far greater degrees of success but also reveal the delicate negotiations between religious and state actors. Hidden behind apartment blocks in the Hongkou district of Shanghai is the Three Outlooks temple (*sanguan tang*). The temple dates back more than three hundred years when it was first built to honor a local Taoist god. After the communists came to power, the temple was officially closed, and all but two of buildings were destroyed to make way for a factory. At the end of the Cultural Revolution, the factory closed, and local residents again began using the space as a makeshift temple. In 1990, the last of the factory equipment was removed, and the Three Outlooks temple reopened but was not registered. In fact, it took more than nine years to formally register with the district RAB and the Shanghai Buddhist Association. During this period of registration limbo, the temple remained open for business, and its following grew. After the temple finally secured registration, it began the petitioning process to reclaim lost religious property – only two of the original halls remained, and the popular neighborhood temple was quickly outgrowing its space.

The Three Outlooks temple's petition was largely successful. The Hongkou government granted the temple permission to reclaim its land, rebuild, and issued a relocation announcement for residents living on the former temple

---

[112] Interview with Catholic priest X, June 2007, Shanghai.
[113] Ibid.

property.[114] However, the support of local authorities was contingent on the temple footing the bill for the relocation of residents and temple renovations. Local authorities agreed to provide land for new apartments for the dislocated residents, but the temple was required to pay for the construction of the apartment building, the costs of moving, and compensation to the residents. The new apartment building meant that the residents were able to exchange their 1960s vintage forty-square-meter apartments for brand new ninety-square-meter apartment just five hundred meters down the road.

In addition to financing the new apartments and the physical costs of the move, the temple was also required to give a fixed sum to each legal resident affected by the move. This created a bureaucratic scramble in the old apartment complex to add family members to household registration cards (*hukou*).[115] Although the temple was dealing with the relocation of only forty-eight people who had local resident cards, each resident card carried the names of multiple people. One temple elder explained that of the forty-eight resident cards, some had up to twenty people on each card.[116] The temple's compensation settlements were to be based on the total number of displaced people, so each resident had a financial incentive to register multiple family members as living within their flat. In the end, one temple elder estimated that they had paid more than ¥58 million RMB ($9 million) to cover the cost of the new apartments, moving expenses, relocation settlements, demolition of the old apartment complex, and construction of the new temple.[117]

Finally, the complexity of property politics in China can also invite third parties to the bargaining table, where real estate developers broker deals between religious and political authorities. Pudong is the eastern financial center of metropolitan Shanghai and the largest of the administrative districts. In the 1990s, Pudong was relatively sparsely populated farmland, but twenty years later, it is now home to some of the priciest real estate in the country. The Pudong boom is driven in part by the construction of gated expatriate communities, complete with two-story villas, lush parks, and international schools. To attract foreigners to these enclaves, developers sought alliances with religious communities to erect new churches.[118] In the past decade, developers sold parcels of land well below market prices to Catholic and Protestant religious bodies for the construction of new churches. More importantly, they have also

---

[114] In December 2006, the Shanghai Hongkou District Housing Administration Bureau (*Shanghaishi Hongkouqu fangwu tudi guanliju*) issued a public announcement permitting the expansion of the temple and relocation of residents. The demolition notice (*fangwu chaiqian gonggao*) was posted on the Hongkou government website until January 2009.

[115] The hukou is the household registration record, which officially identifies a person as a resident of an area. A hukou generally includes identifying information such the name of the person, parents, children, spouse, and date of birth.

[116] Interview with Sanguan tang temple elder Y, July 2007, Shanghai.

[117] Interview with Sanguan tang temple elder G, July 2007, Shanghai.

[118] Developers have sought alliances particularly with Catholics and Protestants in Shanghai because the majority of expatriates are Western and therefore assumed to be Christian.

ILLUSTRATION 4.7. The demolition of apartment complex adjacent to the Three Out-looks temple in 2007. Photo by author.

helped lobby local authorities for the necessary permissions for the con-struction of religious buildings.[119] According to one Catholic priest who brokered an arrangement with a real estate developer, this is a "win-win" (*shuangying*) situation for all parties involved. The Church is able to pur-chase land that they could not otherwise afford and gain assistance from a powerful developer who walks the applications through the bureaucracy. The developer also wins because the developments attract foreigners, who pay substantially higher rents than local Chinese. Finally, the priest explained, local residents benefit from the increase in their property value, while at the same time enjoying the gardens surrounding the churches, the beauty of the cathedral, and the safety of knowing they have "honest Christian neighbors."[120]

Faith-based Tourism

The material interests of religious and state actors also converge around tourism. In this arena, religious-state interaction departs from the quid pro

---

[119] Interview with TSPM Protestant minister X, August 2007, Pudong.
[120] Interview with Catholic priest D, April 2007, Shanghai.

ILLUSTRATION 4.8. The Three Outlooks temple gate in 2007. Photo by author.

quo exchanges often found in property politics, and more closely resembles collaborative and stable exchanges. Tourism, in other words, presents an arena where religious groups and local governments are on a more equal footing, and where both sides can gain significantly from cooperation. For example, entrepreneurial local officials are able to repackage their locales

ILLUSTRATION 4.9. The Three Outlooks temple new gate in 2010. Photo by author.

to attract potential residents, investors, and visitors, and are keenly aware that religious monuments can enhance local appeal and become a point of pride.[121]

For religious communities, collaboration around faith-based tourism is attractive for several reasons. One is that the government usually foots the bills for renovations that the religious community could not otherwise independently afford; a second is religious groups are still able to conduct services, rituals, and ceremonies with little interference, aside from the occasionally obtrusive shuffling of tourists snapping photographs; third, collaboration opens secondary income opportunities for the religious group; and finally, as a designated tourist site, religions may be able to attract and eventually convert those who might otherwise have never set foot inside their walls. This last rationale can be particularly important in China, where there are strict rules against proselytizing beyond the grounds of state-sanctioned religious buildings. As a tourist venue, therefore, some religious groups may also be able to fulfill their evangelizing mission.

---

[121] For the re-inventing of religious activities as tourism, see Wang (1993); Lyons (2000); Yeung (2000); Wu (2000); Huang (2005); Anholt (2007).

What further distinguishes the tourism arena from that of property politics is that significant cooperation is required on both sides. Religious groups must first agree to the transformation of their place of worship into a tourist site and commit to supporting the tourist industry. This means permitting visitors to observe religious activities and employing staff to manage tourists. Such a commitment also comes with risks. As a tourist attraction, religious communities take the chance that their religious lives will be supplanted or marginalized by secular interests, and that they may disenfranchise current believers, especially as places of worship and meditation become commercialized. Local governments must also commit by providing the necessary bureaucratic stamps and helping finance renovations. Such collaboration can be risky – not only must local governments put up the capital, but also they may need to circumvent central policies and laws that mandate a strict separation of religion and state. Local officials also run the risk of seeing a small return on their speculative investment and attract unwanted attention from their respective political Centers. Such religious-state collaboration, after all, falls into a gray area of legality and, if interpreted in a negative light, could end political careers.

To minimize risks and maneuver around secular state policies, local government officials in Russia and China have devised several tools. For instance, although it is illegal for the state to financially support religious groups, there is little concern when a local goverment develops the tourist sector, even if an attraction has strong religious overtones. In this way, local authorities never invest directly in religious communities but rather invest in the commercial enterprise of tourism.[122] This distinction is important because it provides state funds for rebuilding temples, churches, or religious structures. Monies are transferred through various bureaucracies – such as the local ministry of tourism and commerce or through the ministry of culture – where they are earmarked for improving the appearance of religious buildings by adding gardens, statues, restaurants, and more generally for the preservation of cultural relics. A second strategy is to rename places of worship as museums or living cultural centers.[123] Essentially, local governments secularize and desensitize places of worship and in doing so, they circumvent central policies by altogether avoiding the requirement to register places of worship with the religious bureaucracies of the state. These places instead transfer their registration first through other bureaucracies, such as tourism and commerce or culture. Once a religious site has been cleared through these other institutions, the process is expedited through the religious affairs departments.[124]

---

[122] Interview with SARA bureaucrat O, June 2007, Beijing.

[123] Also see Gossaert and Palmer (2011); Borchert (2005); Ji (2004).

[124] Religious sites that are also tourist ventures tend to be registered with multiple departments. Interview with SARA bureaucrat O, June 2007, Beijing.

Russian Faith-based Tourism

In Nizhny Novgorod, the local government and the Russian Orthodox Church have established a collaborative relationship around tourism. *Il'inskaja sloboda* is a boulevard of eighteenth-century wooden houses that runs from the Kremlin through the oldest part of the city. The majority of buildings in this region follow a similar eighteenth-century architectural style – two stories, wooden, and highly decorative. In an attempt to compete with other Russian cities that have capitalized on faith-based tourism, the local government invested heavily in the reconstruction of this historic area, which by 2006 had been designated to include between seven and ten new Orthodox churches. To help legitimize state investment in the project, the Nizhny government declared the street a "historic-cultural treasure" and prohibited the destruction of any of the wooden buildings.[125] A fund for the reconstruction and management of the tourist area was also established, which comprises representatives from the Kremlin, the local government, and the bishop of the Nizhny Novgorod Orthodox Diocese.[126] The fund has received more than 84 million rubles ($2.7 million) from the federal budget to support the project.[127]

It is worth mentioning that the historical accuracy of a tourist joint venture seems to have little relevance. Local officials are willing to designate projects as historical treasures, and religious communities are eager to accommodate. In the interest of turning a profit, local governments are prepared to reinvent their city's image with "conscious and deliberate manipulations of culture in an effort to enhance the appeal and interest of places."[128] As one advisor to the *Il'inskaja sloboda* project explained, the Orthodox presence in this region is not entirely accurate and overemphasizes the dominance of Orthodoxy. Nizhny Novgorod, as an inland port on the Volga, has always had a plural religious population, and the Orthodox monopoly is a recent invention based on close Orthodox-state relations. In fact, according to historical documents, there were only four to five small Orthodox chapels in the *Il'inskaja sloboda* boulevard area, not the seven then under construction.[129]

The intersection of church and state in the arena of tourism is equally present in Tatarstan. In the capital city of Kazan, the local government partnered with the Religious Board of Muslims for the Republic of Tatarstan (*Duhovnoe Upravlenie Musul'man Respubliki Tatarstan; DUMRT*) for the reconstruction of the sixteenth century Kul-Sharif Mosque (*mechet' Kul-Sharif*). The

---

[125] The street was declared a "historic treasure" in February 2004.

[126] Interview with the advisor to the *Il'inskaja sloboda* fund, February 2006, Nizhny Novgorod.

[127] "Il'inskaja sloboda zhdet patriarha Alekseja II i 84 mln rublei iz federal'nogo budget" [Ilinskaja sloboda is awaiting Patriarch Alexsi II and 84 million rubles from the federal budget] (2004: 16).

[128] Philo and Kearns (1993: 3); Hobsbawm (1990).

[129] Interview with advisor to the *Il'inskaja sloboda* Fund, February 2006, Nizhny Novgorod.

ILLUSTRATION 4.10. The Church of the Ascension of Our Lady in the *Il'inskaja sloboda* region, 2012. Photo by author.

Kul-Sharif Mosque is legendary in Tatar history. The mosque was originally located within the Kazan Kremlin,[130] but was destroyed during the final battle of the Russo-Kazan Wars in 1552.[131] During the final days of the siege, the army of Ivan IV (Ivan the Terrible) captured the city and slew most of the inhabitants except for a small group of holdouts led by the Tatar poet Kul-Sharif.[132] Kul-sharif and his students staged their final attack against the Russian invaders from the Kremlin mosque. Although they all perished in the battle, Kul-sharif was memorialized as one of the last defenders of an independent

---

[130] In Russian, the word "kremlin" (*kreml'*) translates to fortress or fortified complex but is often used in reference to the Moscow Kremlin or as a metonym for central authority. Many Russian cities have kremlins that house local government offices. Such is the case in Tatarstan, where the presidential palace and Shaimiev administration is headquartered in the Kazan Kremlin.

[131] The Russo-Kazan wars were a series of wars fought from the fifteenth to sixteenth century between the Kazan Khanate and Muscovite Russia. The wars ended in 1552 with the capture of Kazan.

[132] The siege lasted from September to October 1552, and approximately three hundred to four hundred thousand Tatar-Bashkirs were killed. The forty-thousand resident population of Kazan was reduced to six thousand after the siege. See Devlet (2004).

Tatar state (Kazan Khanate) before the Russian Empire annexed it and forced Orthodox baptism on the survivors.[133]

In the summer of 1990 shortly before Tatarstan proclaimed sovereignty, there was growing public debate surrounding the reclaiming of the Kazan Kremlin. Leaders of the nationalist movement along with local government officials had moved their headquarters into the Kremlin and were searching for a new symbol of Tatar identity – one that evoked images of national heroes defending Tatar culture against imperial Russia. Leaders of the nationalist movement and various Muslim organizations published an open letter to President Shaimiev in a local newspaper with two key demands: first, that a monument be built to commemorate those who died defending the city from the 1552 Russian invasion. The letter reminded the president that the Russians had built such a monument to honor fallen (Russian) soldiers in the city, but there was nothing to honor the thirty thousand massacred Tatars. The second demand was that a mosque be rebuilt within the Kazan Kremlin, asserting that the two Orthodox churches still standing in the Kremlin yard were built "on the graves of Tatars and their mosques."[134]

What followed were many years of public debate as to how to best assert Tatar identity. In 1994, President Shaimiev responded to this debate by declaring the Kazan Kremlin a "Museum Complex and Historical Preserve."[135] The objective of the presidential decree was to reclaim the Kremlin as part of the Tatar nation and to develop it into a place that would attract tourism and international attention.

Shortly after the presidential decree, the local government initiated a petition to designate the Kazan Kremlin a UNESCO World Heritage Site. For the Shaimiev administration, the reconstruction effort was designed to restore "the Kazan Kremlin to a state fitting its significance as an object of historical-cultural importance for the republic, the Russian Federation and the international community."[136] In a nod to the plural nature of Tatarstan, the plans also included a facelift for the two standing Orthodox churches in the Kremlin, a museum of Islamic Culture of the Volga Region, a Museum of the Culture of Slavic Peoples of the Volga, and a National Art Gallery. Yet despite the appeals to multiculturalism, the crowning jewel of project was the reconstructed Kul-Sharif Mosque.

---

[133] The first Tatar state, ancient Volga Bulgaria, converted to Islam in 922. The state was later became the part of the Tatar Kingdom (Kazan Khanate) with Kazan as the capital. The Tatar territory ran from the northern boundaries of Volga Bulgaria to the river Sura in the west and the river Belaya in the east. Following the conquest of Ivan the Terrible, most of the mosques of Kazan Khanate were destroyed or converted to Orthodox Churches. See Bukharaev (2000).

[134] Quoted in Graney (2007: 21).

[135] Presidential Decree President RT (1995).

[136] *Sic*. Quoted in Graney (2007: 21).

The Shaimiev administration and Religious Board of Muslims for the Republic of Tatarstan (*Duhovnoe Upravlenie Musul'man Respubliki Tatarstan; DUMRT*) had hoped to build a mosque that would attract international attention, yet their plans almost derailed the UNESCO petition. This is because UNESCO World Heritage sites are intended to protect existing cultural relics; however, the Kremlin Museum Complex and Historical Reserve required the destruction of a historic building to make way for the new Kul-sharif Mosque. This was a problem for UNESCO officials because the remains of a sixteenth-century "Russian" building were to be razed to rebuild a sixteenth-century "Tatar" mosque.[137] After significant lobbying on the part of the Tatar government and an agreement to adjust the mosque's location in the Kremlin yard, UNESCO was willing to sign off on the project. The only hitch was that the architects were still arguing about how to proceed with the construction of the mosque – there were no images or historical records describing the original mosque, and all that was known of the structure was the number of minarets.[138]

Rather than taking a preservationist's approach and rebuild the mosque in the style of other sixteenth-century Tatar mosques, the local government organized design competitions before a final plan was chosen.[139] Although, there were no records describing the original mosque, the reincarnated Kul-sharif Mosque likely shares little if anything in common with the original. The new mosque is decisively modern, with polished marble floors and multiple crystal and gold chandeliers hanging in a lobby; it is monumental in size, making it the largest mosque in Europe; unsurprisingly, its gleaming eight minarets and turquoise dome look out of place in Tatarstan.

The rebuilding of the mosque was a coup for both Muslim and local politicians on several fronts.[140] First, the new mosque sits within the walls of the Kremlin, which is historically and metonymically the center of power, reinforcing the importance of Tatar sovereignty and national identity. According to Nadir V. Kinossian, "the idea of reconstructing the legendary mosque fit very well into the political agenda. Politicians saw the role of the project as emphasizing the new political status of the republic as a sovereign state as opposed to that of a subject of the Russian federation."[141]

Second, the successful UNESCO petition elevated Tatar cultural heritage to that of other Russian World Heritage sites, including Red Square and the Russian Orthodox cathedrals of Suzdal. Joining this prestigious UNESCO list put Kazan on a tourist map along with other major Russian and global attractions.

---

[137] See Kinossian (2008).
[138] Interview with archaeologist at the Tatarstan Academy of Sciences, Kazan, May 2006.
[139] The design firm that eventually won the contest was Tatinvest-grazhdanproyect. The design is based on composite influences of mosques in Turkey.
[140] Interview with Imam S from the Board of Muslims of the Republic of Tatarstan (*Duhovnoe Upravlenie Musul'man Respubliki Tatarstan; DUMRT*), April 2006, Kazan.
[141] Kinossian (2008: 200).

ILLUSTRATION 4.11. Kul-Sharif Mosque in Kazan, 2006. Photo by author.

As a result, tourism has become an important catalyst for Tatar urban renewal as buses of schoolchildren, domestic tourists, pilgrims, and even heads of state include the Kazan Kremlin on their travel itinerary.

Third, for the Muslim community, the monumental mosque has become a place of pilgrimage for Muslims across the Russian Federation, and many refer to it as "Russia's Mecca." As a place of pilgrimage, Tatar Muslims are also able to use the mosque as a platform to promote Tatar's brand of Islam – "Cosmopolitan" or "Euro-Islam."[142] Cosmopolitan Islam traces its roots to nineteenth-century Tatar intellectuals who called for peaceful integration with their Russian neighbors. They rejected interconfessional violence and Wahhabism, and they considered Turkey an impressive model of how to balance a secular state with religious pluralism. The leaders of this movement, moreover, proposed that Tatarstan should be the model for the rest of Russia, and in fact, for the rest of the world: where Muslim, Christians, and Jews could live together in a secular society without conflict.[143]

Finally, one imam remarked that the greatest benefit to the strategic partnership has been the 400-million ruble ($14.2 million) price tag, which was shared largely by the state and private donors.[144] Tatar Muslims control the largest and most impressive mosque in the country, which is a place of pilgrimage and international importance, and have no financial burden to speak of.

Chinese Faith-based Tourism

Religious-state collaboration in the tourist arena is also quite popular in China. Entrepreneurial local governments and religious communities forge alliances with the shared goal of economic development, and religion is often "big business."[145] For local goverments, faith-based tourism has several advantages. It is a way to showcase local culture, earn extra revenue, and simplify the management of religious communities.[146] For religious groups, collaboration is attractive because it facilitates religious expansion and renovation (often at the expense of the state), as well as opportunities to earn extra revenue from the growing number of pilgrims.

Located forty kilometers to the southwest of metropolitan Shanghai is Songjiang, a district where the local goverment has been extremely active in promoting faith-based tourism. Songjiang has traditionally been seen as a sleepy fishing village on the Wusong River, but in the mid-1980s, the government began to invest in historic preservation as a way to encourage economic growth. Religious groups became one of the primary beneficiaries of this endeavor. In

---

[142] On Euro-Islam, see Hakimov and Jakupov (2004).

[143] To some extent the Euro-Islam model has been successful. Secretary of State Hillary Clinton scheduled a "fact-finding" trip to Kazan in October 2009, and in June 2011, the city hosted peace talks between Armenia and Azerbaijan over Nagorno-Karabakh. However, in August of 2012 violent attacks by Islamic militants in Kazan have called into question Tatarstan's model of religious tolerance and whether Euro-Islam will endure; see Herszenhorn (2012).

[144] Interview with Imam S from the Board of Muslims of the Republic of Tatarstan (*Duhovnoe Upravlenie Musul'man Respubliki Tatarstan; DUMRT*), April 2006, Kazan; also Arsent'eva (2005: 2).

[145] Webster (2008).

[146] The bureaucratic restrictions on tourist sites are more flexible than those for religious ones; interview with SARA bureaucrat O, June 2007, Beijing.

Fangta Park (*fangta gongyuan*), the government converted a Song dynasty tea-house into the Shanghai Mazu Cultural Palace (*Shanghai tianma wenhua guan*).

Shanghai was originally home to three Mazu temples, as it was customary for followers, including government officials, to offer incense at one of the temples before embarking on a sea-faring voyage. The last of the original temples was destroyed during the late Qing dynasty (1883).[147] Nearly a full century later, the Songjiang district government sought to gather the remaining ruins of the Mazu temple and transfer them to Songjiang. The plan was to rebuild a Mazu temple in the center of the Fangta Park.

Building a Mazu temple, however, requires creative bureaucratic stamps, even for local governments. This is because Mazu is not one of the five official religions. Although there are some aspects of Mazu rituals that resemble Taoist and Buddhist practices, it remains classified in both China and Taiwan as a popular religion.[148] Such classification means that Mazu worship is considered illegal. Although it is not impossible to build and register such temples – as there are dozens of Mazu temples lining the coast of Fujian – local governments must first demonstrate a strong demand.[149] However, in Songjiang there was little to no demand for a Mazu temple. In fact, the local government estimated less than ten percent of the population adhered to any religious tradition and perhaps only a handful of migrants in the greater Shanghai area worshiped the Mazu goddess.[150] The question then becomes: why would the Songjiang government go to the trouble of building a temple for a goddess with limited local demand and is considered illegal by Beijing?

The answer is not because the local government is particularly tolerant in its management of religion. Over the past two decades, the Songjiang government has been quite active in targeting illegal religious activity, including shutting down at least thirty-two unauthorized temples; organizing reeducation classes for those taking part in "cultlike" or superstitious activities; warning TSPM churches to rein in their self-appointed missionaries (*zifeng chuandaoren*); closing several Protestant house churches and unauthorized meeting points; issuing administrative warnings to the Catholic Church to cease summer classes and discourage annual pilgrimages to the Sheshan Basilica; and formally warning leaders of the underground Catholic Church to stop their activities.[151]

---

[147] The temple was located on Henan Road next to Suzhou creek.

[148] See especially Watson (1985); Boltz (1986); Sangren (1993, 1988); Pas (1989); Dean (1993); Rubinstein (2003, 1995).

[149] Across Fujian the Mazu cult has strong popular legitimacy, which has encouraged the state to accommodate its worship.

[150] Interview with Mazu Temple worker, May 2007, Songjiang. In 1996–7, for example, 9.67 percent of the local population is reported to be religious; see Songjiang xian difang shizhi bianzhuan weiyuanhui (1997b: 721).

[151] See Songjiang xian difang shizhi bianzhuan weiyuanhui (1997a: 368); Songjiang xian difang shizhi bianzhuan weiyuanhui (1997b: 301, 407); Y. Wang (2000: 219); He (2001: 229, 2005: 307).

Government support for the Mazu temple lies in the fact that local cadres saw the temple as a business opportunity. The Mazu cult is well known along the coasts of China and Asia, with temples scattered along former trade and migration routes to Taiwan, Korea, Japan, and extending farther south.[152] Perhaps more important is the fact that Mazu's largest number of adherents are from Taiwan, and there was hope that a Mazu temple would attract Taiwanese investment to Songjiang. This gamble was partially successful: a wealthy Taiwanese businessman funded part of the restoration, and the Mazu temple officially opened in 2002.

One temple worker was quick to add that although the building looks like a practicing temple – there are altars, incense, and recordings of monks chanting piped in the background – it is not registered with the Songjiang RAB. The temple is officially titled the Shanghai Mazu Cultural Palace (*Shanghai tianma wenhua guan*) and classified as a museum, which places it under the protection of the Ministry of Culture and under the management of the Parks Department. This means that all profits from admission tickets and temple donations go directly to the Parks Department and not to any religious body. Moreover, the temple does not have any priests, and a majority of its visitors do not come to worship the goddess. Yet for the practitioners, like the Taiwanese patron who helped fund the temple, the local authorities import Mazu priests from Fujian annually to conduct religious ceremonies on the birthday and anniversary of the goddess' mortal passing. According to one temple worker, "this is just good business" (*zhe shi bi hao maimai*).[153]

The Songjiang district government has also used faith-based tourism as a springboard for other types of commercial investment. In addition to the Mazu temple, the local government invested heavily in the renovation of the Songjiang Old Town, converting it into a commercial and tourist center. A pedestrian mall has been built lined with retail shops, restaurants, and historic buildings. At one end of the mall is the White Crane in the Clouds Mosque (*Yunjian beihe si*, also called *Songjiang qingzhensi*). In 1985, the mosque entered into a formal partnership with the government.[154] The terms of the agreement were straightforward: the local government would help repair the historic structure to its pre-1949 appearance and relocate the current factory and residents that were occupying part of the mosque's buildings.[155] In return, the mosque would function simultaneously as a museum to support the local regime initiative to revitalize the Old Town.

---

[152] Mazu temples have been estimated at 800 in Taiwan, 57 in Hong Kong and Macau, and 135 in Korea, Thailand, Vietnam, Cambodia, Burma, Japan Malaysia, Indonesia, India, and the Philippines. Mazu temples have additionally been established as far as Paris, New York, San Francisco, and Sao Paulo. See, F. Yang (2004); Nyitray (2000); Li (1995).

[153] Interview with Mazu Temple worker, May 2007, Songjiang.

[154] In 1980, the mosque was registered as a cultural relic under the protection of the Shanghai municipal government; see Sun, Wu and Liu (2001: 262–3).

[155] Sun, Wu and Liu (2001: 450).

To facilitate this process, the district government reinstated the mosque as a local cultural relic under its protection and funded the necessary repairs for the 1989 reopening (more than ¥3.5 million RMB).[156] Local authorities also awarded the mosque an annual stipend of ¥100,000 RMB ($15,700) to help with maintenance costs.[157] Such a large financial contribution was not controversial because the mosque was built during the Yuan dynasty (1314) and was in desperate need of repair. Moreover, the mosque's unique architecture made it a good candidate for cultural (and thus national) preservation – the exterior façade has many characteristics of a Buddhist or Taoist temple, yet within the walls, it has somewhat more conventional Islamic influences – an apt architectural metaphor for the historical adoption of Islam into China.

Both the imam of the mosque and leaders from the Shanghai Islamic Association welcomed partnership with the local government for the simple reason that they would not otherwise have been able to afford the renovations.[158] Part of the agreement allowed the mosque to reclaim some of its prerevolutionary property. Considering the small Muslim population in the city (under three hundred people), rather than expanding the buildings to accommodate more worshipers, the mosque's leadership council took the advice of the district government and leased the property to commercial developers to further the growth of the Old Town.[159] Where gardens once stood before 1949, now restaurants surround the mosque serving halal specialties, as well as shops that sell sporting goods and designer clothes. According to the accountant for the mosque, this was the best financial solution because the government stipend goes almost entirely for maintenance, and the rents from the commercial development turn quite a handsome profit – one that is shared with other less fortunate mosques in the greater Shanghai area.[160]

The transformation of religious landmarks into tourist ventures is not always as smooth as the case of the Songjiang mosque. On a small hill approximately twenty miles west of the mosque is the Catholic Basilica of Our Lady of Sheshan (*Sheshan jin jiaozhi you shengmu dadian*). A Catholic church in some form or another has stood on the hillside in Sheshan since 1863, when Jesuit missionaries seeking shelter from the Taiping Rebellion built the first chapel. The present basilica has gone through several reincarnations; however, most

---

[156] He, Zhang, and Ou (2004: 309); interview with Imam A, May 2007, Songjiang; interview with accountant D for mosque, May 2007, Songjiang.

[157] In 1905, the Shanghai Municipal Administration Commission of Cultural Heritage declared the mosque a cultural relic and under its protection; however, after 1949 the mosque went into disrepair and was almost leveled during the Cultural Revolution.

[158] The foundation has sunk several feet below street level and the mosque needs to be pumped out after each rain. Interview with Imam A, May 2007, Songjiang; interview with accountant D for mosque, May 2007, Songjiang.

[159] Goverment documents estimate the Songjiang Muslim population at less than three hundred in 1998; see Y. Wang (2000: 219).

[160] Interview with accountant D for mosque, May 2007, Songjiang.

ILLUSTRATIONS 4.12 AND 4.13. The exterior of the Songjiang mosque and adjoining shops, 2007. Photos by author.

of the structure was constructed from 1925 to 1935. After the communists came to power, the Sheshan Basilica was confiscated and the acting bishop imprisoned.[161] The basilica remained closed until 1981, when the Chinese Catholic Patriotic Association (CCPA) regained ownership.[162]

In the mid-1980s, the Songjiang government offered to help with the reconstruction of the basilica, which had been badly damaged during the Cultural Revolution. The government had larger plans to develop Sheshan and its surroundings into a tourist attraction, hoping to attract leisure-seeking urban Shanghainese to the more pastoral Sheshan. Plans were underway to create a 401-hectare "Shanghai Sheshan National Holiday Resort" to take advantage of the twelve mountain peaks in the area. However, according to one priest, he suspected that local cadres also hoped to profit from the growing number of Catholic pilgrims.[163]

Although many of the Sheshan priests were suspicious of the commercialization of the basilica, it was eventually incorporated into the holiday resort on the condition that non-Catholic tourists would not be allowed admission to the church during religious activities.[164] Authority for the new park was divided among three separate work units (*danwei*): the CCPA, the Songjiang Parks Department, and the Songjiang Cultural Relics Bureau.[165] As the Parks Department set about developing tourist services, such as erecting a chairlift to take visitors to the top of the peak, tensions rose with the Church. The Parks Department (with the backing of the local government) requested an admissions fee be charged at the base of the peak. This meant that all visitors to Sheshan, both Catholic pilgrims walking up to the fourteen Stations of the Cross and tourists alike would be charged a ¥30 RMB ($4.75) entrance fee. For the Catholic Church, this was unacceptable on both spiritual and financial grounds. Those attending mass should not have to pay to pray, and ¥30 RMB seemed a considerable amount for even the wealthiest parishioners. After extensive negotiations, the Parks Department agreed to have two entrances for the peak – a centrally located gate for tourists with an ¥80 RMB ($12.61) ticket fee and a free, unmarked gate on the opposite, undeveloped side of the mountain for practicing Catholics (and staffed by volunteer gatekeepers who

---

[161] Bishop Gong (Cardinal Ignatius Kung) was sentenced to life in prison for leading a "counterrevolutionary clique under the cloak of religion." In 1979, while still in prison, he was secretly elevated to cardinal by Pope John Paul II; however, this was not made public until he immigrated; see Rosenthal (2000).

[162] He (1991: 961). Again, the Chinese Catholic Patriotic Association (CCPA) is the one of the Religious Patriotic Associations (RPAs) in China. The RPAs were reorganized in the 1980s for each of the five official religions to ensure that religious leaders worked inline with the larger goals of the regime.

[163] Interview with Catholic priest A, July 2007, Shanghai.

[164] Sun, Wu, and Liu (2001: 322).

[165] The term *danwei* refers to one's work unit or place of employment. Before the 1980s, all Chinese were assigned to a work unit, which administered housing, education, medical care, and the like.

ILLUSTRATION 4.14. The Basilica of Our Lady of Sheshan, 2007. Photo by author.

loosely verified guests' religious credentials). As a compromise, the Catholic Church agreed to collect a ¥2 RMB ($0.32) fee to enter the basilica, with the exception of scheduled masses and on holidays.

The Sheshan basilica serves as an interesting comparison with the Songjiang mosque. Both are designated "cultural relics," receive financial support from the state, and are considered "local tourist attractions" by the Songjiang government. Yet there are striking differences in terms of state support and the enthusiasm on the part of religious actors. The basilica's annual stipend is roughly ¥600 RMB ($94.59), whereas the mosque receives approximately ¥100,000 RMB ($15,700). As one priest commented, "the money isn't even enough to pay someone to clean the [basilica's] gutters."[166] This discrepancy may also reflect these communities' larger relationship with the state. Although both Muslims and Catholics are considered foreign religions in China, the Catholics in Shanghai appear to have a more strained relationship with those in power than local Muslims. In the summer of 2012, for example, Bishop Thaddeus Ma Daqin announced at his public ordination ceremony that he was resigning from the government-sponsored Chinese Catholic Patriotic Association (CCPA). He explained, "After you take up the ministry and become

[166] Interview with Catholic priest B, July 2007, Shanghai.

ILLUSTRATION 4.15. The chairlift for the Sheshan Holiday Resort, 2007. Photo by author.

auxiliary bishop of Shanghai, there's a lot going on. . . . Heart and mind should be completely devoted to ministering and spreading the Good Word. Some posts are not convenient to continue to hold. So, from this day, this time of holy celebration, it is no longer convenient for me to continue to be a member of the Patriotic Association."[167] Following this public defection from the CCPA, the regime's response was swift. Bishop Ma was placed into "retreat" at Sheshan, two Shanghai seminaries were temporarily closed, and numerous priests and nuns were required to attend patriotic reeducation classes. This serves as an important reminder of the fluidity of the politics of religion in authoritarian regimes, and how quickly political winds may shift.

[167] Bishop Ma's resignation from the CCPA was quoted in Tejada and Mozur (2012); also see "New Shanghai bishop 'barred from ministry'" (2012).

CONCLUSIONS

The cases presented in this chapter illustrate diverse patterns of interaction between religious and political authorities in which the two sides are actively trading resources to secure strategic needs. In each bargaining matrix, material resources are the currency of exchange – they are a means to an end and are traded to secure specific goals. These exchanges reveal that the nature of interaction is often economic – each has a set of resources that are desired by the other and are open to exchange. Thus, despite the common assumption that religious groups are irrational and only concerned with supernatural forces, this chapter demonstrates that they can be as calculating as their secular peers. It also suggests that religious actors are becoming increasingly important economic and political players.

It would be a mistake, however, to assume that the bargaining games in this chapter are inherently equal. Russia and China are authoritarian regimes, and relations with the state, even at the local level, tend to be asymmetrical with the local political elites usually gaining more. At the same time, the outcome of religious-state interaction is not necessarily zero-sum. A gain for the local government does not mean a loss for religious organizations, or vice versa. Religious groups and local governments provide a service to each other; they offer resources that lessen the other's vulnerabilities, minimize uncertainty, and help achieve strategic goals.

Therefore, it might be useful to think of material bargaining games as developing in two stages within the authoritarian context. In the first stage, religious and local officials negotiate with each other to secure their position and influence. The interactions tend toward give-and-take exchanges in which governments selectively reward religious communities and religious groups attempt to curry favor to ensure their survival. The second stage is more collaborative and durable, in which the two sides become partners around shared material goals. Whether the goals of collaboration are focused on the political economy of reconstructing local identity, faith-based tourism, or attracting commercial investment, cooperation requires a greater commitment on both sides. And although it is fair to say that these collaborative exchanges still favor the state, the playing field is considerably more level. There is a diminished threat of rent-seeking behavior on the part of local cadres because they need compliance from religious communities.

This chapter also suggests that some religious communities are gaining more than others. These are the groups on the receiving end of state patronage; those that have carved out the closest niches with secular power; and those that are able to move from bargaining relationships to collaborative partnerships. This raises the question: why do local officials partner with some religious groups and leave others to wither?

To address this question, it is instructive to return to some of the arguments from earlier chapters that highlight the resources religious actors bring to the table. The expectation here is that cooperation is more likely when religious communities bring valuable commodities to the exchange. The bargaining games presented in this chapter provide support for this argument. Resource endowments do matter, and those groups that are resource rich tend to cooperate more than those that are resource poor. However, it is important to keep in mind that local politics also determines the demand and market value of any given resource. This in turn helps explain why local authorities willingly cooperate with religious communities on the political margins or those that are shunned by Moscow and Beijing – because these religious groups provide attractive resources that address local needs. Recall, for instance, the Chinese cadres who built the Mazu temple on the outskirts of Shanghai, the mega-churches and factory-churches erected by Christian bosses, and the swift re-registration of evangelicals in Kazan who provided much-needed social services. Thus, what seems to be important for the local authoritarian state is what religious communities bring to the exchange, rather than their legal status. Local political elites are willing to navigate around central policies and directives when it is advantageous and when there is a local demand to do so.

The chapter finally suggests that some religious groups are nevertheless cooperating more. To help explain this observation, it is useful to revisit the argument that addresses the cultural capital of religious organizations. Here, the argument is that religious-state cooperation is more likely when religions have indigenous ties to a country, which translate into greater cultural resources. Again, this chapter provides some support to the claim that the insider position of a religion influences material cooperation. Consider, for instance, the tourism arena in China where there is an established market for tourism around Buddhist and Taoist temples. Faith-based tourism for these religions is a relatively safe investment for local cadres on numerous levels, not the least of which is a demand among domestic and foreign tourists, and that these religions are seen as integral parts of Chinese culture. Faith-based tourism for other religious communities such as Protestants, however, is much riskier. Not only is there is little market demand to visit Protestant churches in China, but Christianity is more generally viewed as an outsider religion (and thus somewhat invasive), making it more difficult for even resource-rich Protestants to establish vertical ties with the state.

This same kind of selective collaboration is also observed locally in Russia. Recall, in Nizhny Novgorod where politicians exaggerated a historic presence of the Orthodox Church to compete with other cities that have capitalized on faith-based tourism. This reimagining is possible because of Orthodox Christianity's special place in Russian history and the large population of Orthodox Christians in Nizhny. Similarly, a collaborative relationship between Islam and state is present in Kazan. Again, this partnership is feasible because visitors travel to Kazan to see Tatar Muslims, not Orthodox Christians or other minority religions. Thus, understanding why local governments collaborate with some religious communities and ignore others must take into account not only the resource endowments but also the cultural capital of religious communities. Religious communities that have an insider status or that have local popular legitimacy have a natural advantage in forging alliances and cooperating around shared material goals.

In the next chapter, the discussion turns to how bargaining games play out when nonmaterial resources are at stake and religious groups and their authoritarian overseers negotiate issues of power and prestige. The chapter continues to flesh out the limits, consequences, and costs of religious-state collaboration in authoritarian regimes, as well as highlights the differences on these issues between Russia and China.

5

The Politics of Faith, Power, and Prestige

> At the heart of all Russia's victories and achievements are patriotism, faith and strength of spirit.
>
> – Vladimir Putin[1]

> As long as we are united politically and have mutual respect regarding spiritual beliefs, religion can play a positive role in social harmony.
>
> – Ye Xiaowen, former head of the SARA[2]

The previous chapter demonstrated that the politics of religion in authoritarian regimes is shaped largely by economic concerns in which local government officials and religious communities' material interests have become intertwined and can often translate into "big business." In this chapter, the discussion continues to illustrate the closing gap between the sacred and secular; however, the focus turns to the ongoing process of negotiation over nonmaterial concerns. In addition to seeking material gains, political and religious authorities are simultaneously vying for power and prestige. Governing elites seek power to enhance legitimacy and command respect, and religious leaders attempt to influence political decision making, manipulate the religious landscape, and promote their spiritual agenda.

The chapter proceeds in three steps. The first explores how competition for power and prestige shapes religious-state interaction. Here, I continue the arguments from the previous chapter that resources are bargaining chips offered to the opposing side to achieve strategic needs. However, I suggest that cooperation around issues of power and prestige is a riskier strategy for both parties. Local governments endanger empowering religious communities, who in turn

---

[1] Quoted in Grove (2013).
[2] Reported by *Xinhua* (2011).

could nourish civil society, establish competing centers of power, and at the extremes, "capture" the local state. Religious leaders risk alienating their base by developing "unholy alliances" with those in power and becoming increasingly dependent on state support. The second section introduces the nonmaterial resources that each side brings to the bargaining table and the outcomes of religious-state interaction, including some instance where cooperation backfires. The chapter concludes by analyzing the larger implications of cooperation around power and prestige, addressing which groups are gaining the most, and highlighting the similarities and differences between Russia and China.

THE LOGIC OF NONMATERIAL COOPERATION

Scholars from Niccolo Machiavelli to Hans Morgenthau have understood politics as the struggle for power and prestige.[3] Whether the actor is a newly crowned prince, a nation-state, or an empire, political behavior is driven by the desire to control and influence. The fact that power and prestige also influence the behavior of authoritarian political elites and religious leaders does not need a long introduction. Power, for government officials, is a vehicle to consolidate authority, lengthen time horizons in office, curtail opposition, facilitate governance, and implement political agendas. Although religious groups' goals are weighted toward spiritual concerns, power allows them to further their religious mission, whether that means by growing congregations, promoting a more religiously rooted society, or safeguarding their position in a highly uncertain context.

Similarly, prestige for both religious and political authority is an indirect pathway to increase influence through noncoercive means. Prestige engenders authority, enhances legitimacy, and is tied closely to status. Therefore, religious entities with a surplus of cultural prestige are often in a position to receive state favors as well as use their moral authority and popular legitimacy to influence political decision making. For autocratic elites, prestige feeds directly into the regime's need for legitimacy by giving local authorities a moral authority of their own to govern while giving rise to belief in the regime's institutions and values. Prestige, for that reason, can be particularly valuable in an authoritarian regime where formal mechanisms of accountability are limited and popular support to rule may be weak.[4]

The struggle for power and prestige are particularly acute concerns in contemporary Russia and China, where transition politics have given rise to an ideological vacuum.[5] Power holders are quite aware that the guiding ideologies of the past, including Marxist-Leninism and Maoism in China, and the

---

[3] Machiavelli (1984); Morgenthau (1967).

[4] Lipset (1983).

[5] See especially Sil and Chen (2004); Potter (2003); Colton and McFaul (2002); Gudkov (2001); Tu (1999); Madsen (1993).

more recent experimentations with democracy in Russia have little normative resonance in society.[6] This absence of ideology can be troubling for ruling elites because ideology can be an effective tool of autocratic control. Not only does ideology demobilize citizens by providing an excuse not to rebel, it also rationalizes the existing political order. As Václav Havel writes,

> [ideology] is a very pragmatic, but at the same time an apparently dignified, way of legitimizing what is above, below, and on either side... It is a veil behind which human beings can hide their own "fallen existence," their trivialization, and their adaptation to the status quo. It is an excuse that everyone can use, from the greengrocer, who conceals his fear of losing his job behind an alleged interest in the unification of the workers of the world, to the highest functionary, whose interest in staying in power can be cloaked in phrases about service to the working class. The primary excusatory function of ideology, therefore, is to provide people, both as victims and pillars of the post-totalitarian system, with the illusion that the system is in harmony with the human order and the order of the universe.[7]

Although Russian and Chinese government officials may still give lip service to socialist and democratic ideals, they are quite aware that these moral codes no longer function as a unifying force. As a result, authoritarian elites are seeking alternative ways to enhance loyalty and ensure social stability for those living within their locales to positively position themselves and their allies. In the absence of a compelling ideological frame, local governments may then turn to religious communities for support.

Again, it should come as no surprise that religious cultural capital is sought after by authoritarian elites. History is filled with examples of the "divinity of dictators" in which religion is used to expand support for a regime, demobilize political challengers, and define national identity.[8] As Jeffrey R. Seul suggests, appropriating the cultural capital of religious communities can be an optimal strategy for political elites because "no other repositories of cultural meaning have historically offered so much in response to the human need to develop a secure identity."[9] Thus, close cooperation with religious communities may allow governments to assume the moral authority, respect, and trust that the general public has in religious bodies as their own.

Similarly, in periods of political transition and heightened uncertainty, it may be particularly advantageous for autocratic elites to draw on the cultural capital and symbols of religious organizations to maintain stability. David I. Kertzer explains "new political systems borrow legitimacy from the old by nurturing

---

[6] Ru and Ren (2006); Han (2006). For a more general discussion of antidemocratic discourse in China, see Shambaugh (2008).
[7] Havel (1985: 29).
[8] Smith (1996); Linz (2004 [1996]).
[9] Seul (1999: 558); also Almond and Verba (1963).

the old ritual forms, redirected to new purposes."[10] This helps explain the irony of Soviet-era New Year's trees that were trimmed with photos of Lenin or why communist systems, more generally, canonized their own set of gods (Lenin and Mao), saints (Marx and Engel), sinners (Trotsky and Lin Biao), holy books (*The Communist Manifesto* and *Little Red Book*), hymns ("The International"), and clergy (party members).[11] Local governments can turn to the familiarity of religion and ritual to shore up regime support and enrich their own power and prestige.

The struggle for power and prestige is equally as pressing for religious communities. Since the 1980s, religious communities in Russia and China have been regrouping from under the shadow of state-promoted atheism in which religion was viewed as backward and an instrument of Western imperialism. Religious groups were renounced, activities were driven underground, and many believers had no choice but to hide their religious identities and practices. Although religious freedom has certainly increased in both countries, antireligious propaganda and the legacies of intense secularization still looms in many circles. For instance, interviews with some religious studies experts and Chinese officials charged with managing religious groups frequently made light of the current revival as the "religion problem" (*zongjiao wenti*), which was being fueled by the backward and uneducated (*wenhua shuiping hen di*).[12] Here, the understanding was that an educated and rational individual would never embrace religion. This sentiment also permeates academic literature. For example, a Shanghai Academy of Social Sciences (SASS) survey found "illness" (*shengbing*) as one reason why people were converting to Protestantism.[13]

Some religious communities in Russia also face antireligious sentiment. In particular, the media commonly refers to nontraditional religious groups such as Protestants, Catholics, Baha'i, and Jehovah's Witnesses as "sects" or "cults" (*sekty, kul'ty*).[14] Such pejorative language is reinforced by religious communities with traditional claims, such as Orthodox Christians and Muslims, who

---

[10] Kertzer (1988: 42–3).

[11] See especially Froese (2008: 40–2); Fagan (2013: 127); and Bourdeaux (2000) for discussions of religious symbolism under communism and a reversal of the sacred and profane.

[12] It is not surprising for Chinese government officials to discredit growing religiosity because it parallels the larger state narrative that religion will eventually fade in importance and disappear. However, it was initially puzzling to hear similar responses from religious studies scholars, especially after having participated in hundreds of religious rituals to know that the believers cut across all social stratums. It seems that there is a generation of scholars who study the philosophy of religion and are housed in Marxist theory departments. Many of these scholars had never set foot inside a temple, mosque, or church or interviewed a religious believer. In fact, their research did not require them to do so, and it was better to not associate with such groups and be confused with being sympathetic. For a discussion of the important growth of religious studies in China, see F. Yang (2004, 2012).

[13] J. Liu, Luo, and Yan (1999: 4). For similar arguments, see Yao (2004); Yan, Wu, and Yan (2009); Qiao and Chen (2010).

[14] Fagan (2013: 95–101).

often consider competing religious groups as belonging to "totalitarian sects" (*totalitarnye sekty*).[15] These negative labels have real implications for marginalized religious organizations and their practitioners. In April 2006, the Nizhny Novgorod Buddhist Association invited a Danish practitioner of Tibetan Buddhism, Lama Ole Nedal, to give a public lecture on meditation.[16] The lecture was scheduled to take place in the large concert hall of the Nizhny Kremlin; however, not all members of the local religious community were welcoming. One Orthodox priest from a nearby seminary and several of his students posted signs over the lecture's advertisements warning: "Danger Totalitarian Sect." Moreover, they organized a small protest outside of concert hall warning the roughly four hundred visitors that attending the event would risk their immortal soul. According to the priest organizing the protest, the Kremlin is one of the most sacred places in the city and should not be welcoming of this so-called Buddhist, who was part of a "sect."[17] The priest added that had he learned about this event in advance, he would have made sure it was stopped.[18] Here, of course, the implication is that his contacts in the government would prohibit or relocate the talk.

Exacerbating the tension, Ole Nedal quipped at the beginning of the lecture: "some very serious looking men in black told me that this is a holy place and I should not be here. I told them that I feel pretty holy myself. Then, one priest told me to shut up, and I told him to shut up and walked away. So, I guess, we came to some kind of mutual understanding."[19] However, not all religious minorities are as bold or have the benefit of foreign passports. One Pentecostal pastor in Nizhny, for example, explained that they are often

---

[15] In April 2001, a conference entitled "Totalitarian Cults – Menace of the XXI Century" was held in Nizhny Novgorod. The welcoming remarks were given by Alexander Leonidovich Dvorkin, Ph.D., M. Div., Chairman of the Department of Sectology of St. Tikhon's Orthodox Theological Institute, Chief Editor of the *Prozreniye* (*Recovery of Sight*). Dvorkin identified the following "cults" in Russia: Pentecostals, Moonies, Scientologists, Mormons, Hare Krishna, Jehovah Witnesses, the Anastasia and Radasteya cults (an offshoot of Russian Orthodox Christianity), New Apostolic Church and Church of the Last Testament of Vissarion (charismatic Protestants) and Aum Shinrikyo. Opening remarks of the conference are available at: http://www.lermanet. com/cisar/russia/010423.htm (last accessed August 16, 2013). In 2004, the local government and Nizhny Novgorod Orthodox Dioceses organized a series of roundtables on sect activity in the region. The discussions included representative from three traditional religions, Orthodox Christianity, Judaism, and Islam. Evangelical Protestants were not invited to attend. Participants in the roundtable lumped all other religious communities under the negative umbrella of "sects," defined as: "authoritarian organizations, whose leaders, in their struggle toward absolute power over their followers and their organization, hide their intentions under religious, political-religious, psychotherapeutic, health-improvement, educational, scientific-cognitive, and other covers;" see, Nizhny Novgorod Orthodoxy Diocese (2004).

[16] Nizhny Novgorod Buddhist Association has since been renamed the Diamond Way Buddhist Center [Buddijskij centr almaznogo puti].

[17] Interview with Father Alexander and protesting students, March 2006, Nizhny Novgorod.

[18] Ibid.

[19] Ole Nedal lecture on "Buddhism: A Free Mind," April 4, 2006, Nizhny Novgorod.

ILLUSTRATION 5.1. "Danger Totalitarian Sect" warning posted outside of the Nizhny Kremlin, 2006. Photo by author.

referred to as "foreigners" and "spies" in the local media, and they have no avenues for recourse. This is particularly problematic because these labels make it difficult to attract new members or change negative perceptions.[20] Another pastor remarked that the images of Pentecostalized forms of religion used in the media draw directly on old Soviet propaganda films in which Pentecostals are depicted as "drinking blood" and "sacrificing children." Unsurprisingly, these images make it difficult for charismatic churches to rent rooms for activities and almost impossible to advertise on local television without paying exorbitant prices or bribes.[21]

Therefore, although political elites are turning to religion, many religious associational groups are simultaneously orienting themselves toward the political arena in subtle and not-so-subtle ways. Many religious communities are quite aware that their goals – from evangelizing and improving their image to shutting out the religious competition and influencing government policies – can be best achieved by establishing close relations with the powerful and resourceful. Interviews with religious leaders in both countries revealed that they view the state as a necessary partner who is likely to be around for the long-term. In short, the optimal strategy to enhance their power and prestige is through cooperation with the most powerful and legitimizing institution around: the local regime.

State Capture

The decision by religious and political elites to cooperate around issues of power and prestige is not without risks. When local governments invite religious communities into the political sphere and adopt religious symbolism, they not only violate central policies of secularism but may also contribute to instilling competing sources of authority.[22] For instance, by invoking religious symbols and a religious vocabulary, political elites run the risk of transforming religious bodies into legitimizing institutions, which may in turn embolden religious leaders and provide them with a powerful voice in politics. Without question, vociferous religious critics may be troubling for authoritarian leaders in part because they are perceived as transcending politics and having greater moral authority than those in power. Moreover, once religious bodies are invited into the political realm, there is no guarantee that they will always be supportive of the regime, as was the case of the Catholic Church in Franco's Spain.

[20] Interview with Pentecostal Pastor S, July 2012, Nizhny Novgorod.
[21] Interview with Pastor Igor Voronin, Nizhny Novgorod Bishop of RC XVE (Rossijskaja cerkov' hristian very evangel'skoj), July 2012, Nizhny Novgorod; also interview with member P of a Pentecostal church, June 2012, Nizhny Novgorod.
[22] It is worth mentioning that excluding religious leaders from politics may also result in state capture and politicize religious actors. Reza Shah's promotion of a secular Iran encouraged mobilization among the religious opposition. Also see Wald et al. (2005).

Following the Spanish Civil War, Generalissimo Francisco Franco established a collaborative relationship with the Catholic Church, restoring its
power and religious monopoly across the country. Franco's strategy of church-
state alignment served two purposes. One was that Spain was a predominately
Catholic country, and alignment with the Church provided an opportunity to
consolidate power and expand Franco's political base. The other was that the
moral authority of the Church was appropriated to help protect and legitimize
autocratic rule, particularly after World War II when Spain was facing international isolation.[23] The church-state alliance, however, was not durable. In
1971, after the Second Vatican Council, the Spanish Catholic Church began to
distance itself from the regime, and religious leaders across the country resigned
from their political posts. This signaled a loss of legitimacy in Franco's authority and created an opening for democratic reformers.[24] Furthermore, because
the regime had earlier sought the "blessing" of the Church to build coalitions
of support, the Church was now in a position both to delegitimize the Franco
regime and to endorse the political opposition. A similar story of religious
defection may be told in the Balkans, where after years of loyalty the Serbian
Orthodox Church demanded the resignation of President Slobodan Milošević
and that he hand over power to the opposition.[25]

These examples, therefore, illustrate three potential dangers when an authoritarian leader reaches out to religious communities. One is the danger of
depending on religious organizations for political legitimacy. As Juan Linz
notes, politicized religion is an unreliable basis for legitimation in the long-
run because the values of religion may sooner or later come into conflict
with those of the authoritarian regime.[26] Another danger is the potential
for state capture, in which religious groups set the political agenda and
regime incumbents take a secondary role. A third is the potential for nurturing civil society and political opposition. Recall, for instance, the role of
the Polish Catholic Church under communism in organizing the opposition.
One of the greatest challenges facing any opposition group is coordination –
the ability to come together to determine whether newly unified groups have
the capacity to challenge the ruling elite.[27] In Poland, the Church helped solve
this coordination problem by bridging a variety of dissidents and providing
safe spaces where they could meet, debate, and organize their activities.[28]

Unholy Alliances

Religious communities may also pay a price for collaborating with their authoritarian overseers. When a religious community aligns itself with a regime

---

[23] Linz (2004 [1986]: 109).
[24] Philpott (2005: 107–8); Gill (2008).
[25] Crawshaw and Peric-Zimonjic (2000); see also Silber (1992).
[26] Linz (2004 [1986]: 115).
[27] Olson (1965).
[28] See, for example, Kubik (2000); Osa (1989); Morawska (1987).

they may disenfranchise their constituent base and be perceived as betraying their religious principles. Alexis de Tocqueville warned about religious-state alliances: "when a religion makes such an alliance, I am not afraid to say that it makes the same mistake as any man might; it sacrifices the future for the present, and by gaining a power to which it has no claim, it risks its legitimate authority."[29] Indeed, following the military defeat of France by Nazi Germany, bishops of the French Catholic Church declared Marshal Philippe Pétain as the "legitimate authority" and openly supported the Vichy regime.[30] The Catholic hierarchy had loathed the secular policies of the Third Republic and welcomed the pro-Catholic agenda of Marshal Pétain and his allies.[31] Church support was further pledged because "the heralded values of Vichy, *Travail, Famille, Patrie*, were those of the Church. The adversaries of the Church – Freemasons, communists, and the secular – were 'enemies' of the Vichy, the promoter of Christian Catholic civilization."[32] Yet as the war progressed and French Catholics learned of the mass deportation of Jews, religious-state collaboration damaged the moral authority of the Church and membership waned.[33]

Alignment with state authorities may also lead to public criticism of religious bodies as less than independent or abandoning their religious roots. For example, to celebrate the ninetieth anniversary of the communist party, Chinese authorities launched a "red song" campaign (*hong ge*), which spurred hundreds of local singing competitions of patriotic and revolutionary ballads. Although the campaign was widely popular across the country, videos of clergy participation have been openly criticized as blasphemous in online chat rooms. It is interesting to note that following the online criticism, censors subsequently removed videos of religious personnel participating in the campaign.[34]

Religious communities that are seen as puppets of the regime may also risk disillusioning followers and dividing clergy. During the transition to communist rule in China, Christian elites were divided on how best to ensure their survival and demonstrate that they were not a threat to the new regime. The Three-Self Patriotic Movement (TSPM) was founded by a group of liberal Protestants who hoped to carve out a place for Chinese Christians. It was designed as a nondenominational Protestant organization to serve as a conduit between Protestants and the state. The TSPM leadership was largely successful in its hopes that the organization's three guiding principles of self-governance, self-support, and self-propagation would foster friendly relations with those in power. Not all Chinese Protestants, however, were willing to be incorporated under the new regime umbrella. Theological conservatives and leaders of the indigenous Protestant churches viewed the new atheist regime as overtly

[29] de Tocqueville (2000 [1835]: 297).
[30] Curtis (2003: 327).
[31] Paxton (2001: 149).
[32] Curtis (2003: 327), italics in original.
[33] Paxton (2001: 153).
[34] "Leap of faith: religious red songs go too far, say critics" (2011).

hostile toward Christianity, and the TSPM was seen as nothing more than a state organ to infiltrate churches.[35] The concerns of the dissenting Protestants were warranted. As Jason Kindopp explains, the TSPM "was a monolithic, nationally integrated Leninist mass organization. Formally subordinate to the CCP's ruling institutions ('loyalty' to the party was enshrined in its constitution), the TSPM's affairs were determined by a forty-two-member Standing Committee, led by a chairman and several vice chairpersons."[36] The TSPM-state alliance fractured the Protestant community into those who sought a Chinese Christian future working with the regime and those who viewed the unholy alliance as a betrayal of its religious mission. In fact, many from the latter community went on to become the founders of some of China's house churches.

Thus, when weighing the needs of both local authorities and religious communities alongside the risks associated with nonmaterial cooperation, it is reasonable to expect the strategic interaction around issues of power and prestige to be quite selective and perhaps episodic depending upon the political climate. History teaches political elites that empowering religious associational life today may undermine their authority tomorrow, and religious leaders are quite aware that aligning with an autocratic state may result in co-optation and internal schisms. As a result, the outcomes of nonmaterial cooperation are far more uncertain than the bargaining games presented in the previous chapter. This uncertainty is driven, in part, by the nature of the resources being exchanged – promises of favors, influence, and blessings are far more amorphous than the transfer of bureaucratic stamps and public goods. Moreover, with power and prestige as the desired outcome, the stakes are considerably higher with both parties potentially having more to gain and lose.

NONMATERIAL RESOURCES

Nonmaterial resources can be tricky to identify because we are accustomed to thinking of an organization's resources as being tangible and amenable to quantification, such as money, property, and people. Nonmaterial goods, by contrast, are the assets of an organization, including its symbols, organizational networks, mobilization capacity, and information. In practice, the nonmaterial resources local governments bring to the bargaining table are diverse, including invitations into policy making circles and the elevation of some religious traditions over others. In return, religious communities may draw on their cultural capital and offer it to those in power, including blessings of support, endorsement of state policies, and promises to mobilize on behalf of those in power. For both sets of actors, therefore, nonmaterial resources

---

[35] For a discussion of this tension and indigenous Chinese Christianity, see especially, Bays (2012); Lian (2010); Chao and Chong (1997); Hunter and K.K. Chan (1993).
[36] Kindopp (2004a: 123).

come in a variety of packages, but their negotiation tends to coalesce around three areas: (1) the exchange of symbolic support, both religious and political; (2) direct endorsements; and (3) access to political decision making. As this section details, religious-state cooperation around issues of power and prestige is strategic, but it is far less stable than its material counterpart and often has unintended consequences.

Symbolic Support

Some of the most identifiable nonmaterial resources exchanged between religious and political actors are symbolic. Local governing elites may slip religious symbols and language into politics just as religious groups may incorporate political symbols and rhetoric into ritual. The fact that both regime and religion appropriate the others' symbols and vocabulary to secure power and prestige underscores the argument that "politics is not merely about material interests but also about contests over the symbolic world, over the management and appropriation of meanings."[37] Thus, the appropriation of symbols takes both religious and political forms.

Religious Symbolism

All political elites, even in authoritarian regimes, must build support in the eyes of their public. The inclusion of religious symbols can help political elites strengthen their base by associatively anchoring a religious community to those in power.[38] In Russia, it is common for government officials to invite select religious leaders to participate in the ceremonies of the state, such as national holidays and political rallies. In Nizhny Novgorod, for instance, where the majority of the population is ethnically Russian (and therefore "claimed" by the Orthodox Church), Orthodox hierarchs are generally placed directly next to high-ranking political elites during public ceremonies. In the row behind Orthodox religious leaders are Old Believers priests, and imams are generally seated in the third row back; the final and furthest seat is reserved for the local rabbi. The seating arrangement is determined by the fact that Orthodox Christianity (the Russian Orthodox Church and Old Believers), Islam, and Judaism are considered to be the only religions with native ties to the region, and their position mirrors their relative share of the local population. As one rabbi explained, "our official status [as a traditional religion] is largely symbolic, although we have excellent relations with the local government. Whenever we need help with something, they are willing to offer assistance, if they have the resources. But the [local] government is also struggling financially, and frankly speaking, our official status only gives us symbolic support, never financial."[39]

---

[37] Wedeen (1999: 30).
[38] Ibid., 19.
[39] Interview with Rabbi Simon Bergman, March 2006, Nizhny Novgorod.

This suggests a more general point. Nonmaterial bargaining takes place in a heightened level of uncertainty, which means that symbolic support is selective and not available to all religious actors. Although it may be more difficult for local authorities to exclude religious insiders or those that are considered traditional in the region, such status does not guarantee access to state resources or that these groups will engage in cooperative exchanges. In Nizhny Novgorod, for instance, it is extremely rare for religious outsiders, such as Catholic priests or Baptist, Lutheran, or Seventh Day Adventist ministers to be formally invited to political events. On the one hand, these groups represent a small percentage of the population and the government may not see the need to court them or expand their current base of support. Yet, on the other hand, traditional religions that also represent a small percentage of the population are included. The Jewish population, for example, makes up less than 1 percent of the total population in the region, but the local rabbi is always included.[40] This suggests that the exclusion of some confessions may also be way for regime leaders to informally signal a hierarchy of religious support and indirectly discriminate against some faiths.

In Tatarstan, where the population is more equally divided between ethnic Russians (Orthodox) and Tatars (Muslims), the local government strives to send an equivalently balanced signal. At political events and ceremonies, Muslim clerics generally stand to the right of the President Shaimiev and Orthodox bishops to the left. One government official explained that the Shaimiev administration is deliberate in its positioning of religious leaders at political events – it does not want to aggravate the Russian population nor appear to be privileging Islam, which might lead to interconfessional conflict.[41] One advisor to the president joked that government attempts to orchestrate an "Orthodox-Shaimiev-Islam sandwich" to demonstrate an equal commitment to the two largest religions in the republic and to maintain strong ties with both communities. However, one could also argue that the Tatar government is also calculating its relationship with Moscow. It does not want to be perceived as anti-Orthodox, which would complicate its bargaining position with the Center.

The inclusion of select religious leaders into state ceremonies, however, may have unexpected outcomes for those in power. In Russia, November 4 has been created as a new national holiday, Day of National Unity (*den' narodnogo edinstva*). This day was selected because in 1612, a butcher from Nizhny Novgorod, Kuzma Minin, formed a militia to go to Moscow and fight the Poles occupying the Kremlin. This invented holiday was designed to celebrate

---

[40] The Jewish population of Nizhny Novgorod oblast is estimated to at 12,000, or less than 1 percent of the total population. Interview with Rabbi Simon Bergman, March 2006, Nizhny Novgorod.

[41] Interview with adviser R to President Shaimiev, April 2006, Kazan.

national unity because Minin's militia was multiethnic and multiconfessional.[42] Yet, the Day of National Unity's inaugural celebration did not reflect these ideals.

The patriarch of the Russian Orthodox Church was invited to lead the parade in Nizhny Novgorod, and the festivities began with a long procession of Orthodox icons and political leaders marching around the city. In short, the holiday appeared very ethnically Russian and Orthodox Christian. Although other religious leaders, including Old Believers, Jews, and Muslims were invited to participate, they were placed toward the end of the procession, behind the icons and less-prominent local political figures. Minor religious groups in the region, such as Catholics, Protestants, and Buddhists, were not invited to participate.

According to one former bureaucrat, the Nizhny government knew the procession would be broadcast on local and national media and therefore wanted to exhibit its close relationship with the Orthodox Church.[43] Although this strategy did illustrate a close Orthodox-state alliance, it also singled the new holiday was exclusively for Orthodox Russians. In the weeks following the procession, members of some minority religions protested the Orthodox monopoly, claiming the Nizhny government treated non-Orthodox groups as second-class citizens. In fact, the dissent was so intense that bureaucrats feared that violence might break out between the Tatar Muslims and Russian Orthodox communities.[44]

The frustration felt by the Tatar community over the Orthodox-state alliance again resurfaced several months later during the March 2006 local elections.[45] Two candidates running for seats in the parliament produced campaign literature with their photographs superimposed next to mosques, Nikolai Pyrkov of United Russia (*Edinaja Rossija*) and Valerie Antipov from the Russian Party of Pensioners (*Rossijskaja partija pensionerov*). The literature was then mailed to all potential voters with Tatar surnames, which make up less than 20 percent of the voting bloc.

Pyrkov and Antipov's attempt to court the Tatar Muslim vote backfired. Neither candidate had formal ties with the Tatar Muslim community but instead were infamously known for their close ties to the sale and manufacturing of alcohol, something the Religious Board of Muslims in Nizhny Novgorod (*Duhovnoe upravlenie musul'man Nizhegorodskoj oblasti; DUMNO*) actively

---

[42] For a discussion of invented traditions by the state, see Hobsbawm (1990).
[43] Interview with former bureaucrat C, March 2006, Nizhny Novgorod.
[44] Ibid.
[45] In January 2006, an editorial appeared in *Medina al' Islam* (a widely circulated newspaper among Tatar Muslims) demanding the removal of Orthodox symbols, including crosses, from government institutions. The article suggested that if Russia is for Russians, then Tatarstan is for Tatars and fragmentation and secession is likely; see "Rossija dlja russkih, Tatarstan dlja tatar" [Russia for Russians, Tatarstan for Tatars] (2006: 5).

opposed. Pyrkov, for instance, had sponsored legislation permitting liquor-selling businesses to open next to mosques and Islamic schools (*madrassah*), and before running for office, Antipov served as the chairman of the board of a local vodka distillery, Chugunovskiy.[46] Thus, rather than building alliances with the Muslim community, the campaign's appropriated Islamic imagery had the opposite effect and mobilized opposition against the candidates.[47]

Medina Al-Islam, a widely read Muslim newspaper in the Volga region, ran editorials clarifying that candidates Pyrkov and Antipov had no connections with the Muslim community, exposed the candidates' close ties to alcohol distribution, and chastised them for pretending to be "pseudo-Muslims."[48] The leadership of DUMNO also threatened to publish a "blacklist" of candidates and their party affiliations before the election, which would identify all candidates who were "dishonestly" trying to court the Tatar-Muslim vote. As the election drew near, the DUMNO leaders instead issued a press release identifying the two most egregious offenders, Pyrkov and Antipov.[49] According to one Muslim leader, the decision not to publish the blacklist was due to considerable pressure from local and central party elites, who asserted that a blacklist would both tarnish the reputation of Muslims and ignite interconfessional strife.[50] In the end, Pyrkov and Antipov's superimposed images next to local mosques did not ingratiate themselves with the Tatar Muslim community; nevertheless, both candidates were able to win seats in the local parliament, if only by narrow margins.

Beyond incorporating religious symbols into campaign literature and inviting religious leaders to take part in state events, political elites can also use religious rituals as a platform to reach out to religious constituencies as potential supporters, and in Russia voters. For instance, each January, the Russian Orthodox Church celebrates the Feast of the Epiphany, which signifies Jesus' baptism in the Jordan River by John the Baptist. The religious celebration often includes a reenactment of the baptism where adherents submerge themselves in a body of water, which is believed to provide protection from evil influences throughout the following year. Leading up to the 2006 parliamentary elections in Nizhny, a cohort of candidates publicly reenacted the baptism to demonstrate their piousness. In front of local and national media, an Orthodox cross was cut out of the frozen Volga river, and politicians stripped down to their swimsuits, took a ceremonial shot of vodka, and then submerged themselves

---

[46] Interview with Umar-khazrat Idrisov, Chairman of the Religious Board of Muslims for the Nizhny Novgorod Region (*Duhovnoe upravlenie musul'man Nizhegorodskoj oblasti; DUMNO*), March 2006, Nizhny Novgorod.

[47] Sukhonina (2006).

[48] Muharirova (2006: 4).

[49] Sukhonina (2006).

[50] Interview with Damir-khazrat Mukhetdinov, Religious Board of Muslims for the Nizhny Novgorod Region (*Duhovnoe upravlenie musul'man Nizhegorodskoj oblasti; DUMNO*), March 2006, Nizhny Novgorod.

into the blessed river.[51] With the election only a few months away, participation in the public baptism provided an opportunity for candidates to publically demonstrate their faith and support of the Russian Orthodox Church. Moreover, the striking footage of the Nizhny mayor and other politicians emerging from the icy waters saturated the media for days. This footage was wildly popular among the Orthodox community, especially because the political elites had braved the $-40°F$ ($-40°C$) temperatures to partake in the ritual.[52]

Political Symbolism and Patriotism

Local government officials, however, are not alone in their use of symbolism to generate compliance and build support. Religious communities also appropriate symbols of the state in an attempt to strengthen alliances with those in power, increase their influence, and express their patriotism. Just as local authorities ask religious leaders to take part in state ceremonies, religious leaders return the favor and invite local political elites to play a part in religious events. Where local officials may sometimes find it difficult to actively participate in rituals (for example, party members in China are officially atheists), they are nevertheless given a place of honor at groundbreaking ceremonies, temple banquets, and the openings of refurbished religious venues.[53]

The inclusion of political elites at religious events has several potential advantages for religious groups. One is that it permits religious communities to honor local officials and demonstrate their loyalty to those in power. Political elites often welcome the invitation because it gives them the opportunity to expand their base of support in communities where they may otherwise have few inroads. Another advantage is religious groups demystify their activities and demonstrate that they have nothing to hide or pose any threat to the state and society. A third advantage is to signal to current members or potential recruits that they are legitimate religious organizations. In other words, the presence of the regime representatives at temple and church openings may lend a measure of legitimacy to a religious community as both legal and something that is tolerated (if not officially supported) by those in power. Moreover, because religious openings are generally covered in the local media, a visual linkage of a religious community to those in power can be particularly valuable for religious groups, especially among those that have been labeled as sects and cults in the popular media or are viewed as foreign religions.

Religious communities may also adopt the rhetorical tropes of the regime to strengthen alliances with those in power and communicate that their agenda

---

[51] Some of the participants included the Nizhny mayor, Vadim E. Bulavinov, and national head of the Liberal Democratic Party of Russia, Vladimir V. Zhirinovsky.

[52] Focused discussion group with Orthodox Christians H, L, M, January 2006, Nizhny Novgorod.

[53] Interview with Abbot N at Buddhist temple, July 2007, Shanghai. Interestingly, the abbot explained that to make government officials feel welcome at banquets, the temple even serves a nonvegetarian menu and liquor.

runs parallel to the state. It is interesting to note that the tactic of adopting the rhetoric of the regime is a reoccurring theme among associational groups in authoritarian political settings.[54] Kevin O'Brien and Li Linjiang write of farmers as "rightful resisters," who frame grievances against local cadres by adopting the rhetoric and policies of the state.[55] Likewise, Ching Kwan Lee finds that laid-off workers tend to resurrect Cultural Revolution–era slogans to help legitimate their claims and insulate themselves from state crackdown.[56] By mobilizing behind banners of "Yes to Socialism, No to Capitalism!" and "Long Live the Working Class!" protestors can achieve a talisman effect and send a clear message that they are not challenging the larger authority of the regime. Thus, as Elizabeth J. Perry notes, Chinese protestors tend to "advance their claims within the 'legitimate' boundaries authorized by the central state."[57]

Religious communities in Russia and China are also fluent in the rhetoric of the regime. However, rather than adopting regime rhetoric to protect dissent, religious actors tend to use the language of the state to demonstrate their patriotic credentials.[58] In China, where there are more restrictions on religious actors and government elites are more wary of religion, religious organizations perform their patriotism in subtle ways, such as through the adoption of the party mantra of "harmonious society" (*hexie shehui*). In 2005, President Hu Jintao gave a speech to provincial officials on the importance of building a "harmonious society," a society that achieves balance between economic growth and social development.[59] Following this top-down call for harmony, the phrase harmonious society permeated all aspects of economic, political, cultural, and social life.[60] John Deluhry writes that the viral spread of harmony in China is both obligatory and voluntary: "In the case of the media directly controlled by the government, the quantum leap in allusions to 'harmony' was obligatory. In other instances – for example, academics seeking to influence policymakers – references to 'harmonious society' seem to purchase acceptability at little cost. Who doesn't want harmony, after all?"[61]

It comes as no surprise that religious communities have also adopted "harmonious" language to help pursue spiritual agendas and demonstrate loyalty to the regime.[62] In 2006, China hosted the first World Buddhist Forum titled

---

54 See especially Wedeen (1999: chapter 2).
55 O'Brien and Li (2006); see also O'Brien (1996).
56 Lee (2003: 80–1).
57 Perry (2008: 5).
58 Fagan (2013: 179).
59 See, for example, "Building Harmonious Society Crucial for China's Progress: Hu" (2005).
60 Delury (2008: 39) finds that one Chinese journal database referenced 30 articles on "harmony" in 2003, but following Hu's speech the number jumped to more than 6,600. Also see *Xinhua* (2007: 1); C. Wu (2005: 3); M. Yang (2008).
61 Delury (2008: 40).
62 *Xinhua* (2007); also see Dunch (2008).

"In Search of Peace and Harmony."[63] The theme and opening remarks of the conference advocated a "harmonious coexistence of mankind and nature, a natural extension of President Hu Jintao's 'harmonious world concept.'"[64] The conference additionally focused on the spiritual beliefs of Buddhism, suggesting it might play a geopolitical role as an important bridge between China and other Asian countries. The *China Daily* reported that

> Buddhism could provide this important spiritual link and affinity to transnational Asian societies that seek a better tomorrow, but not just through materialism alone, as the frantic pace of economic growth and development unfortunately dictates today. As Asian societies "modernize," there is an urgent need for them to seek religious directions to fill the moral void. Buddhism, with its philosophy of peace and harmony, could provide this important linkage.[65]

Other religious communities have also "harmonized" their printed materials to show their compatibility with the regime. In fact, in interviews with religious leaders, I frequently inquired about their influence in the local community. Often, the response sounded like preapproved recordings – Christian, Buddhist, Muslim, and Taoist religious personnel alike invariably spoke of their religion "promoting a harmonious society." Like the protesting workers mentioned earlier, this convergence is due in part to the fact that religious communities are aware that adopting the language of the state can help legitimize their goals and limit suspicions of their activities. One Protestant minister explained that when she knew bureaucrats from the Religious Affairs Bureau (RAB) or public security agencies would be visiting her church, she tried to draw on Bible passages that spoke of harmony. Although in her sermons, she never mentions government policies directly, she explained that integrating harmonious themes into her message helped educate the atheist cadres that Christianity is compatible with the agenda of the government. Moreover, she hoped it would send a clear message that Chinese Christians also love their country.[66]

It is striking to note that similar displays of patriotism are also found in unregistered religious groups. A frequent theme among house church leaders was the presence of patriotism within their church. As one house church preacher remarked, even though their churches are unregistered and often targeted by the state, most worship services begin with prayers for China and CCP leaders.[67] Here, the implication is that the church signals its patriotism and informally undergirds the authority of the state.

---

[63] The Buddhist Association of China and the China Religious Culture Communications Association organized the forum. More than 1,250 delegates, including Buddhist leaders, scholars, and government officials from thirty-four countries participated.

[64] Teo (2006: 4).

[65] Ibid.

[66] Interview with Protestant minister N, June 2007, Shanghai.

[67] Interview with house church preacher D, August 2007, Shanghai; also see Koesel (2013).

To be sure, one could argue that religious communities are only adopting a "harmonizing" discourse and performing their patriotism because failure to do so would increase state suspicions and lead to suppression. However, if this were the case, we might expect to find all religious groups invoking the rhetoric of the state equally. Religious communities, in other words, would be the modern-day equivalent of Havel's greengrocer, who hangs a "Workers of the World Unite!" poster in his shop window not because he is compelled to do so, but "simply because it has been done that way for years, because everyone does it, and because that is the way it has to be. If he were to refuse, there could be trouble."[68] Yet religious communities, even in tightly controlled ecologies like China, differ from the greengrocer in at least two respects. First, there is considerable variation in the types of state symbols and slogans that religious groups adopt, and some religions are much more assertive in performing their loyalty than others. Second, the motivation behind invoking symbols is more than simply to avoid conflict or to remain below the state radar. Religious communities are politically savvy actors who understand that adopting the language of the state will allow them to potentially negotiate better with the regime and pursue their spiritual agendas. At the same time, there is also no reason to think that these communities do not love their country.

Thus, although some religious communities hang state slogans in their places of worship, there is yet considerable diversity in the ones they select. In a majority of the mosques in Changchun and Shanghai, for example, religious leaders voluntarily display posters reading: "Love your country, love your religion!" (*aiguo aijiao!*) or "Love your country love your religion, united we progress!" (*aiguo aijiao, tuanjie jinbu!*). Other religious communities are certainly familiar with this slogan, but it was not posted in their churches and temples. This raises the question: When given a menu of state slogans to choose from, why would the Muslim community privilege this slogan over others?

Interviews suggested that "Love your country, love your religion!" holds particular meaning among the Muslim community.[69] In China, Islam is considered to be a minority religion, not only because the number of believers is quite small (less than 2 percent of the population), but because Muslims usually also belong to an ethnic minority.[70] Among these diverse minority populations, relations with the central government range from peaceful and largely assimilated, such as the Hui population, to outright animosity as in cases where the state has linked the Uyghurs to separatism and terrorism. In Shanghai and Changchun, where the majority of the Muslim population is Hui but also includes Muslims from more contentious regions like Xinjiang, one imam

[68] Havel, Keane, and Lukes (1985: 28).

[69] I am grateful to Wang Jianping for pointing out that state slogans "Love your country, love your religion!" began appearing in Chinese mosques in the 1950s. Although there is no direct quotation in the Koran, Wang suggests the idea of submitting to authority is compatible with many Islamic teachings, and therefore, this slogan was widely used in mosques across China.

[70] The Chinese government recognizes 55 minority groups, 10 of which are predominately Muslim, including: Hui, Uyghur, Kazah, Dongxiang, Kyrgyz, Salar, Tajik, Uzeek, Bonan, and Tatar.

ILLUSTRATION 5.2. Propaganda banner at a Shanghai Taoist temple, 2006. The banner reads: "*Guanche shishi zongjiao shiwu tiaoli, weihu zongjiao hemu shehui hexie!*" [Implement and carry out the religious affairs regulations, safeguard religion, peaceful relations and a harmonious society!]. Photo by author.

explained that after the September 11, 2001, attacks, there were heightened suspicions against the Muslim community. Displaying a "Love your country, love your religion" poster helped signal support of the regime and that the mosque was not a front for organizing terrorist or extremist activities.[71]

Buddhist and Taoist temples and monasteries have also adopted the language of the regime to demonstrate their support, yet tend to draw on different slogans. In 2006-2007, several temples across Shanghai displayed large, red banners calling to:

> *Safeguard religion, peaceful relations, and a harmonious society!*
>
> *To implement and carry out the religious affairs regulations is every worker's duty!*
>
> *Encourage the education of law and enhance the quality of law for all citizens!*

When inquiring about the origins of these banners, religious personnel explained that they are provided by the district-level RAB, but it was not mandatory to display the banners. If a temple abbot chooses not to hang a

---

[71] Interview with Imam W, July 2007, Shanghai.

banner, there are no repercussions. Nevertheless, the many temples and monasteries did elect to hang the banners as a way to demonstrate their patriotism and harmony with the state.[72] This suggests that even religious insiders such as Buddhists and Taoists are interested in displaying their alignment with the regime. As for the frequency of the banners, during the summer of 2007, roughly one-third of the Buddhist and Taoist temples and monasteries in Shanghai displayed propaganda banners. However, it is worth mentioning that such banners were more common in active temples than tourist temples. This would imply that the banners are aimed at practitioners and not tourists.

In an interesting point of comparison, many Protestant and Catholic leaders residing in the same districts as the Taoist temple shown above also revealed that they too were offered red banners by the local RABs. Yet not wanting to invite the state propaganda inside their churches, they found ways to politely decline or accepted the banners and never hung them. One Catholic priest recalled a story of being visited by a young bureaucrat several years earlier who presented him with a large red banner reading: "It is good to have just one child!" (*zhi sheng yige haizi hao!*). The bureaucrat was promoting the One-Child Policy and insistent that the priest hang the banner to show support for the national campaign. The priest, who had lived through the Cultural Revolution, politely refused and explained that his church would be a place only for religious worship. Privately, however, the priest also made clear that even though the leadership of the Chinese Catholic Patriotic Association (CCPA) supports the One-Child Policy, he did not wish to promote something that the Vatican openly opposes. Since this encounter, the priest joked that local bureaucrats have simply stopped offering him propaganda posters, knowing he will continue to refuse their "gifts."[73]

All of this points to a more general observation. Both local government officials and religious leaders readily borrow the symbols, rituals, and rhetoric from each other to achieve individual strategic needs. Local government officials invoke religious symbols and participate in rituals to expand their bases of support. At the same time, religious communities adopt the rhetoric of the regime to demonstrate their patriotism and advertise their nonthreatening nature – a kind of Pascal's wager on the subject of state intervention. For both sets of actors, therefore, the exchange of symbolic resources reveals the indirect ways to achieve strategic needs and goals. This exchange, however, is not without risks. Recall the two candidates from Nizhny who miscalculated the effectiveness of campaign literature that superimposed their photographs next to mosques. This example reminds us that the religion-regime transfer of symbols, rituals, and rhetoric requires both a willingness to offer resources and a shared understanding of what these symbolic resources entail.

---

[72] Interview with Buddhist monk A, July 2007, Shanghai; interview with Buddhist monk B, Shanghai; interview with Taoist priest V, July 2007, Shanghai.

[73] Interview with Catholic priest L, July 2007, Shanghai.

Endorsements

Beyond the exchange of symbols, some local political elites and religious leaders bring formal endorsements to the bargaining table. For religious communities, this can include backing a political candidate in an election or outright support for the state and its policies. Alternately, local governments can publically support or prop up a religious community, even when this may go against central policies.

Although central laws and policies in Russia and China strongly discourage religious groups' participation in politics, some religious leaders openly bend the rules. Among the diverse religious communities in Nizhny Novgorod, the Old Believers play one of the most active roles in campaign politics by endorsing candidates and publishing recommended voting lists. Such political savvy is surprising not only because a religious groups' meddling in politics is illegal but also because the Old Believers have a history of denouncing political authority, rejecting modernity, and preferring seclusion.[74] Old Believers are Orthodox Christians who split from the Russian Orthodox Church in the seventeenth century because they rejected the liturgical reforms introduced by Patriarch Nikon.[75] After the split, the dissenters divided into several factions to survive, with some resettling in Siberia, others immigrating as far as Oregon, and most worshiping in secret to avoid persecution. Old Believers remain scattered across Russia, but as a religious community, they are best known for their adherence to tradition, preference for isolation, and deep suspicions of outsiders. Yet since the mid-1990s, a small community of Old Believers in Nizhny has become an important political player.[76] Sergei Rudakov, the editor of the newspaper *Old Believers* (*Staroobrjadec*), explains that after the collapse of the Soviet Union democratic elections and political campaigning were underdeveloped. The newspaper began endorsing candidates not only to demonstrate their support of select political allies but also to educate their community about the most amiable candidates.[77]

The newspaper always endorses political candidates with familial ties to the Old Believers community but sometimes openly supports Russian Orthodox

---

[74] For instance, Old Believers declared Peter the Great the "antichrist" after he imposed a double tax on them for refusing to shave their beards.

[75] Some of the controversial changes included a sign of the cross made with three rather than two fingers, baptisms that did not involve complete submersion in water (e.g., sprinkling of water on children was allowed), and religious processions that moved in a clockwise pattern rather than counter clockwise.

[76] The Old Believers population in the Nizhny Novgorod federal region is approximately eighty thousand. The community has roughly two hundred places of worship, which includes churches, prayer houses, and designated places in the forest. Interview with S.V. Rudakov, editor of *Staroobrjadec* [*Old Believers*] newspaper, March 2006, Nizhny Novgorod.

[77] The endorsements generally provide a brief biographical sketch and highlight the candidate's connections, if any, to the Old Believers community. Interview with S.V. Rudakov, editor of *Staroobrjadec* [*Old Believers*] newspaper, March 2006, Nizhny Novgorod.

candidates as well. For instance, before local parliamentary elections in 1998, the newspaper endorsed two candidates, neither of whom practiced the Old Believers faith but had helped the community secure the bureaucratic stamps necessary to open a printing press.[78] Outside of election cycles, the newspaper is also used as a platform to endorse political elites who have favorable relations with the Old Believers community. In 2001, for example, the newspaper endorsed the vice-governor Alexander Vasil'evich Batyrev, a devout Orthodox Christian, for his support with restoring places of worship.[79] The editor explained that the stereotypes of Old Believers as backward recluses shrouded in mysticism are grossly exaggerated, and the community now needs to be more politically active because they are living in the shadow of the Russian Orthodox Church.[80]

However, the extent of the Old Believers' political activism is unusual among the religious communities in the region. Father Igor, the editor of the Russian Orthodox Nizhny Novgorod Diocese Bulletin (*Nizhegorodskie eparhial'nye vedomosti*), explained that although individual priests may have strong opinions about local politics and particular candidates, the Church and newspaper of the dioceses never endorse candidates or political parties.[81] Rather, as a registered religious publishing house, they print information only about Church activities. In the situation in which believers ask for advice about the elections, such as who to vote for, Father Igor emphasized that a priest should simply encourage education and prayer. He stressed that the Russian Orthodox Church is not in the business of politics, "We were once a state church and have no desire to go back to that."[82]

Along similar lines, one local bureaucrat in charge of managing the religious communities cautioned that religious leaders should not endorse or denounce political candidates.[83] He recalled an example of the Tatar-Muslims' threat to publish a blacklist and the potential fallout of interconfessional conflict. Yet when pressed about the unusual political activism of the Old Believers – the fact that they use their publishing house to endorse candidates and provide voting lists – he suggested that the local government does not have the "willpower" (*sila*) to take on the Old Believers. It is not that they do not have the capability,

---

[78] See, for example, March 1998 issue of *Staroobrjadec* [Old Believers].

[79] "Vice-gubernator Batyr'ev: staroobrjadcy mne stali blizhe i ponjatnee" [Vice-Governor Batyrev: I stand closer to and understand the Old Believers] (2001:2).

[80] Interview with S.V. Rudakov, editor of *Staroobrjadec* [Old Believers] newspaper, March 2006, Nizhny Novgorod. This political activism of the Old Believers community has a long history. In the Nizhny Novgorod elections of 1917, for example, they published a "list" of endorsed candidates from their religious community. See "Vybory i staroobrjadcy" [Elections and Old Believers] (March 2000: 2).

[81] In 2001, the head of the Nizhny Novgorod Diocese openly supported a candidate for mayor; see Kotoshikhin (2002).

[82] Interview with Orthodox Father Igor, editor of the *Nizhegorodskie eparhial'nye vedomosti* [Nizhny Novgorod Diocese Bulletin], March 2006, Nizhny Novgorod.

[83] Interview with N.B. Cheremin, consultant for religious organizations for the Nizhny Novgorod Kremlin, March 2006, Nizhny Novgorod.

because the Old Believers community is quite small (less than 1 percent of the population) but rather that no politician wants to be seen as challenging the moral authority of the Old Believers.[84] This religious community, after all, is the forbearer of the Russian Orthodox Church and seen as an integral part of Russian culture.

State Defender

In addition to endorsements of political elites and championing state policies, some religious leaders are also willing to take on the role of state defender. In response to international reports critical of human rights violations, such as those published by Amnesty International and Freedom House, the Moscow Orthodox Church began publishing its own assessment of domestic human rights. The Church maintains that foreign criticisms are based on Western and secular standards alien to Russian society. In other words, the Universal Declaration of Human Rights does not apply, and in its stead the Church has outlined its own vision that places human rights within the context of Orthodox faith, morality, and patriotism.[85]

Other religious communities also look to the Kremlin to enhance their legitimacy, but these overtures have not met with reciprocal support. In the village of *Bol'shaja El'nja*, in the Nizhny Novgorod region, the Church of Mother Photinia Luminous (*Cerkov' matushki Fotinii Svetonosnoj*) proclaimed Vladimir Putin to be the reincarnation of the Apostle Paul.[86] The Church of Mother Photinia Luminous is a syncretic religious movement that combines Orthodox theology with messianic teachings, and devotes a significant portion of the services to the worship of Putin. Not surprisingly, many Orthodox Christians and church leaders in the region are quite apprehensive of the new local saint and have attempted to evict the "sect" from the village. Local authorities, however, maintain that there is no legal basis for removal of the religious group.[87] One could reasonably assume that this is because they do not want to be responsible for the eviction of "Saint Putin."

In China, religious traditions have also taken on the role of state defender, but in a less formal way. During interviews, it was common for religious leaders to pull well-marked copies of the most recent U.S. Department of States' Report on Freedom of Religion from their desks.[88] Several religious leaders in

---

[84] Ibid.

[85] Zolotov (2008).

[86] "Vy vse eshhe ne verite v apostola Putina? Togda my idem k vam!" [You still do not believe in the apostle Putin? Then we will come to you!] (2005: 8); "Sestra Boga" [God's sister] (2005: 3); "V 'Cerkvi matushki Fotinii Svetonosnoj' Putin ob"javlen apostolom" [In 'the Church of Mother Photinia Luminous' Putin is declared the apostle] (2005).

[87] "Zhiteli poselka Bol'shaja El'nja trebujut vyselit' 'Matushku Fotiniju Svetonosnuju'" [Villagers of Bol'shaja El'nja demand to evict the Mother Photinia Luminous] (2005).

[88] In fact, the week that the 2006 U.S. State Department Report on Freedom of Religion report was published, five religious leaders in Changchun cancelled prearranged interviews and cited the State Department Report as making the meeting "too sensitive."

Changchun and Shanghai complained that the report does not reflect the reality of local religious freedom, and often leads to heightened tensions between religious and state actors. Each year after the report is released, bureaucrats from the RAB also visit religious leaders. One imam in Shanghai explained that the visits usually have two competing goals.[89] The first is genuine concern that the religious group might be experiencing the problems outlined in the report, such as local cadres suppressing legal religious activities. The second goal of the visit is to ascertain whether religious leaders are revealing information to foreigners that might reflect poorly on the regime.[90]

Local Endorsements of Religion

Just as religious communities reward political elites with endorsements and speak out in defense of the state, local governments also find innovative ways to informally endorse religious groups to achieve strategic goals. In Qingpu, the westernmost district of Shanghai, is the rural community of Jinze. Crisscrossed by canals, lakes, and wetlands, Jinze is well known for its historic bridges built during the Song dynasty (960–1279 CE). Among residents, however, Jinze is also known for its active popular religious life.[91] Although the town is home to a newly built Protestant church, Catholic retreat center, and several temples that blend Buddhism, Taoism, and local folk practices, the majority of residents worship a local god who protects the ancient stone bridges, *Tianhuang laoye*.[92] At the base of each bridge, residents have constructed small, informal altars where worshipers offer incense and prayers. Illustrations 5.3 and 5.4 showcase two of Jinze's bridges, the wooden Rainbow Bridge and religious practitioners gathering in front of a Song-era stone bridge. Illustration 5.5 shows the informal incense altars fashioned out of old woks and rice bags stuffed with straw.

During Chinese traditional holidays, such as Spring Festival (*chunjie*) and Tomb Sweeping Day (*qingmingjie*), and particularly before high school and college entrance exams, residents make a pilgrimage through the community offering incense and prayers at each of the forty-nine bridges.[93] This is a large,

---

[89] Interview with Imam W, July 2007, Shanghai.

[90] Despite the motivation behind the visits, religious leaders were both mystified and angered by the inaccuracy of State Department Freedom of Religion Reports and on more than one occasion respondents expressed hope that I was collecting data for next years' report.

[91] A layperson at a Protestant church in Jinze complained that the church mainly serves migrant workers and not locals. She complained that after the new church was built, church leaders tried to hire a local caretaker, but no local residents wanted the job because they all worship the bridge god. Eventually the church hired a Christian from a neighbouring town as the caretaker. Interview with layperson Z at Jinze Protestant church, August 2007, Jinze.

[92] *Tianhuang laoye* is a common title used to refer to gods in Chinese folklore.

[93] Spring Festival is one of the most important Chinese holidays; it begins on first day of the month of the Chinese calendar and lasts 15 days. Tomb Sweeping Day is a traditional festival on the 104th day after the winter solstice (or the 15th day from the Spring Equinox), usually occurring around April 5 of the Gregorian calendar. During this day, family members return to the graves of their ancestors to clean them, offer food, and burn paper money for ancestors to use in the

ILLUSTRATION 5.3. The Rainbow Bridge, 2007. Photo by author.

annual event where those with ancestral ties to Jinze return with their extended families to participate. Although this popular religious practice is technically illegal – because popular religion is not one of the five official state religions – the local government does not interfere in the ritual. In fact, according to several practitioners, local officials take great pride in leading the large processions. Local government support of the folk religion has greatly warmed relations between the two.[94] One practitioner who had traveled from neighboring Anhui province explained that the Jinze cadres were not as corrupt as those in other regions because they honored the bridge god and that the god was watching over them.[95]

Local government support of popular religious activities suggests that relations between the two sides are quite strong. Local cadres are willing to participate in the rituals to demonstrate solidarity with those living in their locale. Perhaps more striking is their willingness to ignore central religious policies, which call for the suppression of popular religious practices, by permitting

---

afterlife. In 2008, the Chinese government declared Tomb Sweeping Day a national holiday. Before this time, activities surrounding this holiday were considered superstitious behavior and illegal; see D. Xin (2008).

[94] Interviews with worshipers T and Y at bridges, August 2007, Jinze.

[95] Interview with worshiper J at bridges, August 2007, Jinze.

ILLUSTRATIONS 5.4 AND 5.5. The stone bridges and informal altars of Jinze, 2010. Photos by author.

the open worship of the bridge god. Local officials rationalize their support of illegal religious activities by referring to the practices as "local culture" (*difang wenhua*). Jinze cadres, in other words, are protecting and preserving local cultural practices and not endorsing popular religion. At the same time, the local authorities have cracked down on other illegal religious activities, including shutting down unregistered folk temples, Protestant meeting points, and qigong groups.[96]

In addition to building solidarity among the local residents, the bridges have also brought a considerable amount of prestige to local cadres. In 1999, local officials welcomed the Public Broadcasting Service (PBS) program *NOVA* to film part of the series "Secrets of Lost Empires." The *NOVA* program assembled a team of Chinese and foreign scholars to reconstruct the wooden Rainbow Bridge from a nine-hundred-year-old painting (shown in Illustration 5.3).[97] *NOVA* brought international recognition to the small town, which according to some local believers helped the government lobby for a designation as a "historic area" for the 2010 Shanghai World Expo. Among thousands of applications, Jinze won one of thirty coveted "historic sites" designations for the World Expo, which meant the municipal government funded a facelift for the town and also capitalized on the local bridge culture.[98] In this case, religious-state collaboration not only strengthens legitimacy of local elites and builds trust among residents but may also have residual material benefits.

It is important to note that local authorities may also prop up religious communities not because they have an interest in actually aligning with the religious group but rather to make an impression on other political players. In preparation for hosting the 2010 World Expo, many religious buildings across Shanghai also received facelifts.[99] One Protestant deacon described the renovations as an unexpected blessing.[100] Dilapidated churches were removed and replaced by buildings twice their original size, complete with carved benches, stained glass windows, lush gardens, and perhaps most importantly, air-conditioning. All of these renovations were courtesy of the government. According to one bureaucrat, "Shanghai is expecting over 70 million visitors and will be on display to the world. Besides, many of the World Expo guests will have strong

---

[96] Qingpu nianjian bianjibu (2002: 106); Qingpu qu shi zhi banggongshi (2001: 49).

[97] Photographs and details of the Rainbow Bridge construction are available at the *NOVA* website: http://www.pbs.org/wgbh/nova/lostempires/china/builds.html (last accessed February 24, 2013).

[98] See press release from the Shanghai Municipal Government, "Suburban Relics Saved," November 21, 2004. Available at: http://www.shanghai.gov.cn/shanghai/node17256/node18151/userobject22ai14923.html (last accessed August 16, 2013).

[99] For the 2010 World Expo, the Shanghai Municipal Government dedicated 5.28 square kilometres in Luwan and Pudong districts.

[100] Interview with deacon C from Protestant church, June 2007, Luwan.

religious beliefs and we do not want to disappoint them by the poor quality of our temples and churches."[101]

Government support for renovating religious buildings can also feed into regional competition. One government official assisting in the overhaul of a Protestant church explained that direct financial support was not unusual, and the Beijing municipal government had similarly revamped many religious buildings in preparation for the 2008 Olympics. The Shanghai government was doing the same because it did not want to "lose face" (*diu mianzi*) to its northern neighbor.[102] This observation suggests that reputation is partly responsible for the endorsement and subsequent renovations of religious organizations. Regardless of the local government's intentions, religious communities affected by the World Expo seemed thrilled with the unexpected renovations and larger facilities, especially because it was all at the government's expense.

Political Decision Making

A final resource local officials bring to the bargaining table is access to political decision making and agenda setting. Governing elites may invite religious leaders into the realm of politics to solidify alliances with a religious group, reward them for their loyalty, or utilize their cultural capital to increase authority. For many religious groups, an invitation into the political sphere is highly sought after because it gives them power to shape the social agenda according to their own values and manipulate the religious marketplace. With a direct line to those in power, a religious group may be able to shut out its competition or make life generally difficult for other faiths. As with other forms of nonmaterial cooperation, inviting religious leaders into political decision making is particularly risky. It not only violates laws that mandate a strict separation of religion and state but can also invite unwanted scrutiny from the Center, lead to political destabilization, and spark interconfessional conflict. Yet, despite these concerns, some local governments selectively invite religious actors into the policy-making process. In general, such invitations are far more evident in Russia where ruling elites have more freedom to openly collaborate with religious actors.

The Orthodox-Kremlin Alliance

Mikhail Gorbachev once claimed that since the collapse of the Soviet Union, the Russian Orthodox Church had become a serious power.[103] Indeed, there is a widespread assumption that a mutually beneficial Orthodox-state alliance emerged, with the Kremlin using the Church to help define the guiding

---

[101] Interview with bureaucrat P from the Religious Affair Bureau, June 2007, Luwan.
[102] Ibid.
[103] "Gorbachev criticizes Putin's party" (2009).

principles of the state and serve as the backbone of Russian nationalism and identity.[104] In return, the Church has reclaimed much of its prerevolutionary hegemonic position but falls shy of being a national religion.[105] On numerous occasions, presidents from Yeltsin to Medvedev have spoken about this alliance and the special role of Orthodox Christianity in Russia. At a 2009 reception honoring the newly elected Patriarch Kirill, Putin declared "the Russian Orthodox Church has always defended and hopefully will continue to defend the national and spiritual identity of Russians."[106] He added that Orthodox Christianity is responsible for Russian statehood. President Dimity Medvedev reinforced these sentiments when suggesting, "the essential truth in our state is Orthodoxy. It helps a huge number of our people not only to find themselves in life but also to understand some seemingly simple things, such as what it means to be Russian, what is our people's mission, what made our people great and unique during a specific period."[107]

Not surprisingly, the Church has also taken an active role in promoting itself as the cornerstone of Russian identity. Not only does the Church draw on its historical role during the prerevolutionary era, it also claims default representation of all ethnic Russians. Here, the assumption is that at birth ethnic Russians "belong" to the Church and baptism and conscious conversion is not compulsory.[108] In staking out this ideational claim, some Church hierarchs have also claimed the Church as an integral component of Russian political and economic strength. One church leader suggested that if Orthodox Christianity was to be replaced by another faith "[p]eople would not be raised with an Orthodox mindset. It would not be Russia, they would not be Russians.... Russia will fall apart. Her political and economic might will simply collapse."[109]

The Orthodox-Kremlin alliance is also replicated on the local level, which has translated into indirect advantages for the Church. As the previous chapter demonstrated, property politics is one of the most contentious issues facing religious communities in Russia. The return of religious land and property is a long and arduous process often spanning several years with uncertain outcomes.

---

[104] On Orthodox-Kremlin alliance, see Knox (2005: 105–31); Richters (2012); Froese (2008: 154–6); Chernyshova (2007); Witte (1999); but also Fagan (2013) who argues that the alliance is less durable than many suggest.

[105] For instance, in 2010 party leaders of United Russia reported the Orthodox Church is the "moral basis and foundation of modernization" in the country; see "Centr social'no-konservativnoj politiki 'Edinoj Rossii' predlozhil pravoslavie v kachestve cennostnogo fundamenta modernizacii" [The center for social and conservative policy of "United Russia" suggested Orthodoxy as the value foundation for modernization] (2010).

[106] Putin (2009).

[107] Quoted in Kolesnikov (2011).

[108] Richters (2012: 63).

[109] Metropolitan Sergei quoted in Fagan (2013: 111).

Religious groups must provide documentation proving ownership of destroyed or confiscated property before local bureaucrats begin the negotiations, and there are no guarantees petitions will be approved. Yet in Nizhny Novgorod, local authorities have given the Orthodox dioceses an unusual power in this arena. When a religious group whishes to open a new church, temple, or mosque, it must first secure the required bureaucratic stamps from local ministries. Once these tasks are accomplished, they must collect one additional stamp: informal approval from the Orthodox bishop.[110]

In the mid-1990s when there were few restrictions on religion a variety of religious groups arrived in the Volga region, including Hare Krishnas, Mormons, Jehovah's Witnesses, Scientologists, Pentecostals, and Buddhists. Among these diverse religious traditions, several had quite attractive proselytizing methods. Charismatic Christians held tent revivals, rock concerts, and screened free movies; Buddhists organized yoga and meditation classes; Hare Krishnas provided free vegetarian meals; Scientologists donated laboratory equipment to local universities and schools; and Mormons canvassed the city, knocking on doors and inviting citizens to worship services. For the Orthodox Church, these newcomers were seen as particularly threatening because their methods of proselytizing were both new and perceived to be extremely effective. Moreover, these religious groups were assumed to have extensive international funding.[111] Orthodox Church leaders were concerned that these newcomers would be able to purchase land, quickly establish a presence in the region, and marginalize the Orthodox Church. Church leaders shared these concerns with the Nizhny government, and an informal "Orthodox stamp" was put in play. Since the late 1990s many non-Orthodox groups wanting to open religious buildings in the city must also receive the informal permission from the Church.

One Protestant minister explained that his small congregation had no problems registering with the local government, but when it came time to physically build a church they were told that they must also get permission from the Orthodox bishop. Yet after six months of unanswered phone calls, the Protestant minister was beginning to wonder if his congregation would ever receive this "blessing." The minister further indicated that the influence of the Orthodox Church extends beyond this elusive blessing. Since the founding of their congregation in the early 1990s, it has become increasingly difficult to find places to rent in the city center. Their last landlord refused to renew their contract because his Orthodox priest had told him that supporting

[110] Interview with Imam S from the Board of Muslims of the Republic of Tatarstan [*Duhovnoe Upravlenie Musul'man Respubliki Tatarstan; DUMRT*], April 2006, Kazan. The unofficial Orthodox stamp was confirmed with several Christian denominations. For a parallel dynamic of "telephone laws" to informally regulate religious groups, see Fagan (2013: 84–8).

[111] Interview with Orthodox Father Andre, January 2006, Nizhny Novgorod; also Filatov (2008); Dvorkin (1998).

Protestants is a sin.[112] The minister explained that without a doubt, the wandering nature of his church had a significant toll on the congregation, and members eventually began attending other churches. This small church ultimately failed.[113]

One bureaucrat rationalized the "unofficial stamp" of the Orthodox Church in three ways. First, the informal arrangement helps maintain interconfessional harmony. By giving the Orthodox bishop an unofficial stamp, the city ensures that religious buildings are evenly distributed and that a respectable buffer zone between confessions is maintained – that is, a Seventh Day Adventist church would not be built across the street from an Orthodox one. Second, the Orthodox Church plays as unique role in Russian culture. Here, the argument is that Orthodox Christianity is the majority religion in the Volga region and culturally important to the country and therefore should have influence over minority religions.[114] Finally, the informal power of the Church helps control the spread of "foreign religions" in the region. It is important to note that for other traditional religions, such as Islam and Judaism, the informal blessings have been forthcoming. However, other Christian denominations that are seen as more direct competitors have had much more difficulty, thus revealing how local governments can bestow informal mechanisms of power on religious actors and the inherent disadvantages to being considered a religious outsider.

Political Agenda Setting

One final resource local bureaucrats may offer a religious community is a voice in setting the political agenda. For religious groups, influence in setting the agenda is highly desirable because it empowers them to push their own spiritual agenda and shut out the religious competition. Again, we see this form of nonmaterial collaboration playing out more prominently in Russia among select confessions.

In the past several years, a controversy has been brewing regarding the appropriate separation of church and state in public education.[115] In 2002, the Russian Education Minister, Vladimir Filippov, sent a memorandum to all regions recommending the introduction of a new course into the national curricula, the "Fundamentals of Orthodox Culture" (*Osnov pravoslavnoj kul'tury'*).[116] According to the memo, the goal of the course is to familiarize Russian students with Orthodox culture, art, music, and ideas. The course also touches on ethics and religious themes, such as the purpose of fasting, baptism,

---

[112] Interview with Protestant Pastor H, March 2006, Nizhny Novgorod.
[113] Interview with Protestant Pastor H, July 2012, Nizhny Novgorod.
[114] Interview with former bureaucrat C, March 2006, Nizhny Novgorod.
[115] Kolymagin (2003).
[116] For a background discussion of the Fundamentals of Orthodox Culture, see especially, Richters (2012: chapter 3) and Fagan (2013: 141–3).

heresy, and schism, as well as identifies "destructive sects and cults."[117] The memorandum advises the Fundamentals of Orthodox Culture to be uniformly adopted in both primary and secondary schools for a minimum of one to two hours per week. In primary schools, the course may be integrated into other core subjects, such as history and reading; and in secondary schools, it may replace or supplement subjects such as philology, ethics, or art.[118] The course is recommended to be divided into several topics, including "the Orthodox Christian picture of the world, history of the Orthodox religion and culture, literary culture of the Orthodox (Orthodox literature), the Orthodox way of life, moral culture of Orthodoxy, and Orthodoxy – the traditional religion of the Russian people."[119] In many ways, the subject matter resembles religious education under the tsars and the compulsory course Divine Law or Law of God (*Zakon Bozhij*).[120]

Not surprisingly, Putin and the patriarch came out in support of teaching the Fundamentals of Orthodox Culture, suggesting that it would provide a much-needed moral compass for Russian youth and strengthen national identity under a shared culture. At the same time, the pro-Orthodox course has been extremely controversial and the focus of intense national debate. Opponents of the course have challenged the expanding presence of Orthodox Christianity in secular schools because it is seen as infringing on the separation of religion and state and equality of all religions enshrined in the constitution (Articles 14, 19, and 28). Others suggest the course also violates the 1997 federal law on religions, which states that religion may only be taught in public schools as an elective course, with the written permission of parents, and if the instructors are nonstate employees (Article 5). Still others argue that the course violates a 1992 education law that prohibits activity by religious groups in public institutions (Article 1).[121]

The chorus of critics also includes some non-Orthodox religious leaders who see the education reforms as an insult to the multiethnic and multireligious reality of the country.[122] Borukh Gorin, a spokesperson from the Federation

---

[117] The memo offers several suggestions for the implementation of the course. For instance, the course will prepare a ninth-grade student to be able to explain, "the Abrahamic religious complex, caesaropapism, clericalism, ecumenism, neopaganism in the Christian world, distinctive of the apocalyptic notions of destructive religious sects"; quoted in Moiseenko and Pavlova (2002).

[118] See "Russia: Public Opinion Divided over Tuition of Orthodox Culture in State Schools," (2002).

[119] Moiseenko and Pavlova (2002).

[120] Richters (2012: 47).

[121] Members of the Russian Academy of Sciences and several Noble Laureates have written an open letter to President Putin expressing concern over the legality of the new course. See "Reading, Writing... and Religion?" (2007); Pavlikova (2007); Baskakov (2002).

[122] See, for example, "Head of Council of Muftis of Russia opposes compulsory study of Orthodoxy in schools" (2002).

of Jewish Communities in Russia, explained, "We oppose the obligatory study of the foundations of Orthodoxy. In the first place, pupils are deprived of the right of choice; in the second, I personally am not convinced that they will get anything out of it. Before the revolution, the Law of God was taught in the schools, but the population did not become more religious because of it. Third, this will require great financial expense; after all, right now there are few competent teachers in any confession."[123] Mindful of these criticisms, the patriarch of the Orthodox Church responded, "We do not at all wish to create our own ideological monopoly in education.... Still less do we wish to transfer the responsibility of the moral and spiritual upbringing of children and teenagers to state schools, as is sometimes alleged."[124]

Locally, the Fundamentals of Orthodox Culture has been equally controversial. In Tatarstan, the local government was caught in a difficult situation. As a minority and largely Muslim republic, the introduction of such a course on Orthodox Christianity would be disastrous for political elites. Yet to ignore the central directive might have equally harmful consequences, especially because the curricula changes have support from the highest levels of government. To navigate these unfriendly waters, the Tatar government formed a working group of religious scholars and representatives from all of the major religions in the republic. After several months the working groups came up with the following recommendations: first, the course title would be changed to "World Religions"; second, the material would be expanded to include all major religious groups represented in the republic (e.g., Islam, Orthodox Christianity, Judaism, Buddhism, Catholicism, and Protestantism); third, the themes of the course would shift from religious doctrine to a largely historical narrative of the origins of each major religion; finally, the course would be an elective, and all pupils would need parental permission to participate.

Central political authorities did not oppose the amendments to the course in Tatarstan, especially because some Church hierarchs had already been advocating for flexibility in minority regions. A spokesperson for the Department of External Church Relations of the Moscow Patriarch stated that although "I consider that it is impossible to understand Russia without knowledge of Orthodox culture.... In some republics, let's say in Tatarstan, it would be possible to introduce the foundations of Muslim culture."[125] One bureaucrat from the Kazan Religious Affairs Department explained that had the Tatar government wanted, they could easily have implemented a "Foundations of Muslim Culture" instead; yet, mindful of the diverse religious landscape, they chose to reach out to the plural religious community to redefine the parameters

---

[123] "Variety of opinions on teaching Orthodoxy – Question of the Day: Do Schools Need Religion Classes?" (2002).

[124] Quoted by Fagan (2007).

[125] Ibid.

of the course, explaining that teaching only Tatar culture would create just as much polarization and intolerance as the proposed Orthodox course.[126] A Tatar Orthodox priest echoed these sentiments, explaining that the republic is not neatly divided between Orthodox Russian and Tatar Muslims, but the communities are mixed and live alongside one another as neighbors. In fact, his church in Kazan serves more than three hundred Krjashens, ethnic Tatars who have been baptized in the Orthodox Church.[127] Moreover, there are at least six other Krjashen churches across the republic.[128]

In contrast, the local government in Nizhny Novgorod took a decidedly different approach to the Fundamentals of Orthodox Culture. Nizhny Novgorod was selected as a test region for the implementation of the new course and shortly following the Ministry of Education's memorandum local educators and religious scholars were invited to a meeting at the Nizhny Kremlin. An official from the Ministry of Education explained that in the following year, eighty-four public schools in the Volga region should test-drive the new course.[129] The meeting attendees were instructed to design a series of training manuals for teachers at various grade levels and suggest suitable materials for the course.

When the group reconvened several weeks later to present their recommendations, members from the local Orthodox dioceses were also present. The educators and scholars presented a united front against the proposed course, arguing that it would not achieve the intended goal of local unity but rather would pit the Orthodox Church against the other unrepresented religious groups. The representative from the Ministry of Education assured them that the course would be optional for students but reinforced the point that as religious experts, they should develop course materials that would not instigate interreligious conflict.

By the time religious leaders and members of the public convened for a third meeting, there was growing opposition to the Fundamentals of Orthodox Culture. Parents had organized suggesting that teaching religion is best left to Sunday school and home. School administrators argued that their teachers were not trained as theologians and students will inevitably have questions the teachers were not qualified or able to answer. Other teachers stated that they were atheist and found it insulting to teach themes such as "the moral culture of Orthodox Christianity."

During the public hearing, it also became clear that the opinions of religious leaders were decidedly mixed. One Catholic priest spoke in favor of

---

[126] Interview with bureaucrat D from Religious Affairs Department, April 2006, Kazan.
[127] Interview with Krjashen priest Pavel, June 2006, Kazan.
[128] Ibid.
[129] Nizhny Novgorod was originally selected as one of the experimental locations to implement the course. The course began in 2006.

the course, agreeing that Orthodox Christianity is an integral part of Russian culture with over a thousand year history. He expressed delight to see people returning to the Orthodox Church, yet also showed concern about how other groups might be portrayed, especially because the course outline called for identifying sects and cults.[130] Leaders of other traditional religions, including those from the Tatar-Muslim and Jewish communities, were far more skeptical of the course, suggesting that other traditional faiths should be given equal treatment and have their own specialized courses.[131] Orthodox Christians also expressed many reservations. Several Orthodox priests and religious studies scholars voiced concerns that the course would be taught by atheists who might actually do more harm than good.[132] One Orthodox priest worried that the course may actually turn youth against the Church.[133]

After considerable public debate, the experimental course in Nizhny was renamed "World Religions" and expanded to include all traditional religions in the Volga region – Orthodox Christianity (Russian Orthodox and Old Believers), Islam, Judaism, and Buddhism. Moreover, the time allotted to the study of each religion would be based on their relative percentage of the population. Finally, to help appease religious leaders' concerns, each religion would be allowed to review the course materials and have the opportunity to provide their own teachers. For the local government and the traditional religious communities this was the best arrangement, even if it still continued to indirectly privilege Orthodox Christianity. For instance, finding qualified religious teachers to meet the demands of the course can be quite taxing for the smaller religious groups. The Russian Orthodox Church has a seminary of potential teachers to draw from, but the Muslims and Old Believers have fewer resources, the Jewish community has only one rabbi in the area, and the Buddhists have no formal representatives at all.

The Foundations of Orthodox Culture provides an important in-country comparison of the Nizhny and Kazan governments on several counts. First, it demonstrates the extent to which local governments are willing to invite select religious communities into the decision-making process and how religious actors can help set the political agenda. Once handed the directive from the Center, officials in Kazan immediately invited a number of religious leaders to participate in redefining the course and setting the agenda. Nizhny officials also

---

[130] Interview with Catholic Father Mario, March 2006, Nizhny Novgorod.

[131] Interview with Damir-khazrat Mukhetdinov, Religious Board of Muslims for the Nizhny Novgorod Region (*Duhovnoe upravlenie musul'man Nizhegorodskoj oblasti; DUMNO*), March 2006, Nizhny Novgorod; also see "Novosti Pravoslavija: Sovet Vaada Rossii protiv 'Osnov pravoslavnoj kul'tury' v shkole" [Orthodox news: The Council of the Vaad in Russia against the "Fundamentals of Orthodox Culture in Schools"] (2003: 2).

[132] Interview with Orthodox Father Andre, January 2006, Nizhny Novgorod.

[133] Interview with Orthodox Father Igor, editor of the *Nizhegorodskie eparhial'nye vedomosti* [*Nizhny Novgorod Diocese Bulletin*], March 2006, Nizhny Novgorod.

took steps to reach out to the academic community and Orthodox Church to implement the course. However, it was only following intense criticism that a select group of other religious leaders were also invited to the discussion.

Second, the final product of the courses reflect local government preferences. The World Religions course developed in Tatarstan focuses equally on all religions in the republic; whereas the course in Nizhny includes only traditional religions, and the course content is apportioned relative to the group's size. This means that roughly 60 percent of the course is dedicated to Orthodox Christianity, 20 percent to Islam, and the remainder reserved for other traditional religions, such as Old Believers, Judaism, and Buddhism. Catholics and Protestants make up the smallest proportion of the population and are thus excluded from the Nizhny course.

Finally, the comparison demonstrates the limited autonomy of local governments in implementing directives handed down from Moscow, especially when the directives come heavily endorsed by Putin and the patriarch. Although the Tatar government was initially opposed to the new course, they chose to implement a pragmatic alternative that would not cause tension among religious communities or with Moscow. The bureaucrats in Nizhny Novgorod, by contrast, were willing to ignore local outcry to ensure that the course followed the spirit of the central directive, which privileged the Orthodox monopoly in the region.[134]

CONCLUSIONS

This chapter demonstrates both the willingness and the ability of religious and authoritarian state actors to cooperate around nonmaterial concerns. Political elites delve into the symbolic world, hoping that the cultural capital of religious communities will allow them to consolidate power and prestige. They invite religious leaders into the political sphere and give them a voice in decision making and influence over the local agenda. In exchange, local officials seek to consolidate authority, broaden their bases of support, curtail opposition, and enhance their prestige. Religious communities are also equally interested in the interplay of power and prestige. They adopt the symbols and discourse of the regime to demonstrate their patriotism, endorse political candidates in elections, defend the state, and champion its policies. In exchange, religious groups may also ensure their own survival, as well as potentially enlarge their community, advance their spiritual agenda, and at times constrain religious rivals.

This chapter indicates that the mixing of religion and politics can be a risky strategy for both sides and that religious-state cooperation around issues of power and prestige operates in a context of greater uncertainty. When local authorities participate in religious rituals and invite religious leaders into the

---

[134] Interview with former bureaucrat C, March 2006, Nizhny Novgorod.

political sphere, they run the risk of inviting scrutiny from above, alienating other religious communities, and creating an opening for religious leaders to undermine their authority. At the extremes, they may even permit hegemonic religions to capture the state. Recall, for instance, the Orthodox monopoly in Nizhny Novgorod, which most closely resembles state capture. Political elites disregarded the principles of secularism and equality of religions enshrined in the constitution to maintain close ties to the Church. Such an alliance has paid off handsomely for the Orthodox Church, allowing it to influence local politics and the religious landscape according to its interests.[135] This monopoly has also meant that the Orthodox Church's major competitors, including Catholics and Protestants, face additional indirect hurdles when advancing their own spiritual missions.

Moreover, the Orthodox-Nizhny alliance has allowed the Church to flex its muscle in the arena of education and steer local curricula in a more spiritual direction. Here, local bureaucrats largely ignored the academic and public criticisms directed at the Fundamentals of Orthodox Culture and proposed a course design that openly favors Orthodox Christianity. A majority of the course content is dedicated to the study of Russian Orthodox Christianity, and even the concerns of many Orthodox priests (i.e., atheist teachers may do more harm than good in presenting the materials) has been rectified by allowing priests into the classroom. Although the invitation is ostensibly open to other religious leaders, no other faiths have the necessary depth of personnel.

The mixing of politics and religion also creates internal problems for religious communities. Religious groups that adopt the symbols and discourse of the state may pay a price for such collaboration. For some religious groups, close relations led to a decline of legitimacy among believers and internal schisms among clergy. For example, in 2011, three priests in Udmurtia formally split from the Russian Orthodox Church on the grounds that church hierarchs had cultivated too close of a relationship with the government.[136] Consider another example of the Shanghai Catholic priest who refused to hang a banner supporting the One-Child Policy. The priest worried that such an open endorsement would give the appearance of an unholy alliance with the regime and the impression that his church was a mouthpiece for the party. In this case, local bureaucrats did little to sanction the priest's behavior, but this is not always the true. One Protestant pastor in China explained that after she chose not to hang a state banner in the main worship hall of her church, she was

---

[135] The Church has other advantages – for instance, at one highway entrance leading into the city, local authorities placed large icons to "bless" visitors. The icons are located in Shcherbinka-2 district, reported on the website Religious Freedom in the Nizhny Novgorod Region [Religioznaja svoboda v nizhegorodskom regione]. Available at: http://religio-nn.narod.ru/ (last accessed April 5, 2013). This website is administered by Igor Siminov, the former chief specialist of the Department for Religious Relations for the Administration of the Nizhny Novgorod Region.

[136] Washington (2011).

surprised to find other pastors critical of her behavior. Some even suggested she was unpatriotic. In her defense, she maintained that the church was very simple with only a painted cross on one wall, and government propaganda would be out of place. However, because of this internal conflict, she eventually resigned her position in the TSPM church and now ministers to an unregistered house church.[137]

This chapter additionally carries several implications for religious-state interaction in authoritarian regimes. First, the chapter reveals that as in most bargaining processes, the state generally has the upper hand; however, the relative power balance begins to tip toward religious actors when nonmaterial resources are the currency of exchange. This is because religious groups are rich in cultural capital, prestige, and moral authority that autocratic elites often lack and seek.

Second, the finding that religious groups of all stripes, including insider, outsider, majority, and minority voluntarily endorse those in power and take on the role of state-defender suggests this interaction is more complex than mere co-optation. In other words, both unregistered house churches and religious monopolies are at the very least supportive of the regime by displaying and promoting patriotism, not fostering dissent.

Third, this chapter demonstrated that nonmaterial collaboration is considerably more selective than its materialistic equivalent. In the previous chapter, local officials forged joint ventures with a variety of religious groups, especially if there was a profit to be made. Yet the risks associated with nonmaterial cooperation make the practice far less frequent and local governments more discriminating. Local officials, especially in China, only invite a select handful of religious communities to the bargaining table, and these groups tend to be limited to religious insiders. This observation is consistent with scholarship on local state-society interaction and the liabilities of some religious associational groups. For instance, Lily L. Tsai finds village cadres do a better job delivering public goods and services when they are embedded in communities with native ties. Tsai writes:

> both temples and churches generally encompass the administrative village in which they are located. They differ, however, in their embeddedness of local officials. The Communist Party's deeply ingrained distrust of Christianity and Christian organizations prevents village officials from participating in village churches even when the majority of the people in the village consider themselves part of the congregation. In contrast, village officials often participate in the activities and rituals of temple groups in their community, which are tolerated by the state as long as they limit their activities to within the village.[138]

For local authoritarians, therefore, some religions are predisposed to nonmaterial cooperation while others carry certain liabilities. Again, in Russia, it comes

---

[137] Interview with house church pastor E, August 2007, Beijing.
[138] Tsai (2007: 253).

as no surprise the Orthodox Church occupies a privileged position and has cornered the market on cultural capital and religious prestige. In China, no single religious community has established this kind of monopoly; yet those with deep historical ties, such as Buddhism, Taoism, and popular religions (as in Jinze), have the most popular legitimacy to offer local elites with the least amount of risk. By contrast, Chinese Protestants and Catholics, despite their deep roots, are still considered religious outsiders, which is the equivalent of possessing cultural stigma in the eyes of many political elites.

This chapter also reveals the imbalance of bargaining games between the two countries, in which nonmaterial cooperation is considerably more pervasive in Russia than in China. The greater frequency of religious-state cooperation in Russia is driven in part because no religion in China can match the power and autonomy of Orthodox Christianity. Although there is evidence that both Buddhism and Taoism were treated as state-religions in Chinese history, the current regime seems less interested in advertising these particular historical ties. In Russia, however, historians and politicians widely credit the Orthodox Church with unifying the state, and Moscow has turned to the Church to help define Russian nationalism and to protect the nation in times of de-democratization. In fact, this turn to the Church for protection is often literal. Katja Richters, for examples, writes that "since the mid-1990s, the sprinkling of holy water on servicemen, weapons, buildings, etc., and display of icons and flags depicting Orthodox saints have become widespread in the Russian Army."[139] Of course, only Orthodox priests are asked to bless nuclear submarines and lend icons to warships, and only the Orthodox Church has a small chapel in FSB (former KGB) headquarters in Moscow.[140] Therefore, it comes as no surprise that the Orthodox-Kremlin alliance has also seeped down into local politics. However, rather than blessing warships, Church leaders in Nizhny have built churches in nearby penal colonies, been given exclusive access to local prisons, and taken on the role of blessing the hometown soccer club and consecrating pharmacies.[141]

This leads to one final point. Religious-state cooperation is further shaped by the differences in the two countries' authoritarian political systems and the comparatively more open political climate in hybrid regimes. Russia is a mixed authoritarian system where political elites have noticeably more freedom in

---

[139] Richters (2012: 62).

[140] Dubas (2009).

[141] In 2006, Orthodox priests consecrated fifty-five pharmacies in Nizhny Novgorod and blessed the local Spartak soccer team before an important game; reported on the website Religious Freedom in the Nizhny Novgorod Region [Religioznaja svoboda v nizhegorodskom regione]. Available at: http://religio-nn.narod.ru/ (last accessed April 5, 2013). In 2007, the Nizhny Dioceses established a formal partnership with the General Directorate of the Federal Penitentiary Service allowing ten churches to be built in the penal colonies of the region. However, the Orthodox Church has informally had access to the penitentiary services since early 1996; see "Cerkovnoe bogosluzhenie v mestah lishenija svobody" [Church services in prison] (2005: 6).

their relations with religious groups than their Chinese counterparts. Russian politicians can, and frequently do, display their religious values and preferences (toward the Orthodox Church), where such action by a Chinese official would likely result in demotion, outright dismissal from her post, or worse.[142] This suggests that the boundaries between the sacred and secular are far more porous in Russia than in China. Addressing the question of why this is the case and the implications are the tasks of the next chapter.

---

[142] A Russian politician advocating for Pentecostal and charismatic Christianity would also likely be sanctioned.

6

Conclusions: Collaboration and Conflict in Comparison

The devil is in the details.

Karl Marx declared religion the "opium of the people," and for decades communist leaders waged a war on religion: churches, mosques, and temples were destroyed; religious leaders were executed; scientific atheism was taught in schools; and ubiquitous propaganda denounced religion as feudal, superstitious, and backward. But in the end, as the Soviet Union collapsed and post-Mao China embraced capitalism, it was clear that another aspect of the great socialist experiment had failed – religion did not die out as Marxist-Leninist and Maoist ideology had predicted. In fact, as Russia and China distanced themselves from their communist pasts, it became increasingly apparent that religious associational life was flourishing.

This book set out to enhance our understanding of the politics of religion in authoritarian regimes by answering a number of questions. Among them, what is the relationship between religious and political authority? Do religious groups function as a constraint on or partner to authoritarian regime leaders? When do religious groups, as members of civil society, encourage political liberalization, and when do they reinforce autocratic traditions of rule? How do different authoritarian contexts affect the development of religious associational life and the prospects of cooperation or conflict with those in power?

APPROACH

I have addressed these questions by constructing three levels of comparison, each of which was designed – through a particular combination of similarities and differences – to address the issues at hand and inform the other levels. Thus, to explain how authoritarian regimes dealt with growing religiosity inside their borders, and how "more" or "less" authoritarianism impacted religious-state interests and interaction, I compared how the central policies in Russia and China have transformed the religious marketplace. This comparison demonstrated, on the one hand, that top-down policies were instrumental in lifting the lid on religion and creating greater space for religious activities in both countries. On the other hand, the same policies were often ambiguous and allowed local authorities to manage religious communities in different ways, ranging from collaborative and mutually empowering to asymmetrical and conflictual.

With the understanding that the politics of religion is a local game, I drew on four city-based case studies – Nizhny Novgorod, Kazan, Changchun, and Shanghai – to explain variation in types of religious-state interaction. Here, I compared how differences in political contexts, economic burdens, and religious landscapes affected relations between religious groups and local governments. What made these comparisons so illuminating is that I was able to account for many likely causes of cooperation and conflict and at the same time maximize variation of one of my dependent variables: types of religious-state cooperation. This intracountry comparison shed light on issues, such as how different pathways of liberalization informed the behavior of political elites and their relationship toward associational life; how and why local governments attempted to exercise control over some religious groups while ignoring or even propping up others; and how differences in regime openness and restrictions on religious liberty shaped religious organizations' interactions with their authoritarian overseers.

A third level of comparison centered on the differences among religious traditions in Russia and China. Here, I was interested in explaining how different religious groups attempted to protect and promote their interests. The goal of this third comparison was to identify which communities were gaining the most from cooperation with those in power and which ones were being excluded. What made this approach so instructive was that it lent itself to numerous fruitful comparisons. For instance, religious actors were grouped according to their faith, such as Muslim or Catholic; they were compared according to their size, such as religious majorities or minorities; religious actors were further categorized as having either insider or outsider status; finally, religious groups were disaggregated according to their material and cultural resources. This multilevel approach testified to the methodological advantages of comparative inquiry and allowed for greater confidence in explaining the patterns of religious-state cooperation and conflict, and the consequences of this interaction.

ARGUMENTS

Throughout this book, I have argued that even in repressive political settings where uncertainty is high and religious freedoms are in flux, religious and political actors have needs that converge in many ways. This is particularly apparent at the local level, where the two sides pursue strategic partnerships.

I presented an interests-based theory that places a combination of uncertainty, needs, and resources at the center of religious-state interaction. In authoritarian political systems, I argued that religious and government actors operate under conditions of uncertainty regarding their position and prospects for survival. Local authorities fear religious groups will encourage instability, incite rebellion against the regime, or otherwise jeopardize their political futures. Religious leaders may fear regime elites will limit religious activities and roll back freedoms. In this uncertain context, I suggested that each side has symmetrical needs that must be met for its survival and prosperity with respect to money, power, and prestige. These needs are not always zero-sum and are often mutually supportive and interdependent. Finally, I argued that religious and state actors both have a distinct set of resources that can be offered to the other side to help meet key needs. The result is best understood as a strategic process of exchange in which religious and state actors become unexpected allies.

To be sure, there are many reasons why this argument is surprising. Tensions have long existed between the sacred and secular (this has been particularly true in Russia and China), and religious-state collaboration does not necessarily follow from other civil society experiences. Authoritarian leaders have a long history of coercing and co-opting religious leaders to serve the interests of the regime. Moreover, religion has proven particularly threatening for dictators because it represents a competing center of power and asserts an authority that transcends their own. Even when civil society is weak, as is the case in many authoritarian regimes, religious organizations tend to have resources other associational groups do not. They are well organized, have dense networks, provide safe and centralized places to gather, and often possess charismatic leaders and devoted followers – all of which make religious organizations particularly threatening to authoritarian leaders and their allies.

This book challenges the assumption that the relationship between religion and the authoritarian state is one of domination and resistance, where the state penetrates and co-opts religious communities, and religious groups in turn mobilize in opposition to the regime. At the same time, the purpose of this book has *not* been to downplay the coercive instruments of autocratic rulers or to suggest that religious-state conflict is absent in Russia and China. Rather, I have argued that the nature of religious-state relations is far more complicated than generally assumed. Although tensions certainly exist between religious and state actors, there is also ample room for mutually beneficial interaction. Local officials and bureaucrats offer crucial resources to religious groups to extend their base of support, ensure compliance, and simplify the management of religious communities. Religious groups use their own economic and cultural capital to cement vertical alliances and safeguard survival and strategic goals. Thus, adaptation and the convergence of interests lay the foundation for religious-state interaction.

This book also tested a number of arguments regarding how regime contexts, including restrictions on religion and constraints on political elites, and variation in religious complexions and resource endowments together informed religious-state behavior. These arguments were designed to shed light on when and how political elites and religious groups cooperate; which set of actors are gaining the most from cooperation and which are gaining the least; and how religious-state relations differ across authoritarian political systems.

This chapter revisits these arguments and presents the major findings of this study, with particular attention paid to the nuances of religious-state collaboration in Russia and China. I discuss the limitations of the theory, and suggest when and where religious-state collaboration is likely to breakdown. The chapter concludes by calling attention to the larger implications for the study of religion and authoritarianism, and suggests how the findings engage several key debates in comparative and international politics.

SUMMARY OF FINDINGS

In this comparative study of religion and contemporary authoritarianism, what stands out most is a strikingly similar story. There is strong evidence that patterns of collaboration reappear and repeat themselves both within and across Russia and China. In fact, cooperation is not only increasingly common, it is also an optimal strategy for both religious and political authorities. Both sides seek stability, influence, and legitimacy, and they understand that these concerns can best be met through cooperative interaction. A religious-state equilibrium, in short, is attainable. Thus, a central finding from this comparative project is the absence of variation between Russia and China. Despite the fact that these countries represent different types of authoritarianism and have heterogeneous political cultures and diverse religious complexions, the dynamics of religious-state collaboration are found in both countries today, just as these patterns were absent in both countries three decades earlier.

This leads to another unexpected finding that travels across the countries and four cases: religious and local regime interaction is rarely based on issues of faith and religious freedom. In fact, spiritual matters only peripherally enter the negotiations and then only among select religious actors. Instead, the bargaining games typically evolve around pragmatic political issues as each side tries to maximize money, power, and prestige. Again, this is not to suggest that ideology is unimportant or that theology does not shape the preferences and behavior of religious communities, but rather that the relationship between local governments and religious leaders tends to be material. As demonstrated in Chapter 4, there is a cash nexus at the center of religious-state interaction.

One possible explanation for this somewhat cynical observation is that the nature of authoritarian politics necessitates that religious groups in the public sphere must first engage the state on more practical issues – for example, reclaiming lost property, rebuilding places of worship, and registration – before considering or pressing for greater religious liberties. It is also quite likely in tightly controlled regimes like Russia and China that most religious communities, excluding perhaps the Russian Orthodox Church, simply do not have the resources and political opportunities needed to push for greater religious freedoms. To do so would likely result in state repression.

Authoritarianism in Russia and China

This study also pointed out important differences in the parameters of religious-state interaction in Russia and China. For one, the pathway of liberalization seemed to define patterns of religious-state cooperation and conflict in important ways. The chapters demonstrated that Russia's flirtation with democratic practices in the 1990s created a sufficiently large liberal opening to allow religious organizations to develop and mature outside of state influence. Although religious actors are required to register with local bureaucracies, the failure to do so does not necessarily result in punitive consequences. In fact, some Russian religious groups openly refuse registration while continuing to open churches and conduct religious activities with little state interference. For example, as I noted in Chapter 5, the Old Believers community in Nizhny Novgorod refused registration on the grounds that the state has no moral authority over the church but is active in electoral politics. In that case, bureaucrats explained that so long as the Old Believers are not harming their members or causing local instability, there is no pressing need to compel registration or official reprise. Moreover, one government official involved commented that forcing the Old Believers to register would be too politically costly. Although Old Believers represent only a small percentage of the population (less than 1 percent), no politician wants to be seen as coercing the moral authority of a religious community that is considered to be the precursor to the Orthodox Church and integral to Russian culture. Thus, it would seem the only negative implication for religious groups opting out of the public sphere is reduced access to government resources.

Similar laissez-faire attitudes toward registration have also been extended to select minority religions in Russia, despite the fact these groups are generally viewed with greater suspicion by both state and societal actors.[1] As I pointed out in Chapter 4, the Jesus Embassy charismatic church in Nizhny was able to evangelize and provide drug rehabilitation counseling for seven years without being registered, not because charismatic Christians were particularly well liked in the region but because the church provided valuable social services that the government and other associational groups were reluctant or unable to take on.[2]

In contrast, China's more restrictive political context makes it much more difficult for religious groups to seek autonomy from the state delineated spaces

---

[1] One bureaucrat explained that during his fifteen years in the Religious Affairs Office he knew of only a handful of religious groups denied registration. Interview with former bureaucrat C, March 2006, Nizhny Novgorod.

[2] Interview with Pastor Paul, March 2006, Nizhny Novgorod.

of "normal" religious activity. Religious communities on the margins, such as the unregistered Protestant house churches or the underground Catholic Church, do not share the same kind of unrestricted autonomy as unregistered groups in Russia. Unregistered religious communities in China operate in a context of greater uncertainty. They have no legal rights, and harsh penalties are regularly enforced for stepping out of state sanctioned spaces, including steep fines and up to three-year sentences at reeducation-through-labor camps (*laodongying*).[3]

To appreciate these national differences, it is instructive to consider more fully an example of an unregistered house church in China. Over the past thirty years, the China Gospel Fellowship (CGF; *Zhonghua fuyin tuanqi*) has grown to become one of the largest house churches in the country.[4] Founded in the 1980s in rural Henan, estimates of membership for this Pentecostal-leaning church number well above 1 million – with one church leader offering a conservative estimate of 3.5 million baptized members.[5] Although it is difficult to know the exact size of the church, CGF is widely recognized as having a significant presence in China, with dense networks that stretch across the country, and its own missionary program.[6]

The sheer size of the unregistered church has made it an obvious target for state suppression. To avoid this outcome, the church has adopted an elaborate organizational strategy for survival. Ironically, this strategy bares close resemblance to the "organizational weapons" used by the Bolshevik and early Chinese communists in their own struggles for power.[7] The church is designed

---

[3] Of course, there is wide variation in how local authorities manage unregistered religious communities. In 2007, for instance, some governments began experimenting with direct registration. One house church minister explained that the municipal government allowed his church to register directly, rather than first affiliating with TSPM churches (interview with house church deacon H, April 2007, Shanghai). Other regions have experimented with different informal arrangements. One local government in Sichuan permitted a large, unregistered church to hold Easter Sunday services for more than five thousand worshipers. Church leaders explained that such permission was granted because cadres were attempting to rebuild legitimacy following the Wenchuan earthquake that killed more than sixty thousand residents; personal correspondence with layperson from the Sichuan church, April 2009. On the coercive tools used against unregistered religious groups, see the U.S. Department of State *China International Religious Freedom Report 2010*. Available at: http://www.state.gov/g/drl/rls/irf/2010_5/index.htm (last accessed August 17, 2013).

[4] For a more detailed discussion of the development of CGF, see Koesel (2013).

[5] Interview with CGF church leader A, September 2006, Beijing. Christian media reports are equally large, estimating CGF membership between 5 and 7 million; see, for example, Lambert (1999: 66); the Voice of the Martyrs. Available at: http://www.persecution.com/public/newsroom.aspx?story_ID=Mjk1 (last accessed August 17, 2013). Academic estimates provide more modest figures between 1 and 4 million. Q. Liu (2009: 82), for example, calculates CGF membership near 1 million, and Kindopp (2004b: 373) places membership at 4 million.

[6] See, for instance, Bays (2012: 195); Lian (2010: 219); Y. Xin (2009: 130); L. Wu (2009: 31); J. Yu (2008); Aikman (2003: 73–133); Xiejiao yanjiu keti zu (1999: 41–8).

[7] Selznick (1952).

to operate in the shadows and on multiple levels. The organizational levels of the church are insulated from each other, with minimal knowledge of the members above and below. In this way, if any one level is raided by the authorities, the others can continue to function with little interruption. What this means in practice is that the lower units come and go, but their departure does not jeopardize the upper levels or the larger mission.[8]

This specific example illuminates that although similar stories of religious cooperation exist in Russia and China, there are also important differences between the two countries – that is, many religious groups in Russia may refuse registration and operate outside the public sphere without suffering negative repercussions. In China, distance from the state not only means the absence of resources, but also the increase of suspicions by political authorities and often repression.

The more general point here is that the greater political openness and corresponding religious freedoms in Russia have made the need for collaboration with local governments far less critical for a religious group's survival. Russian religious communities are less dependent on the state for funding and may effectively seek out alternative resources to pursue their spiritual and strategic goals. One imam in Kazan, for instance, remarked that the growth of Islam in Tatarstan does not necessarily result from the Shaimiev administration's support.[9] Although President Shaimiev has impeded Islam's revival, government resources tend to be directed at large, symbolic projects such as the rebuilding of the Kul-Sharif Mosque. On the contrary, donors in the Middle East support the projects that are fueling the religious revival – including the building of thousands of small mosques and madrasas in villages across the republic.[10] The implication is that religious groups in Russia may distance themselves from the state yet still function and even thrive with external support, making cooperation more of a tactical decision to extract resources and not necessarily one driven by the need to safeguard survival.

In contrast, Chinese religious groups remain far more dependent on the state. For example, the Chinese Religious Affairs Bureaus (RAB) must approve all "sizable" foreign donations, with such approval seldom granted.[11] One Protestant minister whose church is frequented by many foreigners explained that several years ago after a congregant returned to the United States, he was contacted by an American pastor who wanted to "sponsor" his Chinese church. The American church had raised funds for the expansion of the Chinese fellowship hall, which was currently too small to hold entire the congregation. When the Chinese minister approached his local RAB for permission, his request was denied on the grounds that Chinese churches must not open themselves

---

[8] Koesel (2013).
[9] Interview with Imam F, April 2006, Kazan.
[10] Ibid.
[11] See Document 19, section 11.

up to "foreign manipulation."[12] The stated rationale in this case was that a contribution from abroad might give foreign powers influence over the religious community, and thus a foothold in domestic politics. In fact, the only practical way for a Chinese church to receive a foreign financial gift is if the money is donated privately from an individual (rather than an organized church), and given directly to the Three-Self Patriotic Movement (TSPM), the government organization that oversees all Chinese Protestant churches. The TSPM's policy is to redistribute a portion of such gifts according to donors' wishes and then reallocate the remainder to other religious projects. What this example makes clear is that the more restrictive context in China means religious groups operate under greater constraints, are far more dependent on the state for resources, and have less flexibility in defining the terms of their interaction.

Political Autonomy and Political Dependence

What does a more open political context mean for political elites and their interaction with religious communities? Similar to the findings just detailed, the chapters demonstrated that the more open context in Russia has meant local governments have more flexibility in their relations with religious groups than their Chinese counterparts. Russian politicians do not have to be as creative in their support of religion or hide their patronage of religious communities under the cover of preserving local culture. In fact, many flaunt their support by installing plaques next to renovated religious landmarks that name themselves, their department, and the amount contributed. However, Chinese officials (who are usually party members and thus technically required to be atheists), are far more inhibited and as a result are careful to ensure that any collaborative arrangements are justified along politically expedient terms – primarily entrepreneurial, such as investments in the local economy and tourism, but also for the preservation of local culture.

The relative flexibility of local officials in Russia brings us to the issue of political accountability in authoritarian regimes. The more competitive authoritarian system in Russia has made political elites far more accountable to local constituents than their Chinese counterparts. Although Russia is not democratic, many political elites secure and maintain power through elections, whereas Chinese officials remain in power by demonstrating loyalty to the Center, maintaining local order, and delivering economic growth.[13]

These differences in authoritarian power structures have important implications for how religious-state bargaining plays out in the two countries. One implication is that the role of the central government is far less pronounced in Russia than in China. The Kremlin is still powerful and may seek to remove

---

[12] Interview with TSPM Protestant minister X, August 2007, Pudong.
[13] Of course, not all Russian political elites are electorally accountable. From 2004 to 2012, the Kremlin abolished elections for regional governors in favor of direct appointment. Following the 2011–12 popular uprisings, gubernatorial elections were reinstated.

local politicians, but local officials' political futures also rest in the hands of voters who may resent state incursion into religious affairs. To remain in power, Russian politicians must build local bases of support to effectively campaign and win elections. This encourages them to more directly reach out to religious groups, and especially to large religious communities with their strong networks. In contrast, Chinese government officials only collaborate selectively with religious groups to maintain stability and increase local revenues – qualities that are valued by Beijing and secure tenures in office. However, even selective collaboration is tempered by the understanding that too much interaction with religious actors may jeopardize a local official's political future.

Second, the more vertical accountability structures in China limit the collaborative arrangements local officials are willing and able to pursue. As Chapters 4 and 5 detailed, collaborative relations are generally divided between material and nonmaterial bargaining games. Although these categories often overlap, in the first type of bargaining relationship, there is a cash nexus driving the interaction in which tangible and quantifiable material resources are exchanged and money is often the bottom line. In the second type of bargaining game, religious and local regime actors cooperate to secure power and prestige. When comparing these two types of interactions, the chapters demonstrated that nonmaterial cooperation poses greater risks for local governments because the exchange of nonmaterial resources is far less transparent and has the potential to nurture civil society groups, establish competing centers of power, and even result in state capture. Moreover, cooperation around issues of power and prestige may be difficult for political elites to reel in if the relationship goes in the wrong direction.

All of this points to a more general nuance in religious-state bargaining between these two authoritarian regimes: nonmaterial collaboration is much less common in China than in Russia. To echo an earlier point, Chinese political elites are far more beholden to forces above them, making it extremely risky to empower religious communities. Even if a local bureaucrat wanted to invite religious leaders into policy circles or to incorporate religious symbols next to the existing communist ones, it would be difficult to justify these choices to superiors. Thus, the potential risks associated with nonmaterial bargaining and the increased constraints on Chinese officials means that religious-state collaboration tends to center on material concerns, whereas Russian authorities more freely engage in both material and nonmaterial bargaining.

Religious Interaction in Authoritarian Regimes

This study allows us to draw several conclusions about how more or less restrictive political environments have an impact on the interaction among religious groups. In particular, I have made the case that the greater political openness in Russia has permitted a more diverse religious presence in the public sphere than in China. Again, the Chinese government only recognizes five official religions – Buddhism, Taoism, Islam, Catholicism, and Protestantism. One implication of fewer restrictions on religion in Russia is that religious actors more openly compete with one another. As illustrated in Chapter 4, religious groups in Russia actively battle for access to state resources, influence, and followers. Moreover, religious organizations are highly attuned to the types of state support rival religions receive and are not shy about advocating for equal treatment.

The less restrictive context in Russia has also led some religious minorities to band together (something that is prohibited in China), in hope of alerting the local government to their importance and counterbalancing the Orthodox monopoly. For example, in Nizhny Novgorod where the Orthodox Church secured a cozy alliance with the state and established barriers for other religious communities, Protestant ministers formed a coalition to make their claims heard by the local government and counter the Orthodox monopoly. The coalition meets on a monthly basis in the basement of a Baptist Church, shares information and legal expertise, and even elects two representatives who interface with the local government and Orthodox Church.[14]

Religious Insiders and Outsiders in Authoritarian Regimes

Thus far, the discussion has focused primarily on the major differences between Russia and China. The comparative project also permits us to draw some concluding observations about which religious groups are best at navigating restrictive political environments. In other words, assess which religions have carved out the closest relationship with those in power, and which ones are excluded from the bargaining games altogether.

In drawing out differences among religious groups, the empirical chapters lend ample support to the argument that resource endowments increase the frequency of religious-state bargaining. More specifically, insider religious status is a strong predictor of religious-state cooperation.[15] For instance, recall some of the collaborative arrangements in the tourist arena discussed in Chapter 4, including the large Buddhist temple that secured an interest-free loan in Shanghai and the Kul-Sharif Mosque in the Kazan. In these cases and many others, insider status helped with the marketization of religious sites. Cooperation around the rebuilding of the Kul-Sharif Mosque was possible because there was a market demand for Islamic tourism in Tatarstan. A similar argument could be applied to religious insiders in Shanghai whose temples play a role in the local tourist industry.[16] Indeed, it is interesting to note that many religious

---

[14] Interview with Pastor Runov, February 2006, Nizhny Novgorod.

[15] But insider status and resource endowment are correlated.

[16] To be clear, Chapter 4 also presented two examples of religious-state collaboration with religious outsiders, including the Sheshan Catholic basilica and the Songjiang mosque. This chapter suggested that collaboration is possible in these cases because of the historic buildings of each

leaders interviewed in this study distinguished between tourist and nontourist temples. Religious personnel from the historic Buddhist and Taoist temples across the Shanghai – including the Jade Buddha Temple (*Yufo chan si*), the Temple of Peace and Tranquility (*Jing'an si*), and the Shanghai City God's Temple (*Chenghuang miao*) – all made it clear that their temples catered primarily to tourists (domestic and foreign) and nonbelievers.[17] Religious practitioners may visit the temples on major religious holidays to consult with the monks and priests, but they seldom use tourist temples as regular places of worship.

What stands out from the cooperative arrangements I have described, and where the arguments demonstrate some predictive leverage, is in explaining the magnitude of payoffs between insider and outsider religions. Religious insiders tend to make out quite well from the bargaining games and often are the ones being courted by the state rather than the other way around. Among the numerous religious groups surveyed in this study there is no greater insider than the Russian Orthodox Church. Since the early 1990s, the Church has benefited enormously from its insider status and, with the help of the state, reestablished a religious monopoly. This monopoly is visible from the Kremlin all the way down to the local level – Orthodox priests flank politicians at political events, onion-topped cathedrals have been lavishly refurbished, and Orthodox Christianity has become an important cultural marker, defining for the post-Soviet citizen what it means to be Russian.

It is not surprising, therefore, that the Church tends to dominate the bargaining games and is generously rewarded. As detailed in Chapters 4 and 5, for example, the Church has received from among so many benefits free heating, building subsidies, tax-exempt status to import cigarettes and export vodka, authority over the curriculum of public schools, access to prisons and hospitals, and veto power over where rival churches will be constructed. The Church has also used its relationship with the regime to protect its hegemonic status. In June 2013, the Russian Duma passed blasphemy legislation that carries a three-year sentence, fines up to 500,000 rubles (more than $15,000), and compulsory correctional labor for public displays that offend "the feelings of religious believers" and express "disrespect toward society."[18] Here, it is important to note that the blasphemy bill was largely in response to the protest of the feminist punk band Pussy Riot. In February 2012, Pussy Riot briefly occupied the alter of Moscow's Christ the Savior Cathedral and performed their "Punk Prayer," which includes lyrics accusing the patriarch of believing more in Putin than in God.

---

occupy. To my knowledge, no other Catholic or Muslim venues in Shanghai are part of a collaborative tourist arrangement.

[17] In fact, the Jade Buddha monastery has two ticketing systems and charges more expensive prices for tourists. Interview with monk Y from Yufo si, August 2007, Shanghai; interview with monk Q at Jing'an temple, May 2007, Shanghai; interview with Taoist priest C from Chenghuang miao, May 2007, Shanghai.

[18] Kravtsova (2013).

In China, no religious group has the same kind of insider status or comes close to establishing a religious monopoly like the Russian Orthodox Church. Among the five official religions, one could argue that Buddhism is the most favored by the state and receives the most patronage. The chapters support this claim and show that Buddhists have been the beneficiaries of interest-free loans, access to free and discounted land, state-funded restoration of temples and monasteries, and even tuition waivers for abbots to study toward their MBA degrees. However, Beijing has shown little interest in propping up a Buddhist monopoly.

All of this suggests that bargaining games for insider religions tend to involve larger payoffs from political elites, whereas cooperation for outsider religions tends to center on what these groups have to offer to improve their standing with regime representatives. Religious outsiders in both Russia and China – such as Protestants and Catholics, which are considered to be the most threatening to the Orthodox Church and the most foreign in China – tend to be on the supply-side of collaboration with the state. Their role in bargaining games is about providing public goods and welfare services, which they do in no small part out of self-preservation. Thus, although all religious groups must have something to offer local authorities to get an invitation to the negotiating table, religious outsiders generally have to bring more and receive less in return. Their payoffs are considerably attenuated. As a result, the relationship for religious outsiders is far more asymmetric.

This observation takes us back once again to the costs and benefits perceived by political elites. When local governments reach out to religious communities that are considered endemic within local culture, the risks are lower and the potential payoffs usually greater. Therefore, it can be expedient to justify collaboration in terms of supporting local culture when the religious community has native ties. Moreover, religious groups with insider status generally represent a significant proportion of the local population, making collaborative arrangements all the more attractive. Again, it is no coincidence that politicians in Nizhny Novgorod invite Orthodox priests to bless their campaign rallies where the Church claims a majority of the local population.

More important, however, is the role of insider status in explaining why local governments cooperate with select religious minorities or religious groups on the political margins. Recall the cooperative arrangements in Chapter 5 in the small town of Jinze, where local cadres actively promoted the popular religious activities of the local bridge god, even though these activities are considered illegal by Beijing. In this case, local cadres built trust among residents and received some financial payoffs from the annual religious pilgrimages. This relationship, therefore, underscores the localized nature of religious-state collaboration and demonstrates that even in highly restrictive systems like China, local officials are willing to cooperate with religious communities on the political margins, so long as these groups bring valuable resources to the exchange.

The collaboration in Jinze also lends support to an argument that appeared repeatedly throughout the book: bargaining games are relationships of inter-dependence. Cooperation occurs not only because religious communities have insider status but also because the resources they offer are valuable to local governments. This helps explain why local officials in Shanghai welcomed the investment of Christian bosses and then conveniently overlooked the crosses that adorned their illegal church-factories, and why local cadres ignored the underground Catholic Church's much-needed clinic for the disabled. Again, these cases reinforce the argument that cooperation is available to religious groups operating outside of the public sphere, so long as they deliver resources that are locally in demand.

Winners, Losers, and Those in the Middle

If religious insiders gain the most and religious outsiders the least from collabo-ration, where do we situate religious communities that fall in between, such as Muslims in Russia (in Nizhny Novgorod) and China who have deep roots but are not considered to be a native religion? Again, the answer is complex, but their potential for bargaining largely reflects how they court those in power.

There are two mosques in Changchun and seven in Shanghai that serve the local Muslim community. Informants at each of the mosques reflected on their relations with the local government in comparison to those their religious neighbors have with the state. The responses I documented reveal a strikingly similar hierarchy: Buddhists and Taoists are assumed to have the closest rela-tions, Protestants and Catholics have the tensest relations, and Muslims (at least in Changchun and Shanghai) are somewhere in between.[19] To maintain this middle position and improve relations, one imam in Shanghai explained that the mosques in the region try not to attract attention because local authorities reward stability, and that stability indicates harmony with the regime.[20]

Other Muslim leaders explained that they also try to take advantage of their ethnic minority status to extract resources from the state. For instance, Islam is the only official religion in China that is associated with ethnic minority groups. Therefore, when a mosque needs funding for a new roof or seeks permission to expand, religious leaders also play on their rights as minority constituents of the state. As an ethnic minority, they are eligible for certain state assistance and therefore articulate their demands as support for minority development – something that Beijing looks on favorably and local cadres can include in reports to their superiors.[21]

In Nizhny Novgorod, the Muslim community also represents an ethnic minority with deep, historic ties; however, their relationship to power is quite

---

[19] Religious leaders from the other four religions described similar rankings.
[20] Interview with Imam Y, August 2007, Shanghai.
[21] J. Wang (2009) argues that Muslims use their ethnic status to extract state resources; on this point, also see Hillman (2004).

different from Muslims in Shanghai and Changchun. Rather than keeping a low profile, the Muslim community in Nizhny has been one of the most vociferous critics of the local government's close alliance with the Orthodox Church. Among numerous examples, it was the local Board of Muslims (*Duhovnoe upravlenie musul'man Nizhegorodskoj oblasti; DUMNO*) that criticized the free heating for Orthodox churches and requested equal treatment; it was the Muslim community who protested the "Merry Christmas" posters hung across the city at taxpayers' expense and requested that all religious holidays be equally recognized; it was the Muslim community that threatened to publish a blacklist of candidates during the 2006 local elections; and it was the Muslims who suggested that a course on the foundations of Tatar culture be offered as an alternative to the proposed "Foundations of Orthodox Culture" course in public schools.

To be sure, dissent comes at a cost. The Nizhny Muslim community has largely been left out of collaborative exchanges in the city. As one imam explained, "the local government does nothing to directly harm us, but they also do nothing to help us."[22] This statement reinforces an earlier argument about how collaborative arrangements allow the state to reward loyalty and punish those who are disloyal through quiet forms of repression, such as exclusion from state subsidies. In the context in which some religious groups are given state subsidies, the excluded groups are marginalized and subsequently weakened because of their reduced access to resources.

Nizhny Muslims are conscious that their criticisms have limited their access to state resources and have implemented various measures to ensure their dissent cannot be labeled as "extremist" by regime representatives, something that would jeopardize the larger Muslim community. For instance, there are three mosques in Nizhny, and to prevent accusations that some mosques are cultivating extremism, the DUMNO introduced a rotating schedule for imams. The chairman of DUMNO explained that each of the imams has a slightly different style, and some are more outspoken than others. As a result, a rotating schedule has been introduced so that each Friday imams lead prayers at a different mosque.[23] The implication, of course, is that no mosque can be seen as a pocket of extremism and that local Muslims will have exposure to a range of self-moderating styles.

The position of Islam and its relationship to those in power is differently complicated in Tatarstan.[24] Although the majority of the population is

---

[22] Interview with Damir-hazrat Muhetdinov, Religious Board of Muslims for the Nizhny Novgorod Region (*Duhovnoe upravlenie musul'man Nizhegorodskoj oblasti; DUMNO*), March 2006, Nizhny Novgorod.

[23] Interview with Umar-khazrat Idrisov, Chairman of the Religious Board of Muslims for the Nizhny Novgorod Region (*Duhovnoe upravlenie musul'man Nizhegorodskoj oblasti; DUMNO*), March 2006, Nizhny Novgorod.

[24] In the summer of 2012, two moderate Muslim leaders were killed in Kazan, shattering the image of religious tolerance. The Mujahedeens of Tatarstan, a radical Islamic group, claimed responsibility for the attacks.

Tatar-Muslim and the republic is considered the historic homeland of Islam in Russia, the Muslim community has not established a monopoly like the Orthodox Church has in other regions. One plausible explanation is because the local government has gone to great lengths to promote religious tolerance and resist state capture. Local authorities have been cautious about creating the appearance of favoritism in dealing with religious groups, especially Islam, to avoid encouraging Islamic extremism, an image that would endanger the republic's autonomy from Moscow. It is interesting to note that the local government has taken a number of steps to maintain positive interreligious relations, including the creation of a council to manage religious affairs in the republic, the Council of Religious Matters for the Cabinet of the Republic of Tatarstan (*Sovet po delam religij pri kabinete ministrov respubliki Tatarstan*). The function of the council differs from other bureaucratic organs managing religious groups in the country. The office is divided into various departments: Islamic Affairs; Russian Orthodox Christianity; New Religious Movements, Catholicism and Protestantism; and Legal Concerns. Furthermore, each department serves as an intermediary between the religious groups and the local government, with the idea that they will advocate on behalf of their respective religious group. As one minister explained, the council allows each religious community direct access to the government and discourages any one from attempting to control the state.[25]

THE LIMITS OF COLLABORATION

A central argument throughout the chapters is that in authoritarian regimes, the interests of religious and state actors can align so that both sides pursue innovative arrangements. The empirical findings from the two countries and four cases provided ample support for this argument. At the same time, Russia and China are large and diverse countries, and although religious-state cooperation is certainly present in some regions, there is also conflict. The findings of this project are expected to offer substantial insight to many parts of the authoritarian world, but not necessarily among every corner or among every religious group.

Religious-state conflict is likely to occur when religious communities operate outside of the public sphere. In interviews with members from unregistered communities – including Protestants, Catholics, and Buddhists in China, and Baptists, Pentecostals, and Old Believers in Russia – revealed that that many of these groups want nothing to do with the state or with the state-sanctioned religious organizations. They simply want to be left alone. And yet with regard to associational life, being "left alone" in an authoritarian regime is a conscious deviation from the norm and often serves only to heighten government suspicions. Although this project does provide some evidence of unregistered

[25] Interview with adviser R to President Shaimiev, April 2006, Kazan.

religious and local regime cooperation in both countries, these findings should not be interpreted to reflect all religious groups operating on the margins of autocratic rule.

Religious-state conflict is also likely to be present in border regions where religious and minority identities overlap and separatist movements are present. In these areas, the regime's suspicions of religious and ethnic groups – as potential hotbeds for instability or promoters of secession – overshadow any potential payoffs from cooperation for the local governments. Moreover, in these contested regions there is generally greater oversight by the central government, local officials rule with a heavy hand, and local elites are in power because of their demonstrated loyalty. These conditions hardly inspire innovative relations with religious groups, and therefore we would expect local officials to revert to the more coercive instruments in their toolkit.

The Center

Religious and local regime cooperation may further break down with the intervention of the central government. In the early 1990s, when the religious marketplace was largely unregulated, many new religious movements entered Russia, including practitioners of Scientology. In Nizhny Novgorod, Scientologists registered with the local bureaucracies and were able to establish a sizable following within a few short years, including some members from the provincial administration.[26] Part of their recruitment strategy was to invest heavily into local universities, including providing reading rooms and much-needed computer and laboratory equipment. Converts were also encouraged to devote part of their businesses to the expansion of Scientology. For instance, Alexander Kulikov, the director of the Earthling Chemical Factory (*Zemlyn*) established a Hubbard College on the plant's facilities and encouraged employees to attend courses.[27] Across the city, other business ventures promoted Scientology, including a large, pyramid-shaped shopping mall adjacent to the central train station, where employees were required to attend (and pay for) seminars on Dianetics or risk losing their jobs.[28]

The Church of Scientology operated openly in Nizhny Novgorod until the end of the decade when religious freedoms, especially for new religious movements, were tightened.[29] In 1998, the Ministry of Internal Affairs (*Ministerstvo vnutrennih del, MVD*) labeled Scientology a "satanic sect," stating that "[t]he Church of Scientology is one of the many varied satanic sects which have a distinctly criminal tendency and which actively use psychotropic substances in

---

[26] Dvorkin (1998).

[27] Ibid.

[28] Interview with former Scientologist I, February 2006, Nizhny Novgorod. This was confirmed in an interview with former bureaucrat C, March 2006, Nizhny Novgorod.

[29] Dolgov (1999).

order to acquire control over the personality of adepts."[30] The central denunciation sent an unmistakable message to regional political elites that Scientology would no longer be welcome in Russia. Consequently, local governments began revoking the registration of Scientology branches across the country. Although the Nizhny Scientologist community had established almost a decade of positive relations with the local government, they were also refused re-registration. In fact, the local government even initiated an independent campaign against Scientology warning residents of their "cultlike" activities and recommending all municipal agencies and academic institutions immediately break ties.[31]

This rapid reversal of fortunes for Scientology illustrates two important lessons. One is that religious-state relations under authoritarian rule are both fluid and fragile. A cooperative alliance can rapidly become conflictual and vice versa. The other is that the Center remains a key, if sometimes hidden player in the game who may intervene at any point and quickly rewrite the rules.

Falun Gong

The anticult campaign against Falun Gong offers a final test for this study. As detailed in Chapter 3, Falun Gong is a quasi-spiritual movement that emerged in the 1990s on the outskirts of Changchun and claims to synthesize Buddhist and Taoist philosophy with mysticism and the traditional practice of qigong.[32] The crackdown on Falun Gong raises an important question: why was Falun Gong targeted when it is a homegrown movement with presumably deep Chinese ties?

In addition to having insider status, before the crackdown, Falun Gong was operating with considerably more transparency than many unregistered religious groups in China. Falun Gong had joined the state-sponsored National Qigong Research Association; the founder of the movement had cultivated alliances with regime leaders and lectured widely around the country; and local branches of Falun Gong were legally registered across China.[33] Falun Gong would seem, therefore, to be a likely candidate for religious-state cooperation – it was transparent, registered, courting the state, and considered to have

---

[30] "Saentologija: Psevdo-cerkov', psevdo-nauka, psevdo-pravda" [Scientology: Pseudo-church, pseudo-science, pseudo-truth] (1998).

[31] "Religija v Nizhnem Novgorode: Itogi pereregistracii religioznyh ob"edinenij. Administracija Nizhnego Novgoroda ne rekomenduet sotrudnichat' s nekotorymi religioznymi ob"edineni jami" [Religion in Nizhny Novgorod: Results of re-registration of religious associations. Nizhny Novgorod administration recommends noncooperation with several religious associations] (2001).

[32] See, for example, N. Chen (2003a); Palmer (2007).

[33] Because Falun Gong is *not* one of the five official religions, local branches registered under a variety of alternative affiliations including medical organizations, martial arts organizations, youth leagues, and sports clubs; see Palmer (2007: 189). On the links between Falun Gong and People's Liberation Army (PLA) see Ownby (2003).

indigenous roots. More importantly, Falun Gong's large following and diverse and dense networks could provide attractive resources for government officials to exploit.[34] And yet as the movement grew, its relationship to power changed. Rather than cultivating vertical alliances, Falun Gong practitioners took a more confrontational approach. The crackdown, then, was less the result of Falun Gong's characteristics and more about its tactics.

David Palmer finds that between 1998 and 1999, Falun Gong supporters became increasingly militant, organizing numerous protests in front of government offices and media outlets across China.[35] The protests were largely in response to editorials that were critical of the teaching of Falun Gong, referring to its leader as a charlatan, comparing the organization to the Boxer Rebellion, and concluding that it would bring harm to the nation.[36] Angered by the editorials, practitioners picketed media outlets and government offices demanding apologies. According to Palmer, the targeted government offices and newspapers either ignored the protestors or quickly issued apologies to demobilize them.[37] The combination of having their demands met and perhaps the absence of official sanctions seemed to embolden Falun Gong demonstrators. At dawn on April 25, 1999, roughly ten thousand Falun Gong practitioners sat in silent mediation outside of *Zhongnanhai*, the private compound for the top leadership of the CCP.

The response was swift and ruthless. China's leaders made it clear that any cooperation with Falun Gong would not be tolerated. Falun Gong was denounced as an "evil cult" (*xiejiao*), a profound threat to social stability, and citizens (especially party members) were warned not to take part in its beliefs and activities. Those who refused to renounce the spiritual group were removed from their jobs, expelled from universities, had their housing confiscated by the state, sent to reeducation camps, and by some reports even killed.[38]

The April 1999 protests shifted the political dynamic in such a way as to take any form of religious-state cooperation off of the table. The location of the demonstration – at the doorstep of power – signaled that Falun Gong was organized and willing to take political risks to achieve its aims. The timing of the protests – close to the ten-year anniversary of the Tiananmen Square student uprisings – also escalated tensions in the capital and fueled suspicions of Falun Gong's antiregime sentiments. The scale of the protests – over ten thousand participants from all regions and from different social strata – also seemed to take both the party and security forces by surprise.[39] These factors taken together transformed Falun Gong from a homegrown, spiritual movement to an enemy

---

34 Ownby (2008), for instance, estimates that in the mid-1990s qigong practitioners ranged between 60 and 200 million; Tong (2009: 9) reports there were at least 2 million Falun Gong adherents at the time of the crackdown.

35 Palmer (2007: 256).

36 Palmer (2007); Eckholm (2001).

37 Palmer (2007: 256).

38 Palmer (2007).

39 See, for example, Shue (2001); Hu (2003); N. Chen (2003b).

of the state. The protests in many ways sealed the fate of the organization – it was the wrong place and the wrong time to push for greater rights – and even if Falun Gong and local regime cooperation was once possible locally, it ceased to be after the protests.

One final issue arises with respect to Falun Gong. The rise and fall of the group serves as an important warning for other religious minorities. One leader of an unregistered house church remarked that Falun Gong serves as an example of how *not* to engage the state.[40] Many large house churches share striking similarities with Falun Gong, including extensive networks of more than one million members, devoted followers, and strong mobilization capacity. Church leaders are quite aware that these characteristics make their organizations particularly threatening to regime leaders. Indeed, one church leader commented that like Falun Gong, a single phone call could probably activate the dense network of the church to bring tens of thousands to Beijing in a matter of days, if not hours.[41] However, another church leader stressed that such an act is much too political and would only end badly for the church. There are effective ways to build the church in China and mobilizing in Tiananmen Square is *not* one of them.[42]

IMPLICATIONS FOR RELIGION AND AUTHORITARIANISM

This project set out to advance our understanding of the theoretical links between religion and politics in authoritarian regimes. Although it is widely recognized that the two interact, little is known about the theatre where these interactions take place and their political consequences in an authoritarian context. In focusing on how local governments deal with growing religiosity within their borders, and how religious groups attempt to promote and protect their interests from the margins, this study provides a rare window into the inner workings of the contemporary authoritarian project.

By studying authoritarianism locally, this book advances current discussions of contemporary authoritarianism in two distinct ways. One is by opening the "black box" of these regimes and shedding light on the behavior of local government officials and how they ensure stability, legitimacy, and economic vitality. This study reveals, among other things, that local political elites not only use coercive tools to safeguard their rule, but also – and often – use cooperative strategies to secure political and economic returns. Therefore, the authoritarian toolkit, which figures prominently in studies of the strategic foundations of authoritarian rule, needs to be expanded to include cooperative strategies as well. A second way this study advances discussions of contemporary authoritarianism is by bringing two largely understudied and undertheorized sets of actors to the forefront of the analysis – local governments and religious

[40] Interview with house church leader V, October 2006, Beijing.
[41] Interview with house church leader B, September 2006, Beijing.
[42] Interview with CGF church leader A, September 2006, Beijing.

communities – and in the process detailing how they are agile political and economic players who influence politics from the ground up.

The Politics of Postcommunism

For specialists of Russia and China, this project brings a much-needed cultural dimension to the study of contemporary politics. There are few comparative studies of religion and politics in countries undergoing transitions from communism – or for that matter from other forms of authoritarian rule. Much of the literature on contemporary Russian and Chinese politics privileges the political and economic dimensions of reform at the expense of cultural actors. When cultural dimensions are included, culture tends to take center stage in the narrative, while economic and political actors drop out.

Moreover, works that do explore aspects of religion tend to focus on faiths that are either particularly powerful or extremely contentious, such as the Russian Orthodox Church, Falun Gong, and the Protestant house church movement. These studies rarely examine multiple faiths and generally overlook the political economy of religious-state interaction. Such a focus belies the multireligious reality of Russia and China and provides only a narrow and arguably skewed perspective of religious-state interaction in these influential authoritarian regimes.

This project addresses these shortcomings by studying multiple cultural actors, placing them into the context of political and economic change, and analyzing what the different types of authoritarianism mean for religious-state relations. This shift in focus is important because by overlooking the intersection of culture and politics, we leave ourselves ill prepared to explain how religious groups are influenced by the course of political change and how, in turn, such groups shape the course of politics. This book therefore contributes a critical component to both the growing literature on comparative authoritarianism and contemporary Russian and Chinese studies, and in the process bridges two major, but usually competing, approaches in political science – cultural analysis and political economy. It is my hope that this comparison will serve as a bridge between area specialists and the larger comparative community and encourage more conversations between students of Russia and China, who have much to gain from greater interaction.

State and Society

Readers less interested in the politics of postcommunism will still find a number of theoretical arguments and findings that contribute to larger debates in comparative and international politics. For one, this book adds to the extensive scholarship on central-local relations by illustrating the autonomy of local actors, the uneven implementation of central policies, and identifying the creative strategies local governments adopt to facilitate cooperation with unlikely partners. Thus, no matter how encompassing an authoritarian regime tries to be, this study lends support to the argument that at the end of the day there remains a principal-agent problem when translating central control locally.

Another contribution from this analysis is the continued importance of the state. Many have observed that the state has generally been in retreat during the past two decades as a result of a diminished role in the economy and the organization of society – long gone are the days of the Young Pioneers and state-dominated beekeepers associations. However, the continued role of the state speaks to a larger issue of state-society dynamics in autocratic settings. Even as both countries distance themselves from their communist pasts, neither the Russian nor Chinese state has relinquished complete control over associational life. There is still a desire to influence associational groups that organize citizens, take in funds, and make ideological claims; and religious groups are of particular concern because of their emphasis on values not necessarily shared by the regime alongside their ability to provide alternative sources of authority. However, as this study shows, this concern need not always evolve into a hostile threat. Happily enough for all actors, at the local level there is an opportunity to build relationships that might otherwise scale into costly activities for both sides. In this sense, the evidence presented here provides new testing grounds for debates that consider religious diversity a cause for conflict by highlighting plural societies where religious dynamics take place in variable regime contexts, and religion is often a source of cooperation.[43]

Religion, Civil Society and Authoritarian Regimes

This study, along with other recent works on civil society, also helps us rethink, if not amend, our understanding of the role of associational groups under authoritarian rule. Specifically, this project demonstrates that associational groups are both less independent and more supportive of the authoritarian regime than generally assumed. This finding is important because scholars of democracy tend to assume that the purpose of civil society is to act as a check to those in power. Civil society's strength comes from the fact that it can serve as an important mediator between citizens and the state, and helps create important focal points around which the disenfranchised can mobilize.[44]

Along similar lines, scholars (and presidents!) of the postcommunist region such as Václav Havel, laud faith-based groups for their ability to protect society from political chaos, and chip away at the power of the powerful in authoritarian settings.[45] However, the role of civil society within authoritarian regimes is multifaceted. This project provides strong support for a new model of

---

[43] For example, Lijphart's (1977) consociational model of democracy was developed to main-tain stability in plural societies; Juergensmeyer (2003) documents the global rise of religious violence.

[44] See, for example, Diamond (1992: 483, 1999).

[45] Havel et al. (1985).

state-society relations – one where religious communities do not always function as pockets of dissent, nor are they necessarily incubators of democracy who
stimulate political participation and socialize democratic norms. Instead, religious groups forge vertical alliances with those in power, which by accident or
design ultimately reinforces the authoritarian regime.

The observation that associational life can support authoritarian rule travels
to other regions and other associational terrains. For example, in her study of
associational life in Palestine, Amaney A. Jamal finds that civic associations
are not always or even often a force for democratization but tend to reproduce
the elements of the political context in which they exist.[46] In nondemocratic
systems such as Palestine, and as this project confirms in Russia and China,
associational life does not function as a force for destabilization and political
change, but rather reflects and reinforces the authoritarian political status quo.

Within the Middle East and North Africa (MENA), some have also argued
that religious minorities are strategic supporters of authoritarian rule. Fiona
McCallum, for example, suggests that Christian churches in Egypt, Jordan,
and Syria (at least until the Arab Spring) often found common cause with
their respective authoritarian leaders.[47] These are several factors contributing to church-state alliances in this context. First, like many of the religious
actors detailed in this study, Christian churches in the MENA are operating within political contexts that are repressive and religious freedoms are
tightly controlled. Second, Christians represent a relatively small minority in
largely Muslim countries with histories of interreligious tension. Third, there
is an implicit fear for some Christian leaders that regime change would likely
empower a Muslim majority, and Christians would face greater marginalization, if not open persecution, under new leadership. This combination of factors encourages some church leaders to build allies with authoritarian political
elites.

In exchange for open support of authoritarian leaders, Christian churches
may be offered greater state protection and security for their communities.
Thus, like many of the religious groups discussed in this study, carving out
a protected space within the authoritarian regime is strategic and often has
residual advantages. For instance, in return for supporting President Husni
Mubarak, Coptic Orthodox Church hierarchs in Egypt were able to consolidate
their position, claim greater authority in managing their coreligionists, and
occasionally speak out in favor of greater Coptic rights.[48] At the same time,
some authoritarian leaders may also cultivate church-state alliances. Two such
cases occur in Saddam Hussein's Iraq and Hafez al-Assad's Syria. In both
instances, minority religious communities ruled the regimes, Sunni Muslim

---

[46] Jamal (2007: 20).

[47] McCallum (2012), but also see Armanios (2012) on Coptic Christians demonstrating in Tahrir
Square despite Church leaders' calls for Copts to abstain from the protests.

[48] Rowe (2009: 115, 124); McCallum (2012: 118).

in Iraq and Alawite in Syria. To build support for their rule, Hussein and Assad formed tacit albeit variable alliances with religious minorities, including Christians. These alliances rested on the assumption that those in power and Christian minorities share a mutual threat from the more militant Muslim majority. If the Islamist opposition was to come to power, not only would more moderate regime leaders be disposed but Christians would also face greater uncertainity. In short, regime transition, even if it were in a more democratic direction, would introduce new vulnerabilities for Christian churches, making the "authoritarian status quo . . . preferable to democratic uncertainties."[49]

The overall portability of these findings returns us to the issues of authoritarian durability and resilience. Here, the implication is that we should not hastily assume that religious communities, as members of civil society, provide a counter to those in power. Although many have optimistically looked to civil society organizations as agents of collective empowerment in authoritarian settings, these regimes are usually adaptive and remarkably resilient to political change. By way of example, the Soviet Union persisted for more than seventy years, and after its collapse, Russia only briefly flirted with democracy before rejoining the league of authoritarians. In the fall of 2012, the Chinese Communist Party seamlessly ushered in a new generation of leaders, and there are no signs that collapse is on the horizon. As Vikie Langohr reminds us, "it is certainly true that these [civil society] organizations can call attention to and sometimes limit the depredations of authoritarian rule by publicizing abuses such as the torture of political prisoners and limitations on free speech. They can also help lay the foundations of a democratic culture by disseminating values essential to democracy, including respect for human rights and the rule of law. Beyond these contributions, however, lies the Herculean task of replacing current authoritarian regimes with democratic ones."[50] Therefore, we must be cautious when placing too many expectations on religious organizations as agents of political change, especially when they are up against such stubborn and long-lived opponents.

Indeed, this study suggests three cautionary points about the role of religion in advancing democratic change. First, it is important to keep in mind that any group seeking to challenge authoritarian rule requires broad bases of support that often take decades to build.[51] As Nancy Bermeo and Philip Nord have argued, the contours of associational life are not fixed, and organizational groups do not necessarily have thick linkages between them.[52] This point is particularly true among religious actors who often view each other as competitors instead of compatriots. Second, when religious actors have played a role in encouraging political change, they tend to represent large majorities

---

[49] McCallum (2012: 122).
[50] Langohr (2004: 200).
[51] Bunce and Wolchik (2011).
[52] Bermeo and Nord (2002).

that have joined forces with nonreligious associations. For example, the Polish Solidarity movement was comprised of more than just the Catholic Church and over decades grew to include coalitions of intellectuals, workers, farmers, students, and teachers. The Church sheltered the opposition movement but by no means was the sole player. Finally, we cannot assume that religious organizations are naturally democratic or are particularly good at socializing democratic norms. Many religious organizations are extremely hierarchical, possess strong authoritarian tendencies, and tend to be the defenders of the status quo, not the vanguard of liberal social change.

Religion, Politics, and Political Change in Russia and China

Let us return briefly to religion and authoritarianism in contemporary Russia and China and the prospects for political change. For the most part, religious groups in these countries have steered clear of oppositional politics. In China, this seems like a wise decision because the regime has shown little tolerance for any group advocating democratic change. Yet even in Russia, where there is greater space for oppositional politics and religious groups have more autonomy, there has been little to no movement to challenge the system. The Orthodox Church, for example, which has grown significantly in strength and independence over the past three decades, has not openly challenged the state or pushed for greater democratization. Instead, the Church has remained a staunch supporter of the Kremlin and a critic of the West, leading some to rename it the "Kremlin's Ministry for the Salvation of Souls."[53]

In December 2011, for example, as thousands of Russians took to the streets to protest widespread election fraud and growing dissatisfaction with Putin's renewed candidacy for president, Church hierarchs mildly called on the Kremlin to take the demonstrator's concerns seriously.[54] As the protests evolved, the patriarch came out in strong support of Putin, even describing Putin's twelve years of rule a "miracle of God."[55] On the one hand, this is not terribly surprising, as the Church needs the state to ensure its monopoly. Moreover, the Church is a hierarchical organization that has sought to push Russia in a more socially conservative direction.

On the other hand, it is striking how far the Church is willing to go to discourage dissent. For example, one Orthodox priest who spoke out against the imprisonment of Mikhail Khdorokovsky (the former head of YUKOS Oil) was defrocked for disciplinary reasons. Other outspoken clergy have met similar kinds of internal punishment. Mansur Mirovalev notes, "Bishop Diomid of Chukotka, who lambasted Alexy II's alleged subservience to the Kremlin, found himself demoted to the rank of a monk."[56] Similarly, a Church council

---

[53] Mirovalev (2009); see also Knox (2005: 105–31).
[54] Koesel and Bunce (2012).
[55] Bryanski (2012).
[56] Mirovalev (2009).

excommunicated Father Gleb Yakunin and accused him of working for the CIA "after he headed a government commission that concluded that most top clerics, including Patriarch Alexy and his future successor Kirill, were KGB informers."[57]

These conclusions introduce a final set of issues. If a rich religious associational life is not a sign of impending crisis, a constraint on those in power, or a Trojan horse for greater liberalization, are religious-state cooperative relations stable and likely to endure? To be sure, it is a precarious business to predict the future of any regime, and particularly two that have experienced such fundamental change in recent decades and embody characteristics of both democratic and authoritarian life. Nevertheless, one can image two competing scenarios for religion and authoritarianism.

The first scenario reflects the status quo in which change in either direction will be slow and incremental. Gradual reforms may allow for selective liberalization (or even deliberalization), but in either case these reforms are unlikely to disrupt current religious-state interaction. This first scenario does not suggest that religious groups will become the handmaidens of the state or that their interests and goals always align with those in power. Rather, in the current political climate in which there is limited space for associational life to function and regime incumbents appear to have a solid monopoly on power, religious groups will continue to align with the powerful and resourceful. This scenario parallels some arguments made by Dietrich Rueschemeyer, Evelyn Huber Stephens, and John D. Stephens regarding the role of religious groups in the process of political liberalization.[58] They argue that religious groups with strong ties to the state function as conduits for the ruling-class hegemony and regime status quo; whereas, religious communities that are able to distance themselves from those in power serve as "strong breeding grounds for democratic movements."[59] Following this line of thinking, as long as religious communities in Russia and China continue to link their futures to those in power, dramatic (or democratic) changes are unlikely.

The second and more pessimistic scenario is that Russia and China will return to their more autocratic roots. Restrictions on associational life will increase and religious groups will become increasingly dependent on their authoritarian overseers. One could imagine the process of deliberalization playing out slightly differently between Russia and China. For instance, it would be unlikely that the Kremlin would openly challenge the Orthodox Church, but it might take steps to reinstitute the Church's prerevolutionary status. A nationalized Church would not only be easier for regime leaders to manipulate but would also lend greater moral authority to those in power. It would seem that some Russian leaders would like to head in this direction. In July 2009, leaders of United Russia announced that the patriarch would be able

---

[57] Ibid.
[58] Rueschemeyer, Stephens, and Stephens (1992).
[59] Ibid., 275.

to review (and modify) drafts of laws introduced in parliament. According to Aleksei Malashenko, the ruling party is not only trying to share responsibility for potentially unpopular decisions with the Church, but is also seeking respect: "United Russia desperately lacks something despite its triumphs in elections throughout the country and the overwhelming majority in the lower house of parliament... It lacks society's respect. It lacks recognition as a genuine political party and not just as an organization founded and pampered by the Kremlin."[60] The question remains: would the Church embrace this role willingly?

In China, a more autocratic turn would also likely result in greater restrictions on religious life. However, rather than institutionalizing a "national religion" as in Russia, control over the five official religions would mean less autonomy for all religious groups operating in the public sphere and more scrutiny of unregistered religious actors. At the same time, there is unlikely to be a return to the antireligious campaigns of the past. It seems that the lessons of the Cultural Revolution have been internalized, and when religious beliefs are driven underground, they tend to grow stronger, create martyrs, and become more difficult for the state to control.[61] Indeed, Ye Xiaowen, the former head of the State Administration of Religious Affairs, has argued as much: "[r]eligion will last for a long time, outliving countries and states... [and] this is also true in a communist country, so communists as materialists should respect this simple truth and govern religious affairs with foresight."[62] An outright assault on religion would be counterproductive to the larger goal of making religion serve the state, and coercion might turn the more docile religious groups into regime enemies.[63] Thus, we would likely need to look for more quiet forms of repressions that indirectly and informally marginalize religious actors.

Neither of these scenarios is particularly optimistic for the expansion of religious liberty in the authoritarian world. At present, Russian and Chinese leaders seem quite content to allow a limited space for associational life to develop, and local governments benefit from extracting valuable resources from these communities. For religious groups, more religious freedom would certainly be welcomed, but at this point they have more to gain by aligning with those in power than opposing them. And yet even in seemingly stable and resilient authoritarian regimes, religious-state interaction is not frozen. Political change will almost certainly take place in the coming years, but it is likely to continue to be incremental and horizontal. In the short term, religious communities and their authoritarian overseers will continue to find innovative solutions to reduce uncertainty and meet pressing needs. Over the long term, if the religious landscape continues to grow at the same pace it has for the past three decades,

---

[60] Malashenko (2009).
[61] Zhong (1998).
[62] *Xinhua* (2011).
[63] Svolik (2012: 159).

the negotiating power of religious communities will likely increase and transform the current bargaining games from asymmetric to more equitable ones. Although it is doubtful that religion will become the "opiate of the state" anytime soon, it will certainly play a role in shaping the future of politics under autocracy and beyond.

APPENDIX A

Methodology and Data

> Authoritarian regimes don't want to be studied.
>
> – Robert Barros[1]

Conducting research in authoritarian regimes is a tricky business.[2] These regimes lack transparency, their inner workings are hidden from view, political winds shift often, there are limits to the information we can collect, and political elites are seldom "helpful" in the kind of data they provide. Research, in short, rarely goes as planned. These problems tend to be compounded when the topic of interest is considered politically sensitive. This not only heightens the risks for informants and local colleagues, but also discourages regime representatives from proving any information lest they be accused of sharing "state secrets." And yet despite these obstacles, or perhaps even because of them, we are drawn to the study of the authoritarian political project.

To navigate the uncertainty of autocracy and sort out the many factors shaping religious-state interaction, this project draws on several methods including in-depth interviews, participant observation, political ethnography, and archival research.[3] Data was collected during twenty-eight months of site-intensive field research divided between Russia and China from 2005 through 2007 and again in 2010 and 2012. Fieldwork was based primarily in four cities (Nizhny Novgorod and Kazan, Russia; Changchun and Shanghai, China) and includes more than 185 semistructured interviews with local government officials, religious leaders and adherents, representatives of faith-based NGOs, and

---

[1] Barros (2005: 36).

[2] On the challenges of studying authoritarian regimes, see Barros (2005); Carlson et al. (2010); see also the "Symposium on Research under Authoritarian Conditions," *APSA-Comparative Democratization Newsletter* 9, no. 2 (May 2011).

[3] On site-intensive methods and fieldwork, see Read (2010).

religious studies experts.[4] In both countries, I interviewed local government officials and bureaucrats responsible for registering and monitoring religious groups. For instance, in Russia I met with municipal-level bureaucrats from the Ministry of Justice (*Ministerstvo justicii RF*) and the Council of Religious Matters for the Cabinet of the Republic of Tatarstan (*Sovet po delam religij pri kabinete ministrov respubliki tatarstan*), and in China with district-level bureaucrats from the Religious Affair Bureau (*zongjiao ju*).[5] However, because religious management is a sensitive issue in both countries, negotiating access to government officials and bureaucrats at times was limited, and responses rarely strayed from official rhetoric. As a result, interviews were supplemented with additional open sources to better capture the interaction of religious and local governments and how their relationship changed over time, such as government speeches, local newspapers, historical gazetteers, archival materials, legal documents, and religious organizations' printed media.

Given the plural religious landscape of Russia and China, I interviewed a representative sample of all religious communities found in each case study, including Buddhist, Taoist, Muslim, Catholic, Protestant, Orthodox Christian (Russian Orthodox and Old Believers), Jewish, and popular religious communities. In each locale, I compiled data on a comprehensive sample of religious communities from several sources, such as public government records, phone books, and religious groups' internal directories. For example, in Kazan, the sample covered 101 religious organizations. In large municipalities such as Shanghai, where the sample included more than 350 religious organizations, I then disaggregated the organizations by district and religious traditions. Working from this sample, I contacted each religious organization listed in the district and requested an interview. The acceptance rate for interviews was approximately 80 percent in Russia and 45 percent in China. Given the lower acceptance rate for interviews in China, the sensitivity of researching religion, and the importance of social networks, interviews were also arranged following the "snowball" sampling technique.[6] Besides sampling horizontally across different religious traditions, I also took great effort to interview vertically within

---

[4] Shanghai municipality is equivalent to a province in China and is therefore divided into eighteen administrative districts and one county. To encourage comparison among the cases, I focused on religious-state interaction at the district-level (*diqu*). I conducted fieldwork in 13 districts with plural religious profiles, including Changning, Chongming, Fengxian, Hongkou, Huangpu, Jingan, Luwan, Pudong, Qingpu, Songjiang, Xujia, Yangpu, and Zhabei.

[5] The central level organization that oversees all religious affairs in China has gone by several names. From 1951 to 1954, this organization was called the Religious Affairs Office (RAO); the name changed to the Religious Affairs Bureau (RAB) from 1954 to 1998. In 1998, RAB was again renamed as the State Administration of Religious Affairs (SARA). The municipal and district-level extensions of SARA continue to use the name Religious Affair Bureau (RAB). In this project, the term "Religious Affairs Bureau" (RAB) refers to religious affairs offices at the local level, unless otherwise indicated.

[6] On the "snowball" method of sampling and negotiating access to closed communities, see Maginn (2007).

each organization. For example, in Protestant churches I met with ministers, deacons, preachers, and laypersons. Whenever possible, I also met with the legal representatives and accountants of religious organizations.

In addition to the legal or state-approved religious communities, whenever possible I also met with unregistered religious communities, from Old Believers, Baptists, and Pentecostals in Russia to members of the Protestant house church movement and the underground Catholic Church in China. Many of these religious communities for various reasons want no relationship with the state and as a result are unregistered and have no legal protections. They hold services in secret, often changing their location on a regular basis, and observation of their religious activities is through invitation only. Throughout the chapters, interviews with unregistered religious communities are included and reveal that they sometimes actively pursue close relations with authorities. However, given the limited access to these groups, the arguments and analysis of the book apply primarily to those organized and legal religious communities operating in the public sphere – that is, religious groups that are registered or seeking registration with the state. I acknowledge an imbalance in this study: it certainly is highly desirable to compare religious-state relations among multiple, underground religious communities, and across different authoritarian systems. At the same time, interviews with these groups were much less systematic for understandable reasons and therefore less amenable to drawing generalizations.

This study also made use of participant observation in religious services and rituals, philanthropic projects, and religious classes. For instance, after attending religious activities – be it a reading of the Koran in Tatar or a Buddhist ceremony – I held focused discussions with religious practitioners to explore how members perceive their religion in society and to what extent their religious values might influence local government decision making. In all cases, to ensure standardization across interviews and cases, I asked a sequence of standardized, open-ended questions.[7] Interviews were conducted in Russian or Mandarin by the author, handwritten notes were taken, and the location was chosen by the informant. Occasionally, a research assistant joined the interviews in China, particularly when conducting research in rural areas where respondents preferred to speak in the local dialect. In these cases, I asked questions in Mandarin and a research assistant translated the interviewee's responses into either Mandarin or English. On average, interviews lasted two hours; however, many extended over several days. Finally, because researching religion and politics in authoritarian regimes is a sensitive topic – especially in China and for some minority faiths in Russia – the identifying information of those interviewed for this study has been omitted or changed.

---

[7] On the "standardized, open-ended" approach to interviewing, see Patton (1990).

APPENDIX B

Interviews Cited

RUSSIA

Interview with Orthodox Father Andre, January 2006, Nizhny Novgorod.

Focused discussion group with Orthodox Christians H, L, M, January 2006, Nizhny Novgorod.

Interview with Pastor Runov, February 2006, Nizhny Novgorod.

Interview with Baptist church leader F, February 2006, Nizhny Novgorod.

Interview with former Scientologist I, February 2006, Nizhny Novgorod.

Interview with Father Alexander, February 2006 and March 2006, Nizhny Novgorod.

Interview with former bureaucrat C, March 2006, Nizhny Novgorod.

Interview with Rabbi Simon Bergman, March 2006, Nizhny Novgorod.

Interview with Pastor Paul, March 2006, Nizhny Novgorod.

Interview with S.V. Rudakov, editor of *Staroobrjadec* (*Old Believers*) newspaper, March 2006, Nizhny Novgorod.

Interview with O. Senjutkina, historian and advisor to Religious Board of Muslims in the Nizhny Novgorod Region (*Duhovnoe upravlenie musul'man Nizhegorodskoj oblasti; DUMNO*), February 2006, March 2006, and July 2012, Nizhny Novgorod.

Interview with the advisor to the *Il'inskaja sloboda* Fund, February 2006, Nizhny Novgorod.

Interview with Umar-khazrat Idrisov, Chairman of the Religious Board of Muslims for the Nizhny Novgorod Region (*Duhovnoe upravlenie musul'man Nizhegorodskoj oblasti; DUMNO*), March 2006, Nizhny Novgorod.

Interview with Damir-khazrat Mukhetdinov, Religious Board of Muslims for the Nizhny Novgorod Region (*Duhovnoe upravlenie musul'man Nizhegorodskoj oblasti; DUMNO*), March 2006, Nizhny Novgorod.

Interview with N.B. Cheremin, consultant for religious organizations for the Nizhny Novgorod Kremlin, March 2006, Nizhny Novgorod.

Interview with Catholic Father Mario, March 2006, Nizhny Novgorod.

Interview with Protestant Pastor Igor, March 2006, Nizhny Novgorod.

Interview with Orthodox Father Igor, editor of the *Nizhegorodskie eparhial'nye vedomosti* (*Nizhny Novgorod Diocese Bulletin*), March 2006, Nizhny Novgorod.

Interview with Protestant Pastor H, March 2006, Nizhny Novgorod.

Interview with Imam S from the Board of Muslims of the Republic of Tatarstan (*Duhovnoe Upravlenie Musul'man Respubliki Tatarstan; DUMRT*), April 2006, Kazan.

Interview with adviser R to President Shaimiev, April 2006, Kazan.

Interview with Imam F, April 2006, Kazan.

Interview with bureaucrat D from Religious Affairs Department, April 2006, Kazan.

Interview with Father Oleg, Rector of the Cathedral of Epiphany of Our Lord, May 2006, Kazan.

Interview with archaeologist from the Tatarstan Academy of Sciences, May 2006, Kazan.

Interview with Pastor Pavel, June 2006, Kazan.

Interview with Damir Iskhaov, Chairman of the Political Council of the Tatar Public Center and fomer leader of the Tatar nationalist movement, June 2006, Kazan.

Interview with Rashit Akhmetov, Leader of the Tatarstan Branch of the Democratic Party of Russia and former leader of the Tatarstan nationalist movement, June 2006, Kazan.

Interview with Krjashen priest Pavel, June 2006, Kazan.

Interview with Pastor Paul, June 2012, Nizhny Novgorod.

Interview with member P of a Pentecostal church, June 2012, Nizhny Novgorod.

Interview with Pentecostal Pastor I, July 2012, Nizhny Novgorod.

Interview with Protestant Pastor H, July 2012, Nizhny Novgorod.

Interview with Pastor Igor Voronin, Bishop of RC XVE (Rossijskaja cerkov' hristian very evangel'skoj), July 2012, Nizhny Novgorod.

Interview with Pentecostal Pastor S, July 2012, Nizhny Novgorod.

Interview with F. Dorofeev, professor at the State Lobachevsky University, June 2012, Nizhny Novgorod.

Interview with Pentecostal Pastor S, July 2012, Nizhny Novgorod

Interview with Pentecostal Pastor Z, July 2012, Nizhny Novgorod.

Interview with charismatic church leader A, July 2012, Nizhny Novgorod.

Interview with charismatic Pastor V, July 2012, Nizhny Novgorod.

CHINA

Interview with CGF church leader A, September 2006, Beijing.
Interview with house church leader B, September 2006, Beijing.
Interview with Protestant minister H, October 2006, Changchun.
Interview with Protestant minister G, October 2006, Changchun.
Interview with house church leader V, October 2006, Beijing.
Interview with Catholic priest A, April 2007, Shanghai.
Interview with Protestant Pastor D, April 2007, Shanghai.
Interview with Catholic priest D, April 2007, Shanghai.
Interview with Catholic priest W, April 2007, Shanghai.
Interview with house church deacon H, April 2007, Shanghai.
Interview with former TSPM employee F, May 2007, Shanghai.
Interview with accountant A for the temple, May 2007, Shanghai.
Interview with Buddhist monk L, May 2007, Shanghai.
Interview with Buddhist monk D, May 2007, Shanghai.
Interview with Catholic layperson G, May 2007, Shanghai.
Interview with Catholic layperson M, May 2007, Shanghai.
Interview with Catholic priest Z, May 2007, Shanghai.
Interview with Mazu Temple worker, May 2007, Songjiang.
Interview with Imam A, May 2007, Songjiang.
Interview with accountant for mosque D, May 2007, Songjiang.
Interview with Taoist priest C from Chenghuang miao, May 2007, Shanghai.
Focused discussion group with Buddhist monks L, A, O, May 2007, Shanghai.
Interview with Buddhist monk B May 2007 and July 2007, Shanghai.
Interview with Buddhist monk A, May 2007 and July 2007, Shanghai.
Interview with deacon C from Protestant church, June 2007, Luwan.
Interview with Protestant minister N, June 2007, Shanghai.
Interview with monk Q at Jing'an temple, May 2007, Shanghai.
Interview with bureaucrat P from the Religious Affairs Bureau, June 2007, Luwan.
Interview with Christian boss Q, June 2007, Shanghai.
Interview with Christian boss J, June 2007, Shanghai.
Interview with SARA bureaucrat O, June 2007, Beijing.
Interview with Catholic priest X, June 2007, Shanghai.
Interview with Religious Affairs Bureau bureaucrat J, June 2007, Shanghai.
Interview with Peter McInnis, Amity Printing Press general manager 1988–1993, June 2007, Shanghai.
Interview with bureaucrat O from SARA, June 2007, Beijing.
Interview with Dr. Theresa Carino, coordinator of the Amity Foundation Hong Kong Office, June 2007, Hong Kong.
Interview with Buddhist monk C, July 2007, Shanghai.
Interview with Protestant minister A, June 2007, Shanghai.
Interview with Sanguan tang elder Y, July 2007, Shanghai.

Interview with Sanguan tang elder G, July 2007, Shanghai.
Interview with Catholic priest A, July 2007, Shanghai.
Interview with Catholic priest B, July 2007, Shanghai.
Interview with Abbot N at Buddhist temple, July 2007, Shanghai.
Interview with Taoist priest V, July 2007, Shanghai.
Interview with Catholic priest L, July 2007, Shanghai.
Interview with Imam W, July 2007, Shanghai.
Interview with Imam Z, July 2007, Shanghai.
Interview with Religious Affair Bureau bureaucrat S, August 2007, Shanghai.
Interview with monk Y from Yufo si, August 2007, Shanghai.
Interview with layperson Z from Jinze Protestant church, August 2007, Jinze.
Interview with worshiper T at bridge, August 2007, Jinze.
Interview with worshiper Y at bridge, August 2007, Jinze.
Interview with worshiper J at bridge, August 2007, Jinze.
Interview with Imam Y, August 2007, Shanghai.
Interview with TSPM Protestant minister X, August 2007, Pudong.
Interview with Christian Boss B, August 2007, Shanghai.
Interview with B.L., SMIC management, August 2007, Shanghai.
Interview with Protestant minister M, August 2007, Shanghai.
Interview with Protestant minister D, August 2007, Shanghai.
Interview with house church pastor E, August 2007, Beijing.
Interview with house church preacher D, August 2007, Shanghai.
Interview with Protestant minister L, September 2007, Shanghai.
Interview with house church pastor K, September 2010, Shanghai.
Interview with Protestant deacon A, October 2010, Shanghai.

Bibliography

"A sud'i kto?" [Who are the judges?]. *Staroobrjadec* 31, July 2004: 4.

Acemoglu, Daron, and James A. Robinson. *Economic Origins of Dictatorship and Democracy*. New York: Cambridge University Press, 2006.

Aikman, David. *Jesus in Beijing*. Washington, DC: Regnery Publishing, 2003.

Albrecht, Holger. "How Can Opposition Support Authoritarianism? Lessons from Egypt." *Democratization* 12, no. 3 (2005): 378–97.

Alles, Gregory D. "Religious Economies and Rational Choice: On Rodney Stark and Roger Finke, Acts of Faith (2000)." In *Contemporary Theories of Religion: A Critical Companion*, edited by Michael Stausberg, 83–98. New York: Routledge, 2009.

Almond, Gabriel A., and Sidney Verba. *The Civic Culture: Political Attitudes and Democracy in Five Nations*. Princeton: Princeton University Press, 1963.

Anholt, Simon. *Competitive Identity: The New Brand Management for Nations, Cities and Regions*. New York: Palgrave Macmillan, 2007.

"Arhierei seli za party" [Archbishops at their desks]. *Nizhegorodskie eparhial'nye novosti* 21, no. 67 (November 2005): 2.

Armanios, Febe. "Test of Faith." *The Cairo Review of Global Affairs*. August 12, 2012. Available at: http://www.aucegypt.edu/gapp/cairoreview/pages/articleDetails.aspx?aid=205 (last accessed September 5, 2013).

Armes, Keith. "Chekists in Cassocks: The Orthodox Church and the KGB." *Demokratizatsiya: The Journal of Post-Soviet Democratization* 1, no. 4 (1994): 72–83.

Arrow, Kenneth J. *Social Choice and Individual Values*. New Haven: Yale University Press, 1951.

Arsent'eva, Svetlana. "Glavnaja pjatnica dlja musul'man Tatarstana" [The main Friday for Tatarstan's Muslims]. *Respublika Tatartsan*, June 25, 2005: 1–2.

"Article 300: The Criminal Law of the People's Republic of China, 1999." Reprinted in *Chinese Law and Government* 32, no. 5 (September–October 1999): 46–50.

Ashiwa, Yoshiko, and David L. Wank. *Making Religion, Making the State*. Stanford: Stanford University Press, 2009.

Ayoob, Mohammed. *The Many Faces of Political Islam: Religion and Politics in the Muslim World*. Ann Arbor: The University of Michigan Press, 2008.

Barros, Robert. "Secrecy and Dictatorship: Some Problems in the Study of Authoritarian Regimes." Mexico City: The Committee on Concepts and Methods (C&M), April 2005.

Baskakov, Nikolai. "Nuzhny li v shkole osnovy pravoslavnoj kul'tury" [Are fundamentals of Orthodox culture needed in the schools?]. *Pravda severa* 235, December 27, 2002. Available at: http://www.arhpress.ru/ps/2002/12/20/21.shtml (last accessed September 4, 2013).

Bays, Daniel H. *A New History of Christianity in China*. Malden: Wiley-Blackwell, 2012.

———. "China's New Regulations of Religious Affairs: A Paradigm Shift." Testimony for the Congressional-Executive Commission on China, March 15, 2005; transcripts available at: www.cecc.gov/pages/roundtables/031405/Bays.php (last accessed September 5, 2013).

———. "Chinese Protestant Christianity Today." *The China Quarterly* 174 (June 2003): 488–504.

Becker, Garry S. *The Economic Approach to Human Behavior*. Chicago: University of Chicago Press, 1976.

Beissinger, Mark R. *Nationalist Mobilization and the Collapse of the Soviet State*. New York: Cambridge University Press, 2003.

Bellah, Robert, and Phillip E. Hammond. *Varieties of Civil Religion*. New York: Harper & Row, 1980.

Berger, Peter. *The Sacred Canopy*. New York: Anchor, 1967.

Berman, Eli. *Radical, Religious and Violent: The New Economics of Terrorism*. Cambridge: MIT Press, 2009.

Berman, Sheri. "Civil Society and the Collapse of the Weimar Republic." *World Politics* 49 (1997): 401–29.

Bermeo, Nancy, and Philip Nord, eds. *Civil Society before Democracy: Lessons from Nineteenth-Century Europe*. Lanham: Rowman & Littlefield, 2002.

Bernhard, Michael. "Civil Society after the First Transition: Dilemmas of Post-Communist Democratization in Poland and Beyond." *Communist and Post-Communist Studies* 29, no. 3 (1996): 309–30.

———. "Civil Society and Democratic Transition in East Central Europe." *Political Science Quarterly* 108, no. 2 (1993): 307–26.

Besley, Timothy, and Masayuki Kudamatsu, "Making Autocracy Work." *Development Economics Discussion Paper Series (UK)* 48 (May 2007): 1–59.

Boltz, Judith Magee. "In Homage to T'ien-Fei." *Journal of the American Oriental Society* 106, no. 1 (1986): 211–32.

Borchert, Thomas. "Of Temples and Tourists." In *State, Market, and Religions in Chinese Societies*, edited by Fenggang Yang and Joseph B. Tamney, 97–111. Boston: Brill, 2005.

Borer, Tristan Anne. *Challenging the State: Churches as Political Actors in South Africa, 1980–1994*. Notre Dame: University of Notre Dame Press, 1998.

Bourdeaux, Michael. "Religion Revives in All Its Variety: Russia's Regions Today." *Religion, State & Society* 28, no. 1 (2000): 9–21.

———. *Gorbachev, Glasnost and the Gospel*. London: Hodder and Stoughton, 1990.

Brady, Henry E., and David Collier, eds. *Rethinking Social Inquiry: Diverse Tools, Shared Standards*. Lanham: Rowman and Littlefield, 2004.

Brook, Timothy, and B. Michael Frolic, eds. *Civil Society in China*. Armonk: M.E. Sharpe, 1997.

Brown, Deborah A. "The Role of Religion in Promoting Democracy in the People's Republic of China and Hong Kong." In *Church and State in 21st Century Asia*, edited by Beatrice Leung, 79–143. Hong Kong: The University of Hong Kong, 1996.

Brownlee, Jason. *Authoritarianism in an Age of Democratization*. New York: Cambridge University Press, 2007.

Bruce, Steve. "The Social Limits on Religious Markets." In *Salvation Goods and Religious Markets*, edited by Jorg Stolz, 81–100. Bern: Peter Lang, 2008.

———. *God Is Dead: Secularization in the West*. Oxford: Blackwell, 2002.

Bruun, Ole. *Fengshui in China: Geomantic Divination between State Orthodoxy and Popular Religion*. Honolulu: University of Hawaii Press, 2003.

Bryanski, Gleb. "Russian Church: Under Attack after Backing Putin." Reuters (Moscow), April 3, 2012. Available at: http://www.reuters.com/article/2012/04/03/us-russia-church-statement-idUSBRE83214B20120403 (last accessed September 4, 2013).

Buchanan, James M., and Gordon Tullock. *The Calculus of Consent: Logical Foundations of Constitutional Democracy*. Ann Arbor: University of Michigan Press, 1974.

Bueno de Mesquita, Bruce, and George Downs. "Development and Democracy." *Foreign Affairs* 84, no. 5 (2005): 77–86.

Bueno de Mesquita, Bruce, and Alastair Smith. *The Dictator's Handbook: Why Bad Behavior Is Almost Always Good Politics*. New York: Public Affairs, 2011.

Bueno de Mesquita, Bruce, Alastair Smith, Randolph M. Siverson, and James D. Morrow. *The Logic of Political Survival*. Cambridge: The MIT Press, 2003.

"Building Harmonious Society Crucial for China's Progress: Hu." *People's Daily*, June 27, 2005. Available at: http://english.peopledaily.com.cn/200506/27/eng20050627_192495.html (last accessed September 4, 2013).

Bukharaev, Ravil Farida Zabirov, and Airat Sitdikov. "Kazan Kremlin: The White, Fairy-tale Palace on the Volga River." *World Heritage Review* 28 (2000): 52–63.

Bunce, Valerie. "Conclusion: Rebellious Citizens and Resilient Authoritarians." In *The New Middle East: Protest and Revolution in the Arab World, edited by* Fawaz A. Gerges. New York: Cambridge University Press, 2013, forthcoming.

———. *Subversive Institutions*. New York: Cambridge University Press, 1999.

———. "The Political Economy of the Brezhnev Era: The Rise and Fall of Corporatism." *British Journal of Political Science* 13 (1983): 129–58.

Bunce, Valerie, and Sharon Wolchik. *Defeating Authoritarian Leaders in Postcommunist Countries*. New York: Cambridge University Press, 2011.

Burawoy, Michael, and Katherine Verdery, eds. *Uncertain Transitions: Ethnographies of Change in the Post Socialist World*. Lahnam: Rowman and Littlefield, 1999.

Burdo, M., and S. B. Filatov, eds. *Atlas Sovremennaja religioznaja zhizn' rossii: opyt sistematcheskogo opisanija*. Tom I–IV [Atlas of contemporary religious life in Russia. Volumes I–IV]. Moscow: Keston Institute, 2005.

"Byt' li Rossii pravoslavnoj?" [Will Russia be Orthodox?]. *Slovo katehizatora* 1 (January 2004): 9.

Cao, Nanlai. *Constructing China's Jerusalem*. Stanford: Stanford University Press, 2011.

———. "Boss Christians: The Business of Religion and the 'Wenzhou Model' of Christian Revival." *The China Journal* 59 (2008): 63–87.

Carlson, Allen, Mary E. Gallagher, Kenneth Lieberthal, and Melanie Manion, eds. *Contemporary Chinese Politics: New Sources, Methods, and Field Strategies*. New York: Cambridge University Press, 2010.

Casanova, Jose. *Public Religions in the Modern World*. Chicago: University of Chicago Press, 1994.

Cavendish, James C. "Christian Base Communities and the Building of Democracy: Brazil and Chile." In *Religion and Democracy in Latin America*, edited by William H. Swatos Jr., 75–92. New Brunswick: Transaction Publishers, 1995.

"Centr social'no-konservativnoj politiki 'Edinoj Rossii' predlozhil pravoslavie v kachestve cennostnogo fundamenta modernizacii" [The center for social and conservative policy of "United Russia" suggested Orthodoxy as the value foundation for modernization]. SOVA Center, February 17, 2010. Available at: http://www.sova-center.ru/religion/news/authorities/religion-general/2010/02/d18005/ (last accessed September 4, 2013).

"Cerkov' i vlast': my vmeste sluzhim otechestvu" [Church and state: together we serve the fatherland]. *Pravoslavnoe Slovo* 3, no. 160 (February 2000): 4.

"Cerkovnoe bogosluzhenie v mestah lishenija svobody" [Church services in prison]. *Nizhegorodskie eparhal'nye novosti* 11, no. 57 (June 2005): 6.

Chambers, Simone, and Will Kymlicka, eds. *Alternative Conceptions of Civil Society*. Princeton: Princeton University Press, 2002.

Chan, Anita. "Revolution or Corporatism? Workers and Trade Unions in Post-Mao China." *The Australian Journal of Chinese Affairs* 29 (1993): 31–61.

Chan, Kim-Kwong. "The Christian Community in China: The Leaven Effect." In *Evangelical Christianity and Democracy in Asia*, edited by David H. Lumsdaine, 43–86. New York: Oxford University Press, 2009.

Chan, Kim-Kwong, and Alan Hunter. "Religion and Society in Mainland China in the 1990s." *Issues & Studies* 30, no. 8 (1994): 52–68.

Chao, Emily. "The Maoist Shaman and the Madman." *Cultural Anthropology* 14, no. 4 (1999): 505–34.

Chao, T'ien-En (Jonathan), and Rosanna Chong. *Dangdai Zhongguo Jidujiao fazhan shi: 1949–1997* [A history of Christianity in contemporary China, 1949–1997]. Taipei: CMI Publishing Co, 1997.

Chau, Adam Yuet, ed. *Religion in Contemporary China*. London: Routledge, 2011.

———. *Miraculous Response: Doing Popular Religion in Contemporary China*. Stanford: Stanford University Press, 2005a.

———. "The Politics of Legitimation and the Revival of Popular Religion in Shaanbei, North-Central China." *Modern China* 31, no. 2 (2005b): 236–78.

———. "Popular Religion in Shaanbei, North-Central China." *Journal of Chinese Religions* 31 (2003): 39–79.

Chaves, Mark. "On the Rational Choice Approach to Religion." *Journal for the Scientific Study of Religion* 34, no. 1 (1995): 98–104.

Chen, Cunfu. "Impact of China's Economic Development on Christian Communities in Zhejiang Province." In *Zhuanxing qi de Zhongguo Jidujiao – Zhejiang Jidujiao gean yanjiu* [Chinese Christianity in transformation – case studies of Christian communities in Zhejiang province], 135–65. Beijing: Dongfang chubanshe, 2005.

Chen, Cunfu, and Huang Tianhai. "The Emergence of a New Type of Christians in China Today." *Review of Religious Research* 46, no. 2 (2004): 183–200.

Chen, Nancy N. *Breathing Spaces*. New York: Columbia University Press, 2003a.

———. "Healing Sects and Anti-Cult Campaigns." *The China Quarterly* 174 (2003b): 505–20.

———."Urban Spaces and Experiences of Qigong." In *Urban Spaces in Contemporary China*, edited by Debra S. Davis, 347–61. Washington, DC: Woodrow Wilson Center Press, 1995.

Chernyshova, Daria. "The Kremlin and the Church: Historic Ties: How does religion influence civil society and what role does it play in our system of government?" *Moscow News*, December 6, 2007. Available at: http://www.russialist.org/2007-252-30.php (last accessed September 4, 2013).

Chesneaux, Jean, ed. *Popular Movements and Secret Societies in China 1840–1950*. Stanford: Stanford University Press, 1972.

"Chinese Religious Leaders Indignant over 'Falun Gong'" [Zongjiao jie dui 'Falun Gong' zuixing biaoshi qianglie fenkai]. *People's Daily* [overseas edition], February 1, 2001: 4.

Chirot, Daniel. "What Happened in Eastern Europe in 1989?" In *Political Protest and Popular Culture in Modern China: Learning from 1989*, edited by Jeffrey N. Wasserstrom and Elizabeth J. Perry, 215–32. Boulder, CO: Westview Press, 1991.

"Chubajs zamalivaet grehi v Nizhegorodskoj oblasti?" [Chubias atones for sins in Nizhny Novgorod Oblast?]. *Novoe Delo* 32, August 5–11, 2004: 8.

"Circular of the Central Committee of the Chinese Communist (CCP) Party on Forbidding Communist Party Members from Practicing 'Falun Dafa'" [Zhonggong zhongyang guanyu Gongchandangyuan bu zhun xiulian 'Falun Dafa' de tongzhi]. *People's Daily* [overseas edition], July 23, 1999: 1.

Collier, David. "Trajectory of a Concept: 'Corporatism' in the Study of Latin American Politics." In *Latin America in Comparative Perspective: New Approaches to Methods and Analysis*, edited by P. Smith, 135–62. Boulder, CO: Westview Press, 1995.

Collier, Ruth Berins, and David Collier. "Inducements versus Constraints: Disaggregating 'Corporatism'." *American Political Science Review* 73, no. 4 (December 1979): 967–86.

Colton, Timothy J. *Yeltsin: A Life*. New York: Basic Books, 2008.

Colton, Timothy, and Michael McFaul. "Are Russians Undemocratic?" *Post-Soviet Affairs* 18, no. 2 (2002): 91–121.

Crawshaw, Steve, and Vesna Peric-Zimonjic. "Orthodox church tells Milosevic to hand over presidency to rival." *The Independent UK*. September 29, 2000. Available at: http://www.independent.co.uk/news/world/europe/orthodox-church-tells-milosevic-to-hand-over-presidency-to-rival-699599.html (last accessed September 4, 2013).

Cristi, Marcela. *From Civil to Political Religion: The Intersection of Culture, Religion and Politics*. Ontario: Wilfrid Laurier University Press, 2001.

Curtis, Michael. *Verdict on Vichy: Power and Prejudice in the Vichy France Regime*. London: Arcade Publishing, 2003.

de Tocqueville, Alexis. *Democracy in America*. Translated and edited by Harvey Mansfield and Delba Winthrop. Chicago: University of Chicago Press, 2000 [1835].

Dean, Kenneth. *Taoist Ritual and Popular Cults of Southeast China*. Princeton: Princeton University Press, 1993.

Debardeleben, Joan. "The Development of Federalism in Russia." In *Beyond the Monolith*, edited by Peter J. Stavrakis et al., 35–56. Washington, DC: The Woodrow Wilson International Center Press, 1997.

Delury, John. "'Harmonious' in China." *Policy Review* 148 (2008): 38–44.

Devicyn, Viktor. "Svoboda very: horosho ili ploho?" [Freedom of belief: good or bad?]. *Rossijskaja gazeta* 86, April 23, 2004: 6.

Devlet, Nadir. "The Djadid Movement and Institutions of Islamic Education in the Volga-Ural Region." In *Proceedings of the International Symposium on Islamic Civilisation in the Volga-Ural Region: Kazan, 8–11 June 2001*, edited by Ali Çaksu, Radik Mukhammetshin, and Ekmeleddin Ihsanoglu, 65–76. Istanbul: Research Centre for Islamic History, Art and Culture, 2004.

Diamond, Larry. *Developing Democracy: Toward Consolidation.* Baltimore: Johns Hopkins University Press, 1999.

———. "Toward Democratic Consolidation." *Journal of Democracy* 5, no. 3 (1994): 4–17.

———. "Economic Development and Democracy Reconsidered." *American Behavioral Scientist* 35, no. 4/5 (1992): 450–99.

Diamond, Larry, Marc F. Plattner, and Philip J. Costopoulous, eds. *World Religions and Democracy.* Baltimore: Johns Hopkins University Press, 2005.

Dickson, Bruce. J. "Sustainability and Party Rule in China: Coercion, Co-optation and Their Consequences." In *The Dynamics of Democratization: Dictatorship, Development and Diffusion* edited by Nathan Brown, 93–117. Baltimore: Johns Hopkins University Press, 2011.

———. "Cooptation and Corporatism in China: The Logic of Party Adaption." *Political Science Quarterly* 115, no. 4 (2000): 517–40.

Dobson, William J. *The Dictator's Learning Curve: Inside the Global Battle for Democracy.* New York: Doubleday, 2012.

"Document 6: A Circular on Some Problems Concerning the Further Improvement of Work on Religion" [Zhonggongzhongyang Guowuyuan guanyu jinyibu zuo hao zongjiao gongzuo ruogan wenti de tongzhi] (February 5, 1991). Reprinted in *Chinese Law and Government* 33, no. 2 (March/April 2000): 56–63.

"Document 3: Circular on Stepping Up Control over the Catholic Church to Meet the New Situation" [Guanyu zai xin xingshi xia jiaqiang Tianzhujiao gongzuo de baogao] (February 17, 1989) released by the Central Offices of the Communist Party and the State Council. Reprinted in *Chinese Law and Government* 33, no. 2 (March/April 2000): 49–55.

Dolgov, Anna. "Moscow Scientology Center Raided." Associated Press, February 26, 1999.

Dubas, Agata. "The New Patriarch of Moscow and All Russia to Continue the Alliance of Church and State." *Center for Eastern Studies Commentary* 20 (February 9, 2009): 1–6.

Dunch, Ryan. "Christianity and 'Adaptation to Socialism.'" In *Chinese Religiosities: Afflictions of Modernity and State Formation*, edited by Mayfair Mei-hui Yang, 155–78. Berkeley and Los Angeles: University of California Press, 2008.

———. "Protestant Christianity in China Today: Fragile, Fragmented, Flourishing." In *China and Christianity*, edited by Stephen Uhalley Jr. and Xiaoxin Wu, 195–216. New York: M.E. Sharpe, 2001.

Dvorkin, Alexander. "A Presentation on the Situation in Russia: Scientology in Russia." *Spirituality in East & West* 11 (1998): 13–20.

Eckholm, Erik. "The Chinese Professor Who Started a Ruckus." *New York Times*, February 5, 2001. Available at: http://www.nytimes.com/2001/02/05/world/the-chinese-professor-who-started-a-ruckus.html (last accessed September 4, 2013).

Egorov, Georgy, Sergei Guriev, and Konstantin Sonon. "Why Resource-poor Dictators Allow Freer Media." *American Political Science Review* 103 (2009): 645–68.

Elliott, Mark, and Sharyl Corrado. "The 1997 Russian Law on Religion: The Impact on Protestants." *Religion, State and Society* 27, no. 1 (1999): 109–43.

Encarnacion, Omar G. *The Myth of Civil Society: Social Capital and Democratic Consolidation in Spain and Brazil.* New York: Palgrave, 2003.

Esman, Milton J., and Norman T. Uphoff. *Local Organizations: Intermediaries in Rural Development.* Ithaca: Cornell University Press, 1984.

Evans, Peter. "The Eclipse of the State? Reflections on Stateness in an Era of Globalization." *World Politics* 50, no. 1 (1997a): 62–87.

———, ed. *State-Society Synergy: Government and Social Capital in Development.* Berkeley: International and Area Studies, University of California, Berkeley, 1997b.

Fagan, Geraldine. *Believing in Russia: Religious Policy After Communism.* New York: Routledge, 2013.

———. "Russia: Putin sounds final bell for Orthodox culture classes?" *Forum 18* (September 24, 2007). Available at: http://www.forum18.org/Archive.php?article_id=1021&printer=Y (last accessed September 5, 2013).

Fan, Liang. "Fojiao yu shehuizhuyi jingshen wenming jianshe" [Buddhism and the construction of spiritual civilization of socialism]. *Dangdai zongjiao yanjiu* 30 (1998): 9–10.

Froese, Paul. *The Plot to Kill God: Findings from the Soviet Experiment in Secularization.* Berkeley, Los Angeles: University of California Press, 2008.

———. "After Atheism: An Analysis of Religious Monopolies in the Post-Communist World." *Sociology of Religion* 65 (2004): 57–75.

Fandong Hui-Dao-Men jianjie [An introduction to the reactionary sects and societies]. Beijing: Qunzhong chubanshe, 1985, chap. 2. Translated by Robin Munro in *Chinese Sociology and Anthropology* 21, no. 4 (Fall 1988–Summer 1989): 49–84.

"Federalnyi Zakon 'O svobode sovesti i o religioznyh ob"edinenijah'" [Federal law 'On freedom of conscience and on religious associations' No. 135-FZ] September 26, 1997.

Fielder, Katrin. "China's 'Christianity Fever' Revisited: Toward a Community-Oriented Reading of Christian Conversion in China." *Journal of Current Chinese Affairs* 39, no. 4 (2010): 71–109.

Filatov, Sergei B. "Orthodox Church in Russia: Post-Atheist Faith." *Studies in World Christianity* 14, no. 2 (2008): 187–202.

———, ed. *Religija i Obshestvo* [Religion and society]. Moscow: Letnij sad, 2002.

———. "Sects and New Religious Movements in Post-Soviet Russia." In *Proselytism and Orthodoxy in Russia,* edited by John Witte Jr. and Michael Bourdeaux, 163–84. Maryknoll, NY: Orbis, 1999.

Filatov, Sergei B., and Roman H. Lunkin. "Statistika rossijskoj religioznosti: Magija cifr i neodnoznachnaja real'nost'" [Russian religious statistics: The magic of numbers and ambigious reality]. *Sociologija religii* (2005): 2–45.

Finke, Roger, and Rodney Stark. *The Churching of America, 1776–2005: Winner and Losers in Our Religious Economy.* New Brunswick, NJ: Rutgers University Press, 2005.

Fleet, Michael, and Brian H. Smith. *The Catholic Church and Democracy in Chile and Peru*. Notre Dame, IN: University of Notre Dame Press, 1997.

Foster, Kenneth W. "Associations in the Embrace of an Authoritarian State: State Domination of Society." *Comparative International Development* 35, no. 4 (2001): 84–109.

Fox, Jonathan. *A World Survey of Religion and the State*. New York: Cambridge University Press, 2008.

———. *Ethnoreligious Conflict in the Late 20th Century: A General Theory*. Lanham, MD: Lexington Books, 2002.

"Freedom for Religion, No Room for Evil Cults." *People's Daily*, February 20, 2001. Available at: http://english.people.com.cn/200102/20/eng20010220_62831. html (last accessed September 4, 2013).

Froese, Paul. *The Plot to Kill God: Findings from the Soviet Experiment in Secularization*. Berkeley: University of California Press, 2008.

———. "After Atheism: An Analysis of Religious Monopolies in the Post-Communist World." *Sociology of Religion* 65 (2004): 57–75.

Frolic, B. Michael. "State-led Civil Society." In *Civil Society in China*, edited by Timothy Brook and B. Michael Frolic, 46–67. Armonk, NY: M.E. Sharpe, 1997.

Gamzin, Maksim. "Kapkan bezgranichnoj svobody: Ne pora li cekty ob"javit' vne zakona?" [The trap of unlimited freedom: Is it time to outlaw sects?]. *Prospekt* 7, February 17, 2004: 3.

Gandhi, Jennifer. *Political Institutions Under Dictatorship*. New York: Cambridge University Press, 2008.

Gandhi, Jennifer, and Adam Przeworski. "Authoritarian Institutions and the Survival of Autocrats." *Comparative Political Studies* 40, no. 11 (2007): 1279–301.

———. "Cooperation, Cooptation and Rebellion Under Dictatorships." *Economics and Politics* 18, no. 1 (2006): 1–26.

Gandhi, Jennifer, and Ellen Lust-Okar. "Elections Under Authoritarianism." *Annual Review of Political Science* 12 (June 2009): 403–22.

Gautier, Mary L. "Church Attendance and Religious Belief in Postcommunist Societies." *Journal for the Scientific Study of Religion* 36, no. 2 (1997): 289–97.

Ge, Zhuang. "Qianxi xiejiao" [An interpretation of the cults]. *Dangdai zongjiao yanjiu* 28 (1997): 33–7.

Geddes, Barbara. "Authoritarian Breakdown: Empirical Test of a Game Theoretic Argument." Paper presented at annual meeting of American Political Science Association, Atlanta, Georgia, 1999.

Gel'man, Vladimir, and Cameron Ross, eds. *The Politics of Sub-national Authoritarianism in Russia*. Burlington, UK: Ashgate, 2010.

Gibson, James. "Social Networks, Civil Society and the Prospects for Consolidating in Russia's Democratic Transition." *American Journal of Political Science* 45, no. 1 (2001): 51–68.

Gill, Anthony J. *The Political Origins of Religious Liberty*. New York: Cambridge University Press, 2008.

———. "Religion and Democracy in South America." In *Religion and Politics in Comparative Perspective*, edited by Ted Gerard Jelen and Clyde Wilcox, 195–224. New York: Cambridge University Press, 2002.

———. *Rendering unto Caesar: The Catholic Church and the State in Latin America*. Chicago: University of Chicago Press, 1998.

Gilley, Bruce. *The Right to Rule.* New York: Columbia University Press, 2009.

Gladney, Dru C. *Making Majorities.* Stanford: Stanford University Press, 1998.

Goldstone, Jack. "Understanding the Revolutions of 2011: Weakness and Resilience in Middle Eastern Autocracies." *Foreign Affairs* 90, no. 8 (2011): 8–16.

Goodman, Bryna. *Native Place, City, and Nation: Regional Networks and Identities in Shanghai, 1853–1937.* Berkeley: University of California Press, 1995.

Goodman, David S.G., and Gerald Segal, eds. *China Deconstructs: Politics, Trade and Regionalism.* London: Routledge, 1994.

Goossaert, Vincent, and David A. Palmer. *The Religious Question in Modern China.* Chicago: University of Chicago Press, 2011.

"Gorbachev criticizes Putin's party." AP interview by Dan Perry, March 5, 2009.

Graney, Kate. "Making Russia Multicultural: Kazan at Its Millennium and Beyond." *Problems of Post-Communism* 54, no. 6 (2007): 17–27.

Greeley, Andrew. "A Religious Revival in Russia?" *Journal for the Scientific Study of Religion* 33, no. 3 (1994): 253–72.

Gries, Peter Hays. "Narratives to Live By: The Century of Humiliation and Chinese National Identity Today." In *China's Transformations*, edited by Lionel M. Jensen and Timothy B. Weston, 112–28. Lanham: Rowman & Littlefield Publishers, 2007.

Grim, Brian J., and Roger Finke. *The Price of Freedom Denied: Religious Persecution and the Conflict in the Twenty-First Century.* New York: Cambridge University Press, 2011.

Grove, Thomas. "Church should have more control over Russian life: Putin." *Reuters-Moscow.* February 1, 2013.

Grzymala-Busse, Anna. "Why Comparative Politics Should Take Religion (More) Seriously." *Annual Review of Political Science* 15: 421–42.

Gu, Ruizhen. "CPC official calls for positive role of religion in development" [Yu zhengsheng: Fahui zongjiao jiji zuoyong cujin jingji shehui fazhan]. *People's Daily*, January 24, 2013. Available at: http://www.cppcc.people.com.cn/n/2013/0124/c45579-20308181-2.html (last accessed September 5, 2013).

Gu, Yongliang, and Xueyun Zhu, eds. *Jinshan nianjian 2001* [Jinshan yearbook 2001]. Shanghai: Hanyu dacidian chubanshe, 2001.

Gudkov, Lev. "Russia – A Society in Transition?" *Telos* (Summer 2001): 9–30.

Gunn, T. Jeremy. "The Law of the Russian Federation on the Freedom of Conscience and Religious Associations from a Human Rights Perspective." In *Proselytism and Orthodoxy in Russia*, edited by John Witte Jr. and Michael Bourdeaux, 239–64. Maryknoll, NY: Orbis, 1999.

Haber, Stephen. "Authoritarian Government." In *The Oxford Handbook of Political Economy*, edited by Barry R. Weingast and Donald A. Wittman, 693–707. Oxford: Oxford University Press, 2006.

Hakimov, Rafael, and Valiulla Jakupov. "Bor'ba novogo i starogo v Islame" [The struggle between old and new in Islam]. *Minaret* 3 (2004): 53–63.

Hale, Henry E. "The Parade of Sovereignties: Testing Theories of Secession in the Soviet Setting." *British Journal of Political Science* 30, no. 1 (2000): 31–56.

Han, Chengpeng. "'Yansegeming' dui dang de xianjinxing jianshe de qishi" [Reflections on the 'Color Revolutions' for the CCP]. *Zhonggong Tianjin shiwei dangxiao xuebao* 2 (2006): 14–18.

Hardin, Russell. *One for All: The Logic of Group Conflict.* Princeton: Princeton University Press, 1995.

Harrell, Steven, and Elizabeth J. Perry. "Syncretic Sects in Chinese Society: An Introduction." *Modern China* 8, no. 3 (1982): 283–303.

Havel, Václav, John Keane, and Steven Lukes. *The Power of the Powerless: Citizens against the State in Central-Eastern Europe.* New York: M.E. Sharpe, 1985.

Haynes, Jeffrey. "Religion and democratization: An introduction." *Democratization* 16, no. 6 (December 2009): 1041–57.

He, Huiming. *Songjiang nianjian, 2005* [Songjiang yearbook, 2005]. Shanghai: Hanyu da cidian chubanshe, 2005.

_____. *Songjiang nianjian, 2000* [Songjiang yearbook, 2000]. Shanghai: Shanghai shehui kexueyuan chubanshe, 2001.

_____. *Songjiang xianzhi, 1991* [Songjiang county gazetteer, 1991] Shanghai: Renmin chubanshe, 1991.

He, Huiming, Siwei Zhang, and Yue Ou. *Songjiang nianjian, 2004* [Songjiang yearbook, 2004]. Shanghai: Hanyu da cidian chubanshe, 2004.

Henderson, Sarah. *Building Democracy in Contemporary Russia.* Ithaca: Cornell University Press, 2003.

Herszenhorn, David. "Radical Islam Attacks in a Moderate Region Unnerve the Kremlin." *New York Times*, August 25, 2012. Available at: http://www.nytimes.com/2012/08/26/world/europe/radical-islamic-attacks-in-moderate-region-unnerve-kremlin.html?pagewanted=all&_r=0 (last accessed September 4, 2013).

Hertog, Steffen. *Princes, Brokers and Bureaucrats: Oil and the State in Saudi Arabia.* Ithaca: Cornell University Press, 2010.

Hildebrandt, Timothy. "The Political Economy of Social Organization Registration in China." *The China Quarterly* 208 (December 2011): 970–89.

Hillman, Ben. "The Rise of the Community in Rural China: Village Politics, Cultural Identity and Religious Revival in a Hui Hamlet." *The China Journal* 51 (2004): 53–73.

Hlaing, Kyaw Yin. "Challenging the Authoritarian State: Buddhist Monks and Peaceful Protests in Burma." *The Fletcher Forum of World Affairs* 32, no. 1 (2008): 125–44.

Hobsbawm, Eric J. "Introduction: Inventing Traditions." In *The Invention of Tradition*, edited by Eric J. Hobsbawm and Terence Ranger, 1–14. New York: Cambridge University Press, 1990.

Homer, Lauren, and Lawrence Uzzell. "Federal and Provincial Religious Freedom Laws in Russia." In *Proselytism and Orthodoxy in Russia*, edited by John Witte Jr. and Michael Bourdeaux, 284–320. Maryknoll, NY: Orbis, 1999.

Horowitz, Donald L. *A Democratic South Africa?* Berkeley: University of California Press, 1991.

Howard, Marc Morjé. *The Weakness of Civil Society in Post-Communist Europe.* New York: Cambridge University Press, 2003.

Hu, Ping. "The Falungong Phenomenon." *China Rights Forum* 4 (2003): 11–27.

Huang, Xianian. "Dangdai hanchuan dacheng Fojiao yu Zhongguo lvyou – qianxi zhuanxing qi de Zhongguo hanchuan Fojiao lvyou gongneng de bianhua" [The change in the function of Chinese Buddhism tourism]. *Dangdai zongjiao yanjiu* 59 (2005): 5–13.

Huard, Raymond. "Political Association in Nineteenth-Century France: Legislation and Practice." In *Civil Society Before Democracy: Lessons from Nineteenth Century*

Europe, edited by Nancy Bermeo and Philip Nords, 135–53. Lanham, MD: Rowman and Littlefield, 2000.

Hunter, Alan, and Kim-Kwong Chan. *Protestantism in Contemporary China*. Cambridge: Cambridge University Press, 1993.

Huntington, Samuel P. *The Third Wave: Democratization in the Late Twentieth Century*. Norman: University of Oklahoma Press, 1991.

———. "The Clash of Civilizations?" *Foreign Affairs* 72, no. 3 (Summer 1993): 22–49.

Hurst, William. "Cases, Questions, and Comparison in Research on Contemporary Chinese Politics." In *Contemporary Chinese Politics: New Sources, Methods, and Field Strategies*, edited by Allen Carlson, Mary E. Gallagher, Kenneth Lieberthal, and Melanie Manion, 162–77. New York: Cambridge University Press, 2010.

Iannaccone, Laurence R. "Rational Choice: Framework for the Scientific Study of Religion." In *Rational Choice Theory and Religion: Summary and Assessment*, edited by Lawrence A. Young, 25–44. New York: Routledge, 1997.

———. "Voodoo Economics?: Reviewing the Rational Choice Approach to Religion." *Journal for the Scientific Study of Religion* 34, no. 1 (1995): 76–89.

"Il'inskaja sloboda zhdet patriarha Alekseja II i 84 mln rublei iz federal'nogo budget" [Ilinskaja sloboda is awaiting Patriarch Alexsi II and 84 million rubles from the federal budget]. *Kommersant'* 47, March 17, 2004: 16.

Iritani, Evelyn. "China's Next Challenge: Mastering the Microchip." *Los Angeles Times*, October 22, 2002. Available at: http://articles.latimes.com/2002/oct/22/business/fi-china3 (last accessed March 15, 2013).

Jamal, Amaney. *Barriers to Democracy: The Other Side of Social Capital in Palestine and the Arab World*. Princeton: Princeton University Press, 2007.

Ji, Zhe. "Chinese Buddhism as a Social Force: Reality and Potential of Thirty Years of Revival." *Chinese Sociological Review* 45, no. 2 (Winter 2012-2013): 8–26.

———. "Buddhism and the State." *China Perspectives* 55 (2004): 2–12.

Jia, Hao, and Zhimin Lin, eds. *Changing Central-Local Relations in China: Reform and State Capacity*. Boulder, CO: Westview Press, 1994.

Jin, Bp. Aloysius Luxian. "400 Years of Catholicism in Shanghai: A Pastoral Letter Issued at Christmas 2007." Translated by Michael J. Sloboda, M.M., and reprinted in *Tripod* 28, no. 149 (Spring 2008). Available at: http://www.hsstudyc.org.hk/en/tripod_en/en_tripod_149_02.html (last accessed September 5, 2013).

Jin, Hua, Su Kui, Jin Zhou, and Ni Feng. *Jilinsheng zhi, Zongjiaozhi [Jilin Provincial Gazeteer, Religious Gazeteer]*. Changchun: Jilin renmin chubanshe, 2000.

Jin, Luxian. *Jinri Tianzhujiao Shanghai jiaoqu* [Catholic Church in Shanghai today]. Shanghai: Tianzhujiao Shanghai jiaoqu guangqi she, 2000.

Jinshan nianjian bianzuan weiyuanhui. *Jinshan nianjian 1996* [Jinshan yearbook 1996]. Shanghai: Shanghai shehui kexueyuan chubanshe, 1996.

Johnston, Hank, and Jozef Figa. "The Church and Political Opposition: Comparative Perspectives on Mobilization Against Authoritarian Regimes." *Journal for the Scientific Study of Religion* 27, no. 1 (1988): 32–47.

Jowitt, Ken. *The New World Disorder: The Leninist Extinction*. Berkeley: University of California Press, 1992.

Juergensmeyer, Mark. *Terror in the Mind of God*. Berkeley: University of California Press, 2003.

Kääriäinen, Kimmo. *Religion in Russia after the Collapse of Communism*. New York: The Edwin Mellen Press, 1998.

Kahn, Jeff. "The Parade of Sovereignties: Establishing the Vocabulary of the New Russian Federalism." *Post-Soviet Affairs* 16, no. 1 (2000): 58–89.

Kalyvas, Stathis. *The Rise of Christian Democracy in Europe*. Ithaca: Cornell University Press, 1996.

Kamrava, Mehran, and Frank O'Mora. "Civil Society and Democratization in Comparative Perspective: Latin America and the Middle East." *Third World Quarterly* 19, no. 5 (1998): 893–915.

"Karmelitkam ne razreshili zhit" v kottedzhom poselke" [Carmelites are not allowed to live in the cottage settlement]. *Kommersant'* 4, March 4, 2004: 16.

Katzenstein, Peter J. *Small States in World Markets*. Ithaca: Cornell University Press, 1985.

Kennedy, Scott, ed. *Beyond the Middle Kingdom: Comparative Perspectives on China's Capitalist Transformation*. Stanford: Stanford University Press, 2011.

Kertzer, David I. *Ritual, Politics and Power*. New Haven: Yale University Press, 1988.

Kindopp, Jason. "Fragmented yet Defiant: Protestant Resilience under Chinese Communist Party Rule." In *God and Caesar in China*, edited by Jason Kindopp and Carol Lee Hamrin, 122–45. Washington, DC: Brookings Institution Press, 2004a.

———. "The Politics of Protestantism in Contemporary China: State Control, Civil Society, and Societal Movement in a Single-Party State." Ph.D. dissertation, George Washington University, 2004b.

Kindopp, Jason, and Carol Lee Hamrin, eds. *God and Caesar in China: Policy Implications of Church-State Tensions*. Washington, DC: Brookings Institution Press, 2004.

Kinossian, Nadir V. "The Politics of the City Image: The Resurrection of the Kul-Sharif Mosque in the Kazan Kremlin (1995–2005)." *Architectural Theory Review* 13, no. 2 (2008): 190–208.

Kipnis, Andrew. "The Flourishing of Religion in Post-Mao China and the Anthropological Category of Religion." *The Australian Journal of Anthropology* 12, no. 1 (2001): 32–46.

Kirill, Metropolitan of Smolensk and Kaliningrad. "The Russian Orthodox Church and the Third Millennium." Reprinted in *Ecumenical Review* 52, no. 3 (2000): 300–8.

Kirkow, Peter. *Russia's Provinces*. New York: St. Martin's Press, 1998.

Kitschelt, Herbert. "Linkages between Citizens and Politicians in Democratic Polities." *Comparative Political Studies* 33, no. 6/7 (2000): 845–79.

Kitschelt, Herbert, and Steven I. Wilkinson, eds. *Patrons, Clients and Policies: Patterns of Democratic Accountability and Political Competition*. New York: Cambridge University Press, 2007.

Klein, Thoralf, and Christian Meyer. "Beyond the Market: Exploring the Religious Field in Modern China." *Religion* 41, no. 4 (2011): 529–34.

Knox, Zoe. *Russian Society and the Orthodox Church: Religion in Russia after Communism*. London: Routledge Curzon, 2005.

Koesel, Karrie J. "The Rise of a Chinese House Church: The Organizational Weapon." *The China Quarterly* (2013): 1–18.

Koesel, Karrie J., and Valerie J. Bunce. "Diffusion-Proofing: Russian and Chinese Responses to Waves of Popular Mobilizations Against Authoritarian Rulers." *Perspectives on Politics* 11, no. 3 (2013): 753–68.

Koesel, Karrie J., and Valerie J. Bunce. "Putin, Popular Protests, and Political Trajectories: Russia in Comparative Perspective." *Post-Soviet Affairs* 28, no. 4 (2012): 403–23.

Kolesnikov, Andrej. "Voenno-pravoslavnyj uklon" [Military-Orthodox bias]. *Gazeta. Ru.* November 8, 2011. Available at: http://www.gazeta.ru/column/kolesnikov/ 3825730.shtml (last accessed September 4, 2013).

Kolymagin, Boris. "Controversy over Religion in Schools: Law of God in Schools." *Vremia MN*, February 1, 2003.

"Komu meshajut nizhegorodskie katoliki?" [Who is bothered by the Nizhny Novgorod Catholics?]. *Religija* 39, no. 251 (2001): 11.

Kotoshikhin, Grigoriy. "Religija i pervyj tur vyborov glavy goroda Nizhnego Novgoroda" [Religion and the first-round of mayoral elections in Nizhny Novgorod]. September 16, 2002. Available at: http://kotoshihin.narod.ru/art2002/elek2002.htm (last accessed September 5, 2013).

Kravtsova, Yekaterina. "'Blasphemy Bill' Passes Duma Unanimously." *The Moscow Times* 5146, June 11, 2013. Available at: http://www.themoscowtimes.com/news/ article/blasphemy-bill-passes-duma-unanimously/481495.html (last accessed September 9, 2013).

Krishna, Anirudh. "Enhancing Political Participation in Democracies: What Is the Role of Social Capital?" *Comparative Political Studies* 35, no. 4 (2002): 437–60.

"Kruglyj stol s ostrymi uglami" [Roundtable with sharp corners]. *Staroobrjadec* 31, July 2004: 4.

Kubik, Jan. "Between the State and Networks of 'Cousins': The Role of Civil Society and Non-Civil Associations in the Democratization of Poland." *Civil Society Before Democracy: Lessons from Nineteenth Century Europe*, edited by Nancy Bermeo and Philip Nord, 181–207. Lanham, MD: Rowman and Littlefield, 2000.

———. *The Power of Symbols against the Symbols of Power: The Rise of Solidarity and the Fall of State Socialism in Poland*. University Park: Pennsylvania State University Press, 1994.

"Kul't i kul'tura delit imushchestvo" [Cult and culture to divide property]. *Kommersant'* 90, no. 4390, May 24, 2010. Available at: http://www.kommersant.ru/doc.aspx? DocsID=1374481 (last accessed September 4, 2013).

Kuran, Timur. "Now Out of Never: The Element of Surprise in the Eastern European Revolution of 1989." *World Politics* 44, no. 1 (1991): 7–48.

Kuznetsov, Oleg. "Sectarian Revolution." *Zavtra* 49, December 10, 1996. Available at: http://www2.stetson.edu/~psteeves/relnews/sectseng1012.html (last accessed September 4, 2013).

Kuo, Cheng-tian. "Chinese Religious Reform." *Asian Survery* 51, no. 6 (November/December 2011): 1042–64.

Lam, Anthony. "A review of Catholic real estate issues in China." *Tripod* 26, no. 140 (2006). Available at: http://www.hsstudyc.org.hk/en/tripod_en/en_tripod_140_05.html (last accessed September 5, 2013).

Lam, Willy Wo-Lap. "Jiang Compares Sect's Threat to Solidarity." *South China Morning Post*, February 12, 2000: 7.

Lambert, Tony. "Counting Christians in China: A Cautionary Report." *International Bulletin of Missionary Research* 27, no. 1 (2003): 6–10.

_____. *China's Christian Millions*. Oxford: Monarch Books, 1999.

Landry, Pierre F. *Decentralized Authoritarianism in China: The Communist Party's Control of Local Elites in the Post-Mao Era*. New York: Cambridge University Press, 2008.

Lang, Graeme, Selina Ching Chan, and Lars Ragvald. "Folk Temples and the Chinese Religious Economy." *Interdisciplinary Journal of Research on Religion* 1, no. 4 (2005): 1–9.

Langohr, Vickie. "Too Much Civil Society, Too Little Politics." *Comparative Politics* 36, no. 2 (2004): 181–204.

Leahy, Anne. "Putin's Russia." *International Journal* 55, no. 4 (2000): 633–46.

"Leap of Faith: Religious Red Songs Go Too Far, Say Critics." *Want China Times*, July 1, 2011. Available at: http://www.wantchinatimes.com/news-subclass-cnt.aspx?id=20110701000015&cid=1101 (last accessed February 24, 2013).

Lee, Ching Kwan. "Pathways of Labour Insurgency." In *Chinese Society: Change, Conflict and Resistance*, edited by Elizabeth J. Perry and Mark Selden, 71–92. London and New York: RoutledgeCurzon, 2003.

Lemarchand, René. "Political Clientelism and Ethnicity in Tropical Africa: Competing Solidarities in Nation Building." *American Political Science Review* 66, no. 1 (1972): 68–90.

Leung, Beatrice. "China and Falun Gong: Party and Society Relations in the Modern Era." *Journal of Contemporary China* 11, no. 33 (2002): 761–84.

_____. *Sino-Vatican Relations: Problems in Conflicting Authority 1976–1986*. Cambridge: Cambridge University Press, 1992.

Levine, Daniel H. "Conclusion: Evangelicals and Democracy the Experience of Latin America in Context." In *Evangelical Christianity and Democracy in Latin America*, edited by Paul Freston, 207–33. Oxford: Oxford University Press, 2008.

Levitsky, Steven, and Lucan Way. *Competitive Authoritarianism: Hybrid Regimes after the Cold War*. New York: Cambridge University Press, 2010.

Levy, Richard. "Corruption, Economic Crime and Social Transformation since the Reform: The Debate in China." *Australian Journal of Chinese Affairs* 33 (1995): 1–25.

Li, Jinxin. "Guanche dangde zongjiao zhengce, weihu zuguo tongyi he minzu tuanjie" [Adhering to the party's religious policy, maintaining the unification of the motherland and the ethnic cohesion]. *Dangdai zongjiao yanjiu* 27 (1997): 5–9.

Li, Lulu. *Mazu xinyang* [The folk belief of Mazu]. Taipei: Han yang, 1995.

Li, Pingye. "90 Niandai Zhongguo zongjiao fazhan zhuangkuang baogao" [A report on the development of religion in China in the 1990s]. *Journal of Christian Culture* 2 (1999): 201–22.

Li, Shufeng, and Wei Di. "Leaders of Five Major Religious Groups Condemn 'Falun Gong'" [Quanguo wuda zongjiao tuanti fennu shengtao "Falun Gong"]. *People's Daily*, March, 16, 2001: 5.

Li, Si-ming, and Wing-shing Tang, eds. *China's Regions, Polity and Economy: A Study of Spatial Transformation in the Post-Reform Era*. Hong Kong: The Chinese University Press, 2000.

Lian, Xi. *Redeemed by Fire: The Rise of Popular Christianity in Modern China*. New Haven: Yale University Press, 2010.

Lieberthal, Kenneth G. "Introduction: The 'Fragmented Authoritarianism' Model and Its Limitations." In *Bureaucracy, Politics, and Decision Making in Post-Mao China*, edited by Kenneth G. Lieberthal and David M. Lampton, 1–30. Berkeley: University of California Press, 1992.

Lijphart, Arend. *Democracy in Plural Societies*. New Haven: Yale University Press, 1977.

Linz, Juan J. "The Religious Use of Politics and/or the Political Use of Religion: Ersatz Ideology versus Ersatz Religion." In *Totalitarianism and Political Religions*, edited by Hans Maier and translated by Jodi Bruhn, 102–19. London and New York: Routledge, 2004 [1996].

———. *Totalitarian and Authoritarian Regimes*. Boulder: Lynne Rienner Publishers, 2000.

Linz, Juan J., and Alfred Stepan. *Problems of Democratic Transition and Consolidation: Southern Europe, South America, and Post-Communist Europe*. Baltimore: Johns Hopkins University Press, 1996.

Lipset, Seymour Martin. *Political Man: The Social Bases of Politics*. London: Heinemann, 1983.

Liu, Guojian. "Zhonghua fuyin tuanqi huodong de xin tedian" [New characteristics of China Gospel Fellowship's activities]. *Tiedao jingguan gaodeng zhuanke xuexiao xuebao* 19, serial 79, no. 1 (2009): 79–82.

Liu, Jian, Weihong Luo, and Kejia Yan. "Jidujiaotu de xinyang yu xingwei – Shanghai Jidujiao xintu qingkuang diaocha wenjuan fenxi" [The belief and behaviors of Protestants: A survey on the Protestants in Shanghai]. *Dangdai zongjiao yanjiu* 36 (1999): 3–8.

Liu, Peng. "Church and State Relations in China: Characteristics and Trends." *Journal of Contemporary China* 5, no. 11 (1996): 69–79.

Liu, Qiu. "A Closer Look into an Immigrant Workers' Church in Beijing." *Nova Religio* 12, no. 4 (2009): 91–8.

Lorentzen, Peter. "Regularized Rioting: Permitting Public Protest in Authoritarian Regimes." Unpublished manuscript, University of California, Berkeley, June 9, 2010.

Lozada, Eriberto P. *God Aboveground: Catholic Church, Postsocialist State, and the Transnational Process in a Chinese Village*. Stanford: Stanford University Press, 2001.

Luo, Weihong. "Wuyi shenhan huodong hui bu hui fazhan chengwei xin zongjiao?" [Will the activities of witch doctors and wizards grow into new religions?]. *Dangdai zongjiao yanjiu* 27 (1997): 28–32.

Luo, Zhufeng, ed. *Religion under Socialism in China*. Armonk: M.E. Sharpe, 1991.

Lust-Okar, Ellen. "Elections under Authoritarianism: Preliminary Lessons from Jordan." *Democratization* 13, no. 3 (2006): 456–71.

———. "Divided They Rule: The Management and Manipulation of Political Opposition." *Comparative Politics* 36, no. 2 (2004): 159–79.

Lyons, Thomas P. "Regional Inequality." In *Fujian: A Coastal Province in Transition and Transformation*, edited by Y.M. Yeung and David K.Y. Chu, 327–52. Hong Kong: Chinese University of Hong Kong, 2000.

Ma, Qiusha. *Non-Governmental Organizations in Contemporary China: Paving the way to civil society?* New York: Routledge, 2006.

Machiavelli, Niccolo. *The Prince*. New York: Bantam Classics, 1984 [1532].

MacInnis, Donald E. *Religion in China Today: Policy and Practice*. Maryknoll, NY: Orbis 1989.

Madsen, Richard. "Religious Renaissance in China Today." *Journal of Current Chinese Affairs* 40, no. 2 (2011): 17–42.

———. "The Upsurge of Religion in China." *Journal of Democracy* 21, no. 4 (October 2010): 58–71.

———. "Catholic Conflict and Cooperation in the People's Republic of China." In *God and Caesar in China*, edited by Jason Kindopp and Carol Lee Hamrin, 93–106. Washington, DC: Brookings Institution Press, 2004.

———. *China's Catholics: Tragedy and Hope in an Emerging Civil Society*. Berkeley: University of California Press, 1998.

———. "The Public Sphere, Civil Society and Moral Community: A Research Agenda for Contemporary China." *Modern China* 19 (April 1993): 183–98.

Magaloni, Beatriz. *Voting for Autocracy: Hegemonic Party Survival and Its Demise in Mexico*. New York: Cambridge University Press, 2006.

Maginn, Paul J. "Negotiating and Securing Access." *Field Methods* 19, no. 4 (November 2007): 425–40.

Mainwaring, Scott. *The Catholic Church and Politics in Brazil, 1916–1985*. Stanford: Stanford University Press, 1986.

Mainwaring, Scott, and Alexander Wilde. "The Progressive Church in Latin America: An Interpretation." In *The Progressive Church in Latin America*, edited by Scott Mainwaring and Alexander Wilde. Notre Dame: University of Notre Dame Press, 1989.

Makarskov, Nikolaj. "So svoim monastyrem v chuzhuju eparhiju" [With his monastery into a stranger's dioceses]. *Nizhegorodskij rabochij* 37, no. 15454, February 27, 2004: 3.

Malashenko, Aleksei. "Politizacija patriarha" [Politicization of patriarch]. *Nezavisimaya Gazeta, Nizhny Novgorod*, July 10–11, 2009: 139–40.

Malashenko, Aleksei, and Sergei Filatov. *Religija i globalizacija na prostorah evrazii* [Religion and globalization across Eurasia]. Moscow: Moskovskij centr karnegi, 2005.

Manion, Melanie. "The Behavior of Middlemen in the Cadre Retirement Policy Process." In *Bureaucracy, Politics, and Decision Making in Post-Mao China*, edited by Kenneth G. Lieberthal and David M. Lampton, 216–44. Berkeley: University of California Press, 1992.

Markeev, J. "Ugrozhaet li borchanam nashestvie sekt?" [Does the invasion of sects threaten Bor residents?]. *Pravoslavnoe slovo* 15, no. 220 (August 15, 2002): 4.

Marsh, Christopher. *Religion and the State in Russia and China: Suppression, Survival and Revival*. New York: Continuum, 2011.

Marsh, Christopher, and Paul Froese. "The State of Freedom in Russia: A Regional Analysis of Freedom of Religion, Media and Markets." *Religion, State & Society* 32, no. 2 (2004): 137–49.

McCallum, Fiona. "Religious Institutions and Authoritarian State: Church-state relations in the Middle East." *Third World Quarterly* 33, no. 1 (2012): 109–24.

Mertha, Andrew. "'Fragmented Authoritarianism 2.0': Political Pluralization in the Chinese Policy Process." *The China Quarterly* 200 (2009): 995–1012.

"Method for the Annual Inspection of Places of Religious Activity, released by the Religious Affairs Bureau of the State Council, July 29, 1996." Reprinted in *Chinese Law and Government* 33, no. 2 (March/April 2000): 71–4.

Milner, Helen V. *Interests, Institutions and Information: Domestic Politics and International Relations*. Princeton: Princeton University Press, 1997.

"Ministry of Personnel Issues Notice Stipulating that State Functionaries May Not Practice Falun Dafa" [Renshi bu fachu tongzhi guiding guojia gongwuyuan bu zhun xiulian "Falun Dafa"]. *People's Daily* [overseas edition], July 24, 1999: 3.

Mirovalev, Mansur. "Russian Orthodox Church a growing political force." *Moscow (AP)*, April 4, 2009. Available at: http://www.huffingtonpost.com/huff-wires/2009 0404/eu-russia-orthodox-church/ (last accessed September 4, 2013).

Mitrokhin, L.N. "Filosofiia religii: novye perspektivy" [The philosophy of religion: New perspectives]. *Voprosy filosofii* 8 (2003): 18–36.

Moen, Matthew C., and Lowell S. Gustafson, eds. *The Religious Challenge to the State.* Philadelphia: Temple University Press, 1992.

Moiseenko, Andrei, and Tatiana Pavlova. "Will the Bible Become a School Textbook?" *Komsomolskaya Pravda*, November 19, 2002. Available at: http://www.portal-credo. ru/site/?act=monitor&id=748 (last accessed September 5, 2013).

Morawska, Ewa. "Civil Religion Versus State Power in Poland." In *Church-State Relations*, edited by Thomas Robbins and Roland Robertson, 221–32. New Brunswick, NJ: Transaction Books, 1987.

Morgenthau, Hans J. *Politics Among Nations: The Struggle for Power and Peace.* New York: Alfred A. Knopf, 1967.

Muharirova, Aliy. "Kandidaty – psevdomulsul'mane" [Candidates – pseudo-Muslims]. *Medina* 2, no. 15, issue 1427 (2006): 4.

Muhetdinov, D.V. *Azan nad Volgoj* [Azan over the Volga]. Nizhny Novgorod: Izd-vo NIM "Mahinur," 2005.

"Head of Council of Muftis of Russia Opposes Compulsory Study of Orthodoxy in Schools." December 23, 2002. *Portal-credo.ru.* Available at: http://www2.stetson. edu/~psteeves/relnews/0212e.html (last accessed September 4, 2013).

Nathan, Andrew. "China's Changing of the Guard: Authoritarian Resilience." *Journal of Democracy* 14, no. 1 (2003): 6–17.

Nedostup, Rebecca. *Superstitious Regimes: Religion and the Politics of Chinese Modernity.* Cambridge: Harvard University Asia Center, 2009.

Neitz, Mary Jo, and Peter R. Mueser. "Economic Man and the Sociology of Religion: A Critique of the Rational Choice Approach." In *Rational Choice Theory and Religion*, edited by Lawrence A. Young, 106–18. New York: Routledge, 1997.

"New Shanghai bishop 'barred from ministry'." *UCA News*, July 9, 2012. Available at: http://www.ucanews.com/news/new-shanghai-bishop-barred-from-ministry/ 54911 (last accessed September 5, 2013).

Nielsen, Niels. *Revolutions in Eastern Europe: The Religious Roots.* Maryknoll, NY: Orbis, 1991.

Nizhny Novgorod Orthodoxy Diocese. "Zasedanie Kruglogo stola po antisektantskoj dejatel'nosti" [Round-table meeting on the antisectarian activity], April 22, 2004. Available at: http://www.nne.ru/news.php?id=524 (last accessed February 24, 2013).

"Nizhegorodskoe katoliki podveli pravoslavnyh" [Nizhny Novgorod Catholics let the Orthodox down]. *Kommersant'* 33, February 25, 2004: 16.

"Notice on Various Issues Regarding Identifying and Banning of Cultic Organizations," from the Ministry of Public Security of the People's Republic of China." Reprinted in *Chinese Law and Government* 36, no. 2 (2003): 22–38.

"Novosti Pravoslavija: Sovet Vaada Rossii protiv 'Osnov pravoslavnoj kul'tury' v shkole'" [Orthodox news: The Council of the Vaad in Russia against the "Fundamentals of Orthodox Culture in Schools"]. *Pravoslavnoe slovo* 1, no. 230 (January 2003): 2.

Nyitray, Vivian-Lee. "Becoming the Empress of Heaven." In *Goddesses Who Rule*, edited by B. Moon and E. Benard, 166–80. New York: Oxford University Press, 2000.

"O religioznyh konfessijah" [About religious confessions]. *Pravoslavnoe slovo* 18, no. 103 (September 1997): 3.

"O svobode sovesti i religioznykh organizatsiiakh" [On freedom of conscience and religious organizations]. *Vedomosti SSSR* 41, item no. 813 (1990).

Oakes, Tim. "China's Provincial Identities: Reviving Regionalism and Reinventing 'Chineseness'." *The Journal of Asian Studies* 59, no. 3 (2000): 667–92.

"Obrashchenie svjashchennosluzhitelja k pravoslavnomu narodu Pravoslavnoe slovo" [Orthodox priest appeals to Orthodox people]. *Pravoslavnoe slovo* 18, no. 55 (April 1995): 7.

O'Brien, Kevin J. "Rightful Resistance." *World Politics* 49, no. 1 (1996): 31–55.

———. "Chinese People's Congresses and Legislative Embeddedness: Understanding Early Organizational Development." *Comparative Political Studies* 27, no. 1 (1994): 80–109.

O'Brien, Kevin J., and Lianjiang Li. *Rightful Resistance in Rural China*. Cambridge: Cambridge University Press, 2006.

"Obsuzhdaetsja programma vozrozhdenija" [The discussion of the revival program]. *Pravoslavnoe Slovo* 60, no. 23 (December 1995): 1.

O'Donnell, Guillermo, and Philippe C. Schmitter. *Transitions from Authoritarian Rule*. Baltimore, MD: Johns Hopkins University Press, 1986.

Oi, Jean C. "Fiscal Reform and the Economic Foundations of Local State Corporatism in China." *World Politics* 45, no. 1 (October 1992): 99–126.

Oldmixon, Elizabeth Anne. *Uncompromising Positions: God, Sex and the US House of Representatives*. Washington, DC: Georgetown University Press, 2005.

Olson, Mancur. *The Logic of Collective Action*. Cambridge: Harvard University Press, 1965.

"Order 144: Regulations on the Supervision of the Religious Activities of Foreigners in China" [Zhonghua Renmin Gongheguo jingnei waiguoren zongjiao huodong guanli guiding]. Released by the State Council January 1994 and reprinted in *Chinese Law and Government* 33, no. 2 (March/April 2000): 64–8.

"Order No. 145: Regulation Regarding the Management of Place of Religious Activities" [Zongjiao huodong changsuo guanli tiaoli]. Released by the State Council January 1994 and reprinted in *Chinese Law and Government* 33, no. 2 (March/April 2000): 64–8.

Osa, Maryjane. "Resistance, Persistence, and Change: The Transformation of the Catholic Church in Poland." *Eastern European Politics and Societies* 3 (1989): 268–99.

Ottaway, Marina, and Thomas Carothers, eds. *Funding Virtue: Civil Society Aid and Democracy Promotion*. Washington, DC: Carnegie Endowment for International Peace, 2000.

Owens, Michael Leo. *God and Government in the Ghetto: The Politics of Church-State Collaboration in Black America*. Chicago: The University of Chicago Press, 2007.

Ownby, David. *Falun Gong and the Future of China*. New York: Oxford University Press, 2008.

──────. "The Falun Gong in the New World." *European Journal of East Asian Studies* 2, no. 2 (2003): 303–20.

──────. "Chinese Millenarian Traditions: The Formative Age." *The American Historical Review* 104, no. 5 (1999): 1513–30.

Palmer, David A. *Qigong Fever: Body, Science, and Utopia in China*. New York: Columbia University Press, 2007.

Parsons, Talcott. *The Social System*. Glencoe, IL: Free Press, 1951.

Pas, Julian F., ed. *The Turning of the Tide: Religion in China Today*. Oxford: Oxford University Press, 1989.

Patel, David, and Valerie J. Bunce. 2012. "Turning Points and the Cross Diffusion of National Protests" *APSA – Comparative Democratization* 10 (January): 1–11.

Patton, Michael Quinn. *Qualitative Research and Evaluation Methods*. Newbury Park, CA: Sage, 1990.

Pavlikova, Olga. "Edinoobrazie shkol'nyh programm pod voprosom" [Uniformity of curricula in question]. *Gazeta*, October 4, 2007: 21.

Paxton, Robert O. *Vichy France: Old Guard and New Order, 1940–1944*. New York: Columbia University Press, 2001.

Pei, Minxin. *China's Trapped Transition*. Cambridge: Harvard University Press, 2006.

Perry, Elizabeth J. "Popular Protest in China: Playing by the Rules." Paper prepared for the conference sponsored by the Pardee Center of Boston University, "Three Decades of Reform and Opening: Where China Is Headed?" December 8, 2008.

Perry, Elizabeth J., and Mark Selden, eds. *Chinese Society: Change, Conflict and Resistance*. New York: Routledge, 2003.

Petro, Nicolai. "The Novgorod Region: A Russian Success Story." *Post-Soviet Affairs* 15, no. 3 (1999): 235–61.

Pew Research Center. "The Global Religious Landscape: A Report on the Size and Distribution of the World's Major Religious Groups as of 2010." Washington, DC: Pew Research Center, 2012.

Pfaff, Steven, and Guobin Yang. "Double-edged Rituals and the Symbolic Resources of Collective Action: Political Commemorations and the Mobilization of Protest in 1989." *Theory and Society* 30, no. 4 (2001): 539–89.

Philo, Chris, and Gerry Kearns. "Culture, History, Capital." In *Selling Places: The City as Cultural Capital, Past and Present*, edited by Gerry Kearns and Chris Philos, 1–32. Oxford: Pergamon Press, 1993.

Philpott, Daniel. "Explaining the Political Ambivalence of Religion." *American Political Science Review* 101, no. 3 (2007): 505–25.

──────. "The Catholic Wave." In *World Religions and Democracy*, edited by Larry Diamond, Marc F. Plattner, and Philip J. Costopoulos, 102–16. Baltimore: Johns Hopkins University Press, 2005.

Piattoni, Simona, ed. *Clientelism, Interests and Democratic Representation: The European Experience in Historical and Comparative Perspective*. Cambridge: Cambridge University Press, 2001.

Pius XII. "Ad Apostolorum Principis Encyclical of Pope Pius XII on Communism and the Church in China." *Papal Encyclicals Online*. Given on June 29, 1958. Available at: http://www.vatican.va/holy_father/pius_xii/encyclicals/documents/hf_p-xii_enc_29061958_ad-apostolorum-principis-en.html (last accessed September 5, 2013).

Pontusson, Jonas. "Labor, Corporatism, and Industrial Policy: The Swedish Case in Comparative Perspective." *Comparative Politics* 23, no. 2 (1991): 163–79.

Potter, Pitman B. "Belief in Control: Regulation of Religion in China." *The China Quarterly* 174 (2003): 317–37.

Powell, David. "The Effectiveness of Soviet Anti-Religious Propaganda." *The Public Opinion Quarterly* 31, no. 3 (Autumn 1967): 366–80.

Presidential Decree President Republic of Tatarstan. "O Kontseptsii sohranenia, razvitiya i ispolzovaniya ansamblja Kazanskogo Kreml" [On the concept of preservation, development and usage of the ensemble of the Kazan Kremlin]. November 13, 1995.

Przeworski, Adam. "The Game of Transition." In *Issues in Democratic Consolidation: The New South American Democracies in Comparative Perspective*, edited by Scott Mainwaring and Guillermo A. O'Donnell, 105–52. Notre Dame: University of Notre Dame Press, 1992.

"Putin Congratulates Patriarch Kirill on His Name Day with the Order on Real Estate Transfer to Church." *Interfax*, May 25, 2010. Available at: http://www.interfax-religion.com/?act=news&div=7295 (last accessed September 5, 2013).

Putin, Vladimir. "Russian Orthodox Church to Work for Russian identity." *Interfax*, February 3, 2009. Available at: http://www.interfax-religion.com/?act=news&div=5662 (last accessed July 9, 2013).

Putnam, Robert D. *Making Democracy Work*. Princeton: Princeton University Press, 1993.

——. "Diplomacy and Domestic Politics: The Logic of Two-Level Games." *International Organization* 42, no. 3 (Summer 1988): 427–60.

Putnam, Robert D., and David E. Campbell. *American Grace: How Religion Divides and Unites Us*. New York: Simon & Schuster, 2010.

Qiao, Hongming, and Xuejiao Chen. "Zhuanxing qi dongbei nongcun Jidujiao jiating jiaohui shengxing de yuanyin tanxi" [Causes for the prevalence of Christian house churches in the northeastern rural area during transition]. *Gaige yu kaifang* 22 (November 2010): 189–90.

Qingpu nianjian bianjibu. *Qingpu nianjian 2002* [Qingpu yearbook 2002]. Shanghai: Shanghai shehui kexueyuan chubanshe, 2002.

Qingpu qu shi zhi banggongshi. *Qingpu nianjian 2001* [Qingpu yearbook 2001]. Shanghai: Shanghai shehui kexueyuan chubanshe, 2001.

"Quanguo renmin daibiao dahui changwu weiyuanhui guanyu qudi xiejiao zuzhi, fangfan he chengzhi xiejiao huodong de jueding" [Decision of the NPC Standing Committee on Outlawing heretical organization and guarding against and punishing heretical activities]. October 30, 1999. Reprinted in *Chinese Law and Government* 32, no. 5 (September–October 1999): 46–50.

Quinlivan, James T. 1999. "Coup-proofing: Its Practice and Consequences in the Middle East." *International Security* 24, no. 2 (Fall 1999): 131–65.

Ramet, Sabrina Petra, ed. *Adaptation and Transformation in Communist and Post-Communist Systems*. Boulder, CO: Westview Press, 1992.

——. *Nihil Obstat: Religion, Politics and Social Change in East-Central Europe and Russia*. Durham, NC: Duke University Press, 1998.

Read, Benjamin L. "More than an Interview, Less than Sedaka: Studying Subtle and Hidden Politics with Site-Intensive Methods." In *Contemporary Chinese Politics: New Sources, Methods, and Field Strategies*, edited by Allen Carlson, Mary E. Gallagher,

Kenneth Lieberthal, and Melanie Manion, 145–61. New York: Cambridge University Press, 2010.

"Reading, Writing... and Religion?" *RFE/RL*, July 27, 2007. Available at: http://www.rferl.org/content/article/1077844.html (last accessed September 5, 2013).

"Regarding the Wanted Order Issued for the Suspect of Li Hongzhi" [Zhongguo Gong'an bu fabu tongji ling chaji Li Hongzhi]. *People's Daily* [overseas edition], July 30, 1999: 1.

"Registration Procedures for Venues for Religious Activities." Released by the State Council May 1, 1994) and reprinted in *Chinese Law and Government* 33, no. 2 (March/April 2000): 69–70.

"Regulations on Religious Affairs" [Zongjiao shiwu tiaoli]. Promulgated by the State Council of the PRC March 1, 2005. Reprinted in *Chinese Journal of International Law* 5, no. 2 (2006): 475–85.

"Religija v Nizhnem Novgorode: Itogi pereregistracii religioznyh ob"edinenij. Administracija Nizhnego Novgoroda ne rekomenduet sotrudnichat' s nekotorymi religioznymi ob"edinenijami" [Religion in Nizhny Novgorod: Results of re-registration of religious associations. Nizhny Novgorod administration recommends noncooperation with several religious associations]. *Sobornost*, March 6, 2001. Available at: http://orthodox.etel.ru/2001/07/novg.htm (last accessed September 4, 2013).

Richters, Katja. *The Post-Soviet Russian Orthodox Church*. New York: Routledge, 2013.

Riley, Dylan. "Civic Association and Authoritarian Regimes in Interwar Europe: Italy and Spain in Comparative Perspective." *American Sociological Review* 70, no. 2 (April 2005): 288–310.

Rosenthal, Elisabeth. "Cardinal Ignatius Kung, 98, Long Jailed by China, Dies." *New York Times*, March 14, 2000. Available at: http://www.nytimes.com/2000/03/14/world/cardinal-ignatius-kung-98-long-jailed-by-china-dies.html (last accessed September 5, 2013).

"Rossija dlja russkih, Tatarstan dlja tatar" [Russia for Russians, Tatarstan for Tatars]. *Media al' Islam* 1, no. 14 (January 2006): 5.

Rowe, Paul. "Building Coptic Civil Society: Christian Groups and the State in Mubarak's Egypt." *Middle Eastern Studies* 45, no. 1 (January 2009): 111–26.

Ru, Yanxia and Zhongping Ren. "'Yansegeming' gei Zhongguo Gongchandang jianquan zhizheng hefaxing de qishi" [Lessons for the CCP from the 'Color Revolutions': Do better in building legitimacy and maintaining power]. *Neijiang shifan xueyuan xuebao* 1, no. 21 (2006): 34–7.

Rubinstein, Murray A. "Medium/Message in Taiwan Mazu-Cult Centers: Using Time, Space, and Word to Foster Island-Wide Spiritual Consciousness and Local, Regional, and National Forms of Institutional Identity." In *Religion and the Formation of Taiwanese Identities*, edited by Paul R. Katz and Murray A. Rubinstein, 181–218. New York: Palgrave Macmillian, 2003.

————. "The Revival of the Mazu Cult and of Taiwanese Pilgrimage to Fujian." Paper presented at the Taiwan Studies Workshop in Harvard Studies on Taiwan, 1995.

Ruble, Blair A., Jodi Koehn, and Nancy E. Popson, eds. *Fragmented Space in the Russian Federation*. Baltimore: Johns Hopkins University Press, 2001.

Rudolph, Susanne Hoeber. "Introduction: Religion, States and the Transnational Civil Society." In *Transnational Religion and Fading States*, edited by Susanne Hoeber Rudolph and James Piscatori. Boulder, CO: Westview Press, 1997.

Rueschemeyer, Dietrich, Evelyne Huber Stevens, and John D. Stevens. *Capitalist Development & Democracy*. Chicago: University of Chicago Press, 1992.

"Russia: Public Opinion Divided over Tuition of Orthodox Culture in State Schools." *Keston News Service*, December 4, 2002. Available at: http://www.religioscope.com/ articles/2002/031_russia_schools.htm (last accessed August 16, 2013).

"Saentologija: Psevdo-cerkov', psevdo-nauka, psevdo-pravda" [Scientology: Pseudo-church, pseudo-science, pseudo-truth]. *Gorodovoi* (Kirov), April 3, 1998. Available at: http://www2.stetson.edu/~psteeves/relnews/9804a.html (last accessed September 4, 2013).

Samarina, Aleksandra. "Iisus i Edinaja Rossija" [Jesus and United Russia]. *Nezavisimaya Gazeta*, January 21, 2009. Available at: http://www.ng.ru/politics/2009-01-20/ 3_bible.html (last accessed September 5, 2013).

"Samoe dushevnoe stroitel'stvo" [Most spiritual construction]. *Birzha pljus svoj dom* 30, August 12, 1999: 3.

Sangren, Steven P. "Power and Transcendence in the Ma Tsu Pilgrimages of Taiwan." *American Ethnologist* 20, no. 3 (1993): 564–82.

_____. "History and the Rhetoric of Legitimacy: The Ma Tsu Cult of Taiwan." *Comparative Studies in Society and History* 30, no. 4 (1988): 674–97.

Sarotte, M. E. "China's Fear of Contagion: Tiananmen Square and the Power of the European Example." *International Security* 37, no. 2 (Fall 2012): 156–82.

Savadove, Bill. "Buddhism Put to the Service of Tourism." *South China Morning Post*, August 8, 2012. Available at: http://www.scmp.com/article/489484/ buddhism-put-service-tourism (last accessed September 5, 2013).

Schedler, Andreas. *The Politics of Uncertainty: Sustaining and Subverting Electoral Authoritarianism*. Oxford, UK: Oxford University Press, 2013.

Schmitt, Karl. "Church and State in Mexico: A Corporatist Relationship." *The Americas* 40, no. 3 (1984): 349–76.

Schmitter, Philippe C. "Civil Society East and West." In *Consolidating the Third Wave Democracies: Themes and Perspectives*, edited by Larry Diamond, Mark F. Plattner, Yun-han Chu, and Hung-mao Tien, 239–62. Baltimore, MD: Johns Hopkins University Press, 1997.

_____. "Sectors in Modern Capitalism: Modes of Governance and Variations in Performance." In *Labor Relations and Economic Performance*, edited by Renato Brunetta and Carl Dell'Aringa, 3–39. New York: New York University Press, 1990.

_____. "Still the Century of Corporatism?" *Review of Politics* 36, no. 1 (1974): 85–131.

Scott, James C. *Weapons of the Weak*. New Haven: Yale University Press, 1997.

_____. "Patron-Client Politics and Political Change in Southeast Asia." *American Political Science Review* 66, no. 1 (1972): 91–113.

Scott, Thomas. *The Global Resurgence of Religion and the Transformation of International Relations*. New York: Palgrave Macmillian, 2005.

Seiwert, Hubert. *Popular Religious Movements and Heterodox Sects in Chinese History*. Leiden, the Netherlands: Brill, 2003.

Sells, Michael A. *The Bridge Betrayed: Religions and Genocide in Bosnia*. Berkeley: University of California Press, 1996.

Selznick, Philip. *The Organizational Weapon: A Study of Bolshevik Strategy and Tactics*. Santa Monica, CA: The Rand Corporation, 1952.

Senjutkina, O. N. "Jarmarochnaja mechet' – centr obshhenija musul'man Rossii" [Yarmaka Mosque – the center of interaction for Muslims in Russia]. *Medina al'-Islam* No. 6(9) (2005a): 14.

———. "Pervyj s'ezd musul'man Rossii – k 100-letiju provedenija" [The first congress of Muslims in Russia – for the 100th anniversary]. Nizhny Novgorod: Izd-vo NIM "Mahinur," 2005b.

"Sestra Boga" [God's sister]. *Nezhegorodskie novosti*, April 8, 2005: 3.

Seul, Jeffery R. "'Ours Is the Way of God': Religion, Identity, and Intergroup Conflict." *Journal of Peace Research* 36, no. 5 (1999): 553–69.

Seymour, James D., and Eugen Wehrli. "Religion in China." *Chinese Sociology and Anthropology* 26, no. 3 (1994): 3–59.

Shambaugh, David. *China's Communist Party: Atrophy and Adaptation*. Washington, DC: Woodrow Wilson Center Press; Berkeley: University of California Press, 2008.

Shek, Richard. "Sectarian Eschatology and Violence." In *Violence in China: Essays in Culture and Counterculture*, edited by Jonathan N. Lipman and Stevan Harrell, 87–114. New York: State University of New York, 1990.

Shterin, Marat S., and James T. Richardson. "Effects of the Western Anti-Cult Movement on Development of Laws Concerning Religion in Post-Communist Russia." *Journal of Church and State* 42 (2000): 247–71.

———. "Local Laws Restricting Religion in Russia: Precursors of Russia's New National Law." *Journal of Church and State* 40 (1998): 319–42.

Shue, Vivienne. "State Legitimization in China: The Challenge of Popular Religion." Paper presented at the American Political Science Association annual meeting, San Francisco, CA, 2001.

———. *The Reach of the State: Sketches of the Chinese Body Politic*. Stanford: Stanford University Press, 1988.

Sil, Rudra, and Cheng Chen. "State Legitimacy and the (In)significance of Democracy in Post-Communist Russia." *Europe-Asia Studies* 56, no. 3 (2004): 347–68.

Silber, Laura. "Serb Regime Rebuked by Church: Bishops' Letter Seen as Blow to Milosevic." *Washington Post*, May 29, 1992: A28.

Smith, Christian. *Disruptive Religion: The Force of Faith in Social Movement Activism*. New York: Routledge, 1996.

Solnick, Steven L. "Will Russia Survive? Center and Periphery in the Russian Federation." In *Post-Soviet Political Order*, edited by B.R. Rubin and J. Snyder, 58–80. New York: Routledge, 1998.

———. "The Political Economy of Russian Federalism." *Problems of Post-Communism* 43, no. 6 (1996): 13–26.

Solomon, Peter. "Courts and Judiciaries in Authoritarian Regimes." *World Politics* 60, no. 1 (October 2007): 122–45.

Songjiang xian difang shizhi bianzuan weiyuanhui. *Songjiang nianjian (1994–1995)* [Songjiang yearbook (1994–1995)]. Shanghai: Shanghai shehui kexueyuan chuban-she, 1997a.

Songjiang xian difang shizhi bianzuan weiyuanhui. *Songjiang nianjian (1996–1997)* [Songjiang yearbook (1996–1997)]. Shanghai: Shanghai shehui kexueyuan chuban-she, 1997b.

Spence, Jonathan D. *God's Chinese Son: The Taiping Heavenly Kingdom of Hong Xiuquan*. New York: Norton, 1996.

Spiegel, Mickey. "Control and Containment in the Reform Era." In *God and Caesar in China*, edited by Jason Kindopp and Carol Lee Hamrin, 40–57. Washington, DC: Brookings Institution Press, 2004.

———, ed. *China: State Control of Religion*. New York: Human Rights Watch, 1997.

Stark, Rodney, and Roger Finke. *Acts of Faith: Explaining the Human Side of Religion*. Berkeley: University of California Press, 2000.

Stark, Rodney, and William Sims Bainbridge. *The Future of Religion: Secularization, Revival, and Cult Formation*. Berkeley: University of California Press, 1985.

Steen, Anton, and Vladimir Gel'man. *Elites and Democratic Development in Russia*. New York: Routledge, 2003.

Stern, Rachel, and Jonathan Hassid. "Amplifying Silence: Uncertainty and Control Parables in Contemporary China." *Comparative Political Studies* 45, no. 10 (October 2012): 1230–54.

Stockmann, Daniela, and Mary Gallagher. "Remote Control: How the Media Sustains Authoritarian Rule in China." *Comparative Political Studies* 44 (2011): 436–67.

Stoner-Weiss, Kathryn. "Central Weaknesses and Provincial Autonomy: Observations in the Devolution Process in Russia." *Post-Soviet Affairs* 15, no. 1 (1999): 87–106.

———. *Local Heroes*. Princeton: Princeton University Press, 1997.

Sukhonina, Julia. "Vodka pretknovenija" [The vodka stumbling block]. *Kommersant'* 9 (Nizhny Novgorod), January 20, 2006. Available at: http://www.kommersant.ru/doc-rss/642394 (last accessed September 5, 2013).

Sun, Jinfu, Mengqing Wu, and Jian Liu, eds. *Shanghai zongjiao zhi* [Shanghai religious gazetteer]. Shanghai: Shanghai shehui kexueyuan chubanshe, 2001.

Swidler, Ann. "Culture in Action: Symbols and Strategies." *American Sociological Review* 51, no. 2 (1986): 273–86.

Svolik, Milan W. *The Politics of Authoritarian Rule*. New York: Cambridge University Press, 2012.

"Symposium on Research under Authoritarian Conditions." *APSA-Comparative Democratization Newsletter* 9, no. 2 (May 2011).

Szyoni, Michael. "The Virgin and the Chinese State: The Cult of Wang Yulan and the Politics of Local Identity on Jinmen (Quemoy)." *Journal of Ritual Studies* 19, no. 1 (2005): 87–98.

Tarrow, Sidney. "The Strategy of Paired Comparison." *Comparative Political Studies* 43, no. 2 (2010): 230–59.

———. "Expanding Paired Comparison: A Modest Proposal." *American Political Science Association – Comparative Politics Newsletter* 10, no. 2 (Summer 1999): 9–12.

———. *Power in Movement: Social Movements, Collective Action, and Politics*. New York: Cambridge University Press, 1994.

Taylor, Brian D. *State Building in Putin's Russia: Policing and Coercion after Communism*. New York: Cambridge University Press, 2011.

Tejada, Carlos and Paul Mozur. "Bishop's Exit Tests Vatican Relations." *Wall Street Journal*, July 10, 2012. Available at: http://online.wsj.com/article/SB10001424052702303292204577518553244967064.html (last accessed September 5, 2013).

Teo, Eric Chu Cheow. "Buddhism May Act as a 'Harmonious Bridge'." *China Daily*, August 26, 2006: 4.

Ter Haar, B. J. *The White Lotus Teachings in Chinese Religious History*. Leiden, the Netherlands: Brill, 1992.

"The Gorbachev Visit, Excerpts from Speech to UN on Major Soviet Military Cuts." *New York Times*, December 8, 1988: A16.

Toft, Monica Duffy. "Getting Religion? The Puzzling Case of Islam and Civil War." *International Security* 31, no. 4 (2007): 97–131.

Toft, Monica Duffy, Daniel Philpott, and Timothy Samuel Shah. *God's Century: Resurgent Religion and Global Politics*. New York: W.W. Norton, 2011.

Tong, James. *Revenge of the Forbidden City: The Suppression of Falungong in China, 1999–2005*. New York: Oxford University Press, 2009.

————. "An Organizational Analysis of the Falun Gong: Structure, Communications, Financing." *The China Quarterly*, no. 171 (2002): 636–60.

"Totalitarnye sekty – ugroza bezopasnosti Rossii" [Totalitarian sects – a threat to Russian security]. *Nizhegorodskie novosti*, April 30, 2004: 4–5.

Treisman, Daniel S. *After the Deluge*. Ann Arbor: University of Michigan Press, 1999.

————. "Russia's Ethnic Revival: The Separatist Activism of Regional Leaders in a Post-Communist Order." *World Politics* 49, no. 2 (1997): 212–49.

Tsai, Lily L. *Accountability without Democracy*. Cambridge: Cambridge University Press, 2007.

Tsebelis, George. *Nested Games: Rational Choice in Comparative Politics*. Berkeley: University of California Press, 1990.

Tu, Weiming. "The Quest for Meaning: Religion in the People's Republic of China." In *The Desecularization of the World: Resurgent Religion and World Politics*, edited by Peter L. Berger, 85–101. Washington, DC: The Ethics and Public Policy Center, 1999.

————. "Introduction: Cultural Perspectives." *Daedalus* 122, no. 2 (1993): vii–xxiv.

Tullock, Gordon. *Autocracy*. Boston: Kluwer Academic, 1987.

"U.S. Commission on Security and Cooperation in Europe (Helsinki Commission) on Hearing of Unregistered Religious Groups in Russia," April 14, 2005. Transcript available at: http://csce.gov/index.cfm?FuseAction=ContentRecords.ViewDetail&ContentRecord_id=343&ContentType=H,B&ContentRecordType=H&Region_id=101&Issue_id=0&CFId=46506569&CFToken=25821487 (last accessed September 5, 2013).

Uzzell, Lawrence A. "Letter from Moscow." *First Things* 79 (1998): 17–19.

"V 'Cerkvi matushki Fotinii Svetonosnoj' Putin ob"javlen apostolom" [In 'the Church of Mother Photinia Luminous' Putin is declared the apostle]. *Komsomolskaya pravda*, April 11, 2005. Available at: http://www.kp.md/online/news/24541/ (last accessed September 7, 2013).

"V Nizhegorodskoj oblasti 850 religioznyh kul'turno-istoricheskih ob"ektov" [Nizhny Novgorod region has 850 religious sites of cultural-historical importance], May 12, 2006. Posted by the Spiritual Administration of Muslims of the Nizhny Novgorod city and the Nizhny Novgorod region. Available at: http://content.mail.ru/arch/21151/1140230.html?print (last accessed September 4, 2013).

"V Nizhnem Novgorode vosstanovjat Jarmarochnuju mechet'" [Yarmarka Mosque to be restored in Nizhny Novgorod]. *Golos Islama*, September 29, 2011. Available at: http://golosislama.ru/news.php?id=2599 (last accessed September 5, 2013).

"V Sajanogorske pod ugrozoj snosa okazalsja zhiloj dom pastora Cerkvi hristian very evangel'skoj 'Proslavlenie'" [The house of the pastor of the Evangelical Christian

Gospel Church in Sayanogorsk is under the threat of demolition]. *Slavjanskij pravovoj centr*, July 11, 2010. Available at: http://www.sclj.ru/news/detail.php?SECTION_ID=230&ELEMENT_ID=2913 (last accessed September 4, 2013).

Vala, Carsten T. "Pathways to the Pulpit: Leadership Training in 'Patriotic' and Unregistered Chinese Protestant Churches." In *Making Religion, Making the State*, edited by Ashiwa and Wank, 96–125. Stanford: Stanford University Press, 2009.

Vala, Carsten T., and Kevin J. O'Brien. "Attracting without Networks: Recruiting Strangers to Unregistered Protestantism in China." *Mobilization: An International Quarterly* 12, no. 1 (2007): 79–94.

"Variety of opinions on teaching Orthodoxy – Question of the Day: Do Schools Need Religion Classes?" *Komsomolskaya pravda*, November 20, 2002. Available at: http://www2.stetson.edu/~psteeves/relnews/0211b.html (last accessed September 5, 2013).

"Vice-gubernator Batyr'ev: staroobrjadcy mne stali blizhe i ponjatnee" [Vice-Governor Batyrev: I stand closer to and understand the Old Believers]. *Staroobrjadec* 2, April 2001: 2.

"Vopros reshaetsja mgnovenno" [The problem is solved immediately]. *Pravoslavnoe Slovo* 19, no. 128 (October 1998): 4.

"Vstrecha v kremle" [Meeting in the Kremlin]. *Staroobrjadec* 12, April 1999: 1.

"Vybory i staroobrjadcy" [Elections and Old Believers]. *Staroobrjadec* 16, March 2000: 2.

"Vy vse eshhe ne verite v apostola Putina? Togda my idem k vam!" [You still do not believe in the apostle Putin? Then we will come to you!]. *Novoe delo* 7, February 17–24, 2005: 8.

Wah, Poon Shuk. "Refashioning Festivals in Republican Guangzhou." *Modern China* 30, no. 2 (2004): 199–227.

Wald, Kenneth D., Adam L. Silverman, and Kevin S. Fridy. "Making Sense of Religion in Political Life." *Annual Review of Political Science* 8 (June 2005): 121–43.

Walder, Andrew. "The Decline of Communist Power." *Theory and Society* 23, no. 2 (1994): 297–323.

Walters, Philip. "The Russian Orthodox Church and Foreign Christianity." In *Proselytism and Orthodoxy in Russia: The New War for Souls*, edited by John Witte Jr. and Michael Bourdeaux, 31–50. Maryknoll, NY: Orbis Books, 1999.

Wang, Jianping. "Struggle for the Rights: Revival of Islam in China." Paper presented at the seminar of Near East Studies, Cornell University, April 13, 2009.

Wang, Mingming. "Flower of the State, Grasses of the People: Years Rites and Aesthetics of Power in Quanzhou Southeast China." Ph.D. dissertation, Department of Anthropology, University of London, 1993.

Wang, Xu. "Mutual Empowerment of State and Society: Its Nature, Conditions, Mechanisms and Limits." *Comparative Politics* 31, no. 2 (January 1999): 231–49.

Wang, Yaohua. *Fujian wenhua gailan* [An overview of Fujian culture]. Fujian: Fujian jiaoyu chubanshe, 1994.

Wang, Yongshun. *Songjiang nianjian (1998–1999)* [Songjiang yearbook (1998–1999)]. Shanghai: Xuelin chubanshe, 2000.

Wang, Zhaoguo. "Notification from Wang Zhaoguo Regarding the Essence of the Central Government Document on Handling the Falun Gong Issue." *People's Daily* [overseas edition], July 24, 1999. Reprinted in *Chinese Law and Government* 32, no. 5 (September–October 1999): 22–5.

Ware, Timothy. *The Orthodox Church*. Suffolk, England: Penguin, 1997.

Warner, Carolyn M. *Confessions of an Interest Group: The Catholic Church and Political Parties in Europe*. Princeton: Princeton University Press, 2000.

Washington, Tom. "Angry Priests Damn Church's Relationship with the State." *Moscow News*, June 3, 2011. Available at: http://themoscownews.com/society/20110603/188723288.html (last accessed September 4, 2013).

Watson, James L. "Standardizing the Gods: The Promotion of T'ien Hou [Empress of Heaven] Along the South China Coast, 960–1960." In *Popular Culture in Late Imperial China*, edited by David Johnson, Andrew J. Nathan, and Evelyn S. Rawski, 292–324. Berkeley: University of California Press, 1985.

Webster, Paul. "Religious Revival: Buddhism Is Big Business in China." *Canadian Business*, December 8, 2008. Available at: http://www.canadianbusiness.com/business-strategy/religious-revival/ (last accessed September 4, 2013).

Wedeen, Lisa. "The Politics of Deliberation: Qat Chews and Public Spheres in Yemen." *Public Culture* 19, no. 1 (2007): 59–84.

———. *Ambiguities of Domination: Politics, Rhetoric, and Symbols in Contemporary Syria*. Chicago: University of Chicago Press, 1999.

Weigel, George. *The Final Revolution: The Resistance Church and the Collapse of Communism*. Oxford, UK: Oxford University Press, 1992.

White, Gordon, Jude Howell, and Xiaoyuan Shang, eds. *In Search of Civil Society: Market Reform and Social Change in Contemporary China*. New York: Clarendon Press, 1996.

Wielander, Gerda. "Bridging the Gap? An Investigation of Beijing Intellectual House Church Activities and the Implications for China's Democratization." *Journal of Contemporary China* 18, no. 62 (2009): 849–64.

Wiest, Jean-Paul. "Setting Roots: The Catholic Church in China to 1949." In *God and Caesar in China*, edited by Jason Kindopp and Carol Lee Hamrin, 77–92. Washington, DC: The Brookings Institute, 2004.

Wiktorowicz, Quintan. *The Management of Islamic Activism: Salafis, the Muslim Brotherhood and State Power in Jordan*. Albany: State University of New York Press, 2001.

Wilkinson, Steven I. *Votes and Violence: Electoral Competition and Ethnic Riots in India*. New York: Cambridge University Press, 2004.

Wintrobe, Ronald. "Dictatorship: Analytical Approaches." *The Oxford Handbook of Comparative Politics*, edited by Carles Boix and Susan C. Stokes, 363–94. New York: Oxford University Press, 2007.

———. "How to Understand and Deal with Dictatorship: An Economist's View." *Economics of Governance*, no. 2 (2001): 35–58.

———. "The Tinpot and the Totalitarian: An Economic Theory of Dictatorship." *American Political Science Review* 84, no. 3 (1990): 849–72.

Witte, John Jr. "Soul Wars: The Problem and Promise of Proselytism in Russia." *Emory International Law Review* 12, no. 2 (1998): 1–42.

———. "Introduction." In *Proselytism and Orthodoxy in Russia: The New War for Souls*, edited by John Witte Jr. and Michael Bourdeaux, 1–27. Maryknoll, NY: Orbis, 1999.

Witte, John Jr., and Michael Bourdeaux, eds. *Proselytism and Orthodoxy in Russia: The New War for Souls*. Maryknoll, NY: Orbis, 1999.

Wittenberg, Jason. *Crucibles of Political Loyalty: Church Institutions and Electoral Continuity in Hungary*. New York: Cambridge University Press, 2006.

Wood, James E. "Public Religion vis-à-vis the Prophetic Role of Religion." In *The Power of Religious Publics*, edited by William H. Swatos Jr. and James K. Wellman Jr., 33–51. Westport, CT: Praeger, 1999.

Wright, Teresa. *Accepting Authoritarianism: State-Society Relations in China's Reform Era*. Stanford: Stanford University Press, 2010.

Wu, Chong. "Interpreting a Call for 'Harmonious Society.'" *China Daily* [overseas edition], August 3, 2005. Available at: http://www.chinadaily.com.cn/english/doc/2005-03/08/content_422680.htm (last accessed September 4, 2013).

Wu, Jiao. "Religious Believers Thrice the Estimate." *China Daily*, February 7, 2007. Available at: http://www.chinadaily.com.cn/china/2007-02/07/content_802994.htm (last accessed July 31, 2013).

Wu, Longsheng. "Jiating jiaohui yu hexie shehui goujian wenti tanxi" [A probe into house churches' adaption and the construction of a harmonious society]. *Tiedao jingguan gaodeng zhuanke xuexiao xuebao* 19, serial 80, no. 2 (2009): 30–4.

Wu, Yaozong. "My Recognition of the Communist Party" [Wo dui Gongchandang de renshi]. *Tian Feng*, 1958.

Wu, Yakui. "Zhujiajiao de zongjiao – Jiantan zongjiao hudong changsuo de lvyou jingguan gongneng" [Religions in Zhu Jia Jiao – the role of religious places in tourism and sight-seeing]. *Dangdai zongjiao yanjiu* 41 (2000): 20–4.

Xia, Ming, and Shiping Hua, eds. "The Battle between the Chinese Government and the Falun Gong." *Chinese Law & Government* 32, no. 5 (September–October 1999a): 5–104.

———. "The Falun Gong: Qigong, Code of Ethics, and Religion." *Chinese Law & Government* 32, no. 9 (November–December 1999b): 5–101.

Xiao, Hongyan. "Falun Gong and the Ideological Crisis of the Chinese Communist Party." *Journal of East Asia* 19, no. 1/2 (Spring–Summer 2001): 123–43.

Xiejiao yanjiu keti zu. "'Zhonghua fuyin tuanqi' de fazhan zhuangkuang ji fangzhi duice" [Report of CGF development situation and measures of dealing with CGF]. *Tiedao jingguan gaodeng zhuanke xuexiao xuebao* 3 (1999): 41–8.

Xin, Dingding. "New Holiday System Set for First Test." *China Daily*, March 26, 2008. Available at http://www.chinadaily.com.cn/china/2008-03/26/content_6565344.htm (last accessed September 5, 2013).

Xin, Yalin. *Inside China's House Church Network*. Lexington, KY: Emeth Press, 2009.

Xinhua. "NPC deputy proposed inking 'harmonious society' into Constitution." August 3, 2005. Available at: http://news.xinhuanet.com/english/2005-03/08/content_2668397.htm (last accessed September 5, 2013).

Xinhua. "China's Religious Leaders Urged to Play 'Active Role' in Achieving Social Harmony." February 13, 2007. Available at: http://english.peopledaily.com.cn/200702/13/eng20070213_349522.html (last accessed September 4, 2013).

Xinhua. "Buxin shen de Gongchandang weisheme neng tuanjie xinjiao qunzhong" [Atheist Communist Party can unite God's followers]. June 7, 2011. Available at: http://news.xinhuanet.com/politics/2011-06/07/c_121500546.htm (last accessed March 1, 2013).

Xinhua. "CPC official calls for positive role of religion in development," January 1, 2013. Available at: http://news.xinhuanet.com/english/china/2013-01/24/c_132123529.htm (last accessed July 31, 2013).

Xu, Hongbao. "Gaigekaifang xingshi xia de Songjiang Tianzhujiao" [The Catholic Church of Songjiang in Opening and Reform]. *Dangdai zongjiao yanjiu* 4 (1990): 1–7.

Yan, Peijing, Yan Wu, and Bingxi Yan. "Xian jieduan Jidujiao fazhan zhuangkuang qianxi" [A brief analysis of the current situation of Christian development]. *Fazhi yu jingji* 209 (July 2009): 131.

Yang, C. K. *Religion in Chinese society.* Berkeley: University of California Press, 1961.

Yang, Fenggang. *Religion in China: Survival and Revival Under Communist Rule.* New York: Oxford University Press, 2012.

——. "Market Economy and Revival of Religions." In *Chinese Religious Life*, edited by David Palmer, Glenn Shive, and Philip L. Wickeri, 209–26. New York: Oxford University Press, 2011.

——. "Religious Awakening in China under Communist Rule: Political Economy Approach." In *The New Blackwell Companion to the Study of Religion*, edited by Bryan S. Turner, 431–55. Oxford: Wiley-Blackwell, 2010.

——. "The Red, Black and Gray Markets of Religion in China." *Sociological Quarterly* 47 (2006): 93–122.

——. "Lost in the Market, Saved at McDonald's: Conversion to Christianity in Urban China." *Journal for the Scientific Study of Religion* 44, no. 4 (2005): 423–41.

——. "Between Secularist Ideology and Desecularizing Reality: The Birth and Growth of Research in Communist China." *Sociology of Religion* 65, no. 2 (2004): 101–19.

Yang, Mayfair Mei-hui. *Chinese Religiosities: Afflictions of Modernity and State Formation.* Berkeley: University of California Press, 2008.

——. "Goddess across the Taiwan Strait: Matrifocal Ritual Space, Nation-State, and Satellite Television Footprints." *Public Culture* 16, no. 2 (2004a): 209–38.

——. "Spatial Struggles: Postcolonial Complex, State Disenchantment, and Popular Reappropriation of Space in Rural Southeast China." *The Journal of Asian Studies* 63, no. 3 (2004b): 719–55.

——. "Putting Global Capitalism in Its Place: Economic Hybridity, Bataille, and Ritual Expenditure." *Current Anthropology* 41, no. 4 (2000): 477–509.

Yao, Li. "Woguo gaigekaifang yilai Jidujiao fazhan de yuanyin tanxi" [Reasons for the growth of Christianity in China after Opening and Reform]. *Dangdai zongjiao yanjiu* 11, no. 3 (May 2004): 73–4.

Yeung, Y.M. "Meizhou Bay as a Growth Center." In *Fujian: A Costal Province in Transition and Transformation*, edited by Y. M. Yeung and David K. Y. Chu, 353–74. Hong Kong: Chinese University of Hong Kong, 2000.

Ying, Fuk-tsang. *Dangdai Zhongguo zhengjiao guanli* [The management of church and state relations in contemporary China]. Hong Kong: Jiandao shenxueyuan, 1999.

Young, Lawrence A., ed. *Rational Choice Theory and Religion: Summary and Assessment.* New York: Routledge, 1997.

Yu, Jianrong. "Wei Jidujiao jiatingjiaohui tuomin" [The desensitization of Christian house churches]. December 11, 2008. Available at: http://www.sachina.edu.cn/Htmldata/article/2008/12/1696.html (last accessed September 5, 2013).

————. "Religious Demography and House Churches, 2008." *Compass Direct News Service*, July 3, 2009.

Yu, Wangge. "Yifa dui zongjiao shiwu jinxing guanli zhiwojian" [My view on administrating religious affairs by law]. *Dangdai zongjiao yanjiu* 15 (1994): 1–3.

Yuan, Heping. *Xiandaiyan kan Mazu* [A contemporary look at Mazu]. Taipei: Youshi wenhua, 1997.

"Zachem Nizhnemu katolicheskij monastyr'?" [Why does Nizhny need a Catholic monastery?]. *Golos veterana* 7, no. 126, February 19–25, 2004: 15.

"Zakon 'o svobode i religioznyh ob"edinenijah' i staroobrjadchestve" [Law 'on the freedom and religious associations' and the Old Believers]. *Staroobrjadec*, November 1997: 2–3.

"Zakon o svobode veroispovedenii" [Law on the freedom of religion], Vedomosti RSFSR 21, no. 267–1, 240 (1990).

Zartman, William. "Opposition as Support of the State." In *Beyond Coercion: The Durability of the Arab State*, edited by Adeed Dawisha and William Zartman, 61–87. London, New York: Croom Helm, 1998.

Zhang, Liwei, ed. *The Amity Foundation 2006 Annual Report*. Nanjing: Amity Foundation, 2006.

Zhao, Ying and Zhiming Yu. "Forum Opposing Falun Gong Cult Held at Sacred Buddhist Site Nan Putuo" [Zhongguo fan xiejiao renshi juhui Fojiao shengdi Nan Putuo]. *People's Daily*, April 26, 2002. Available at: http://www.people.com.cn/GB/shizheng/19/20020426/718136.html (last accessed March 5, 2013).

"Zhiteli poselka Bol'shaja El'nja trebujut vyselit' 'Matushku Fotiniju Svetonosnuju'" [Villagers of Bol'shaja El'nja demand to evict the Mother Photinia Luminous]. *Novye izvestija*, March 24, 2005.

Zhong, Guofa. "Shilun 'jiji yindao zongjiao yu shehuizhuyi shehui xiang shiying' de chuangxin yiyi" [The Importance of Positively Promoting Religion's Adaption to Socialist Society]. *Dangdai zongjiao yanjiu* 31 (1998): 10–16.

"Zhonggong zhongyang guanyu woguo shehui zhuyi shiqi zongjiao wenti de jiben guandian he jiben zhengce (wenjian no. 19)" [Document 19: The basic viewpoint and policy on the religious question during our country's socialist period]. Reprinted in *Feiqing yuebao* 10 (April 1983): 82–91.

"Zhongyang bangongting diaocha zu guanyu luoshi dang de zongjiao zhengce ji youguan wenti de diaocha baogao" [Report concerning the implementation of the party's religious policies and related issues], December 10, 1985. Examined and approved by the Committee on Legal Work of the Standing Committee of the National People's Congress. Reprinted in *Zhonghua Renmin Gongheguo falu quan shu* [The complete laws and regulations of the People's Republic of China] vol. 10: Civil Law, Beijing: China Democratic Legal System Printing House, 1994: 1099–101.

Zolotov, Andre Jr. "The Church's New Teaching: The Russian Orthodox Church Affirms Values of Freedom and Human Rights." *Russia Profile*, June 30, 2008. Available at: http://russiaprofile.org/culture_living/a1214839164.html (last accessed September 5, 2013).

Index